THE POLITICAL ECONOMY OF THE STATE

THE POLITICAL ECONOMY OF THE STATE

Québec / Canada / U.S.A.

edited by
Dimitrios I. Roussopoulos

BLACK ROSE BOOKS   -   Montréal

BLACK ROSE BOOKS No. D8

First Edition 1973

Hard cover — ISBN : 0-919618-02-2

Paper back — ISBN : 0-919618-01-4

BLACK ROSE BOOKS Ltd.

3934 rue St. Urbain

Montréal 131, Qué

Printed and bound in Québec, Canada.

CONTENTS

CONTENTS

PREFACE

"The more powerful the state and hence the more *political* a country is, the less it is inclined to seek the basis and grasp the *general* principles of *social* ills in the principle of the state itself, thus in the existing organisation of society, of which the state is the active, self-conscious, and official expression. *Political* thought is *political* precisely because it takes place within the bounds of politics. The more acute and vigorous it is, the more it is incapable of comprehending social ills ... The principle of politics is *will*. The more one-sided and thus the more perfected political thought is, the more it believes in the omnipotence of will, the blinder it is to *natural* and spiritual *restriction* on the will, and the more incapable it is discovering the source of social ills."

"We have seen that a *social* revolution involves the standpoint of the *whole* because it is a protest of man against dehumanised life even if it occurs in only one factory district, because it proceeds from the standpoint of the *single actual individual,* because the community against whose separation from himself the individual reacts, is the *true* community of man, *human* existence. The *political soul* of a revolution on the other hand consists in the *tendency* of politically uninfluential classes to end their *isolation* from the state, and from power. Its standpoint is that of the state, an *abstract* whole, which exists only through the separation from actual life and which is *unthinkable* without the *organised* antithesis between the universal idea and the individual existence of man. Hence a revolution of the *political soul* also organises, in accordance with the *narrow* and split nature of this soul, a ruling group at the expense of society."

Karl Marx, in Critical Notes on "The King of Prussia and Social Reform" (1844). Original italics.

"The state organisation, having been the force to which the minorities resorted for establishing and organising their power over the masses, cannot be the force which will serve to destroy these privileges. ... The economic and political liberation of man will have to create new forms for its expression of life, instead of those established by the State.

Peter Kropotkin, Modern Science and Anarchism.

"Today, the State has succeeded in meddling in every aspect of our lives. ... It regulates all our actions. It accumulates mountains of laws and ordinances in which the shrewdest lawyer is lost. Each day it creates new gears to awkwardly patch up the broken old watch, and it comes to create a machine so complex, so inferior, so obstructive, that it revolts even those who are charged wih running it.

It creates an army of employees, spiders with hooked fingers, who know the universe only through the dirty windows of their offices, or by their obscure, absurd, illegible old papers, an evil band who have only one religion, that of the buck; only one care, that of hooking up with any party whatever in order to be guaranteed maximum political appointments for a minimum of work.
The resuls we know only too well."

Peter Kropotkin, Words of a Rebel, 1885.

7

In all modern societies the State is an every-growing network of institutions perpetuating hierarchy and existing social and economic classes. The bureaucratic network has an inherent tendency towards centralisation, cemented by a secret police, a mass standing army, an industrial-scientific autocracy, and a huge propaganda and communications complex at its heart.

While the ownership and control by a small elite of the economic life of a society sets the pattern of exploitation, the State sets the pattern of domination. No revolutionary change in the ownership and control of the economy is possible without an equally revolutionary change in hierarchical relations : the very existence of the State must be questioned in the same way the very existence of private property and manipulation is questioned. In advanced capitalist societies, the question of State and Capital is inter-locked, and so is the radical answer.

The development of a contemporary theory of the State has had a major obstacle. This obstacle however can be changed into an advantage. Marx and Engels, and Marxists since then, have had no worked-out theory of the State. The gargantuan increase in State power in capitalist societies as well as in "socialist societies" gives the anti-statist critique of anarchism a renewed relevance. The anarchist critique of centralisation, bureaucracy, lack of participation and control in the workplace and in the community at large, the centrifugal tendencies of state directed technology must be integrated ino our new studies.

The State is — always has been and always will be as long as it continues to exist — a social instrument of repression. On this basic proposition Marxism and anarchism are in accord. There is also accord on the fact that there is an umbilical cord between the existence of the State and a society divided into classes. Indeed the State is a product of this division, which inturn is based on a society of material scarcity, and the manipulation of this scarcity by a ruling class and power elite.

Nevertheless tremendous differences arose between Marxism, especially Marxism-Leninism and anarchism in the last one hundred years. But many changes have taken place in society during the last century, and many lessons have still to be drawn from the experience of the revolutionary socialist movement. We are not proposing here some new eclecticism or a shot-gun marriage. What we are suggesting however is that among creative Marxists and anarchists, common research and discussion would be useful.

The areas of research include the many new developments in social analysis and social theory. Some of these developments include a fundamental re-examination of the relationship of 'structure' (the economic mode of production) and 'super-structure' (the State, science, technology). This important examination can have wide-ranging consequences. As one group of Marxist researchers put it with regard to one aspect of this question : "The function of various public institutions in maintaining ideological hegemony has produced different consequences in the development of class consciousness. The interpenetration of the base and superstructure in the modern epoch has changed the ideological function of the State — for example, there has been an interpenetration of norms that govern activity at the base and norms that inform activity in the superstructure." (From Introduction to KAPITALISTATE, an international bulletin of Studies on the Capitalist State). By now most revolutionaries working in industrial/technological societies assume as self-evident that the nationalisation of property and the means of production does *not* fundamentally in itself alter the basic inequality between those who exercise power and those who are subject to it. That is, we are beginning to understand anew the different relationship between the realities called exploitation and domination, and that social revolution today must mean not only an end of exploitation of one person by another, *but also* and simultaneously, the end of domination of one person by another. We no longer believe that 'bureaucracy', 'the State', will 'wither away'. The dogma that the 'super-structure' merely reflects the economic mode of production is no longer supportable in the face of the assertion that the phenomena constituting the super-structure shape history separately and decisively. Thus, Rudolf Hilferding, a noted Marxist economist has written : "It is the essence of a totalitarian state that it subjects the economy to its aim ... the Marxist sectarian cannot grasp the idea that present day state power, having achieved independence is unfolding its enormous strengths according to its own laws, subjecting other social forces and compelling them to serve its ends ..." Even the question of what today constitutes 'the mode of production' is being re-examined, also from *within* the Marxist tradition.

The State, irrespective of social origin, class situation and ideological dispositions, is subject to the structural constaints of the system. Nevertheless Nicos Poulantzas is correct when he rejects the "long Marxist tradition (which) has considered that the State is only a simple tool or instrument manipulated at will by the ruling class." Instead, he stresses the "relative autonomy of the state". Poulantzas along with many other Marxists condemns the "economism" of the Second and Third Internationals and attributes to it their neglect of the State. The anarchist tradition has never neglected the State, although it has neglected the study of other aspects of class society.

This brings us finally to another area is need of research. The rapid post-1945 organisational expansion of multi-national corporations has brought into question the analytical primacy of certain basic factors used up until now in social analysis. The whole question of the relationship between political and economic organisation, especially in Canada and Québec has to be sorted out. There is clearly no longer a one-to-one relationship between the two forms.

This book attempts among other things to move away from the predominatly political treatment of the State. Until recently it was primarily the repressive role of the State in capitalist society which has been emphasized. THE POLITICAL ECONOMY OF THE STATE tries to discuss the ideological function of the State, the economic role of the State in capitalist societies, and the ways inwhich the State participates in the reproduction of the class structure of society.

The critique offered in this book is not only a critique of the State but equally a critique of the current conception of "the political" which defines itself in terms of the State.

Montréal, April 1973   *Dimitrios I. Roussopoulos*

INTRODUCTION

We would like to maintain with this book that the liberals and the political Left in Canada and Québec have no coherent theory of the State. The present poverty of 'political science' as taught in our schools of 'higher learning' need not surprise us, but this attitude on the part of establishment academia has important social consequences. The current orthodoxy in 'political science' has turned on the claims (which have become unexamined articles of faith) of a pluralist-democratic view of society. Therefore the State is not a special institution whose essential purpose is to defend and perpetuate the present class structure.

On the other hand, "... Marxist political analysis, notably in relation to the nature and role of the state, has long seemed stuck in its groove, and has shown little capacity to renew itself." In "The State in Capitalist Society", Ralph Miliband not only shatters the myth of pluralistic democracy but goes on to admit that Marxism has made no substantial contributions to our understanding of the State for a very long time. Indeed we might add that the cancerous growth of the State both in capitalist and 'socialist' societies, as well as the new relevance of the anarchist critique of the State, has forced many radicals to re-open the question in a fundamental way. Miliband adds,

"Marx himself, it may be recalled, never attempted a systematic study of the state." He goes on to say,

"For the most part, Marxists everywhere have been content to take this thesis as more or less self-evident ; (referring to the thesis in the **Communist Manifesto** — the editor) and to take as their text on the state Lenin's **State and Revolution,** which is now half a century old and which was in essence both a restatement and an elaboration of the main view of the state to be found in Marx and Engels and a fierce assertion of its validity in the era of imperialism. Since then, the only major Marxist contribution to the theory of the state has been that of Antonio Gramsci, whose illuminating notes on the subject have only fairly recently come to gain a measure of recognition and influence beyond Italy. Otherwise, Marxists have made little notable attempt to confront the question of the state in the light of the concrete socio-economic **and** political **and** cultural reality of actual capitalist societies. Where the attempt has been made, it has suffered from an over-simple explanation of the interrelationship between civil society and the state. Even though that 'model' comes much closer to reality than democratic-pluralist theory, it requires a much more thorough elaboration than it has hitherto been given ; Paul Sweezy was scarcely exaggerating when he noted some years ago that 'this is the area in which the study of monopoly capitalism, not only by bourgeois social scientists but by Marxists as well, is most seriously deficient.' "

Our analysis of the State in this book, is far from complete and is only a beginning. Hopefully with the encouragement of our readers and other researchers we will advance the study. We do not for instance deal with the question that Miliband raises in his book as to whether we can speak of a 'ruling class' in relationship to countries of advanced capitalism, as contrasted with the existence of economic elites which, 'by virtue of ownership or control or both, do command many of the most important sectors of economic life.' An investigation of this question is crucial if we are to understand the degree to which the State has an independent and separate institutional role and function in our type of society. We do not deal with the whole range of institutions related to the 'state system' — public corporations, central banks, regulatory commissions ; that is the vast administrative function of the State which reaches way beyond the traditional bureaucracy associated with government. Nor do we deal with the social composition of the 'state elite'. We also do not deal with the role, function and enormous growth of the civil service, the judiciary including the police and prison system, and the military and para-military. We have not dealt with the role of the State in the competition between different 'interests' in capitalist

society. Finally we have not dealt with the mass media and the extensive educational system as the central agencies that legitimize the system along with the political parties and legislative assemblies. In a word what we have done is to survey the major economic and social characteristics of the State in our advanced capitalist society and submitted to detailed analysis the pattern of economic power and relationship of the State to the political economy. Without however continuing the study of the above enumerated questions, and without undertaking a similar study of the role and function of the State in 'socialist' countries, not only will our understanding of the processes of centralisation, bureaucracy and authoritarianism be limited, but the revolutionary alternative will itself be limited and consequently its programmatic and strategic potential.

The growth of the State apparatus in capitalist society has not escaped the attention of radical observers. Yet while it is universally admitted that Western economies are characterized by a form of State capitalism, the theoretical and strategic conclusions to be drawn from this fact have often not been drawn. Too frequently we act according to an outmoded conception of the structure of capitalist society and the means of transforming it, even when we know that structure has been substantially changed.

A major cause of our weakness in this area of research is that not enough detailed material has been gathered describing the extent and form of the role of the State in capitalist society and analysing its origins and patterns of development. This has been particularly the case in Canada and in Québec. The essays in this book, we believe, make a vital contribution to knowledge in this essential area.

From the kind of analysis presented, a new strategy and concept of organizing a socialist movement must be fashioned. Our theoretical inadequacy grows more apparent every day; and as militancy among governmental and para-governmental workers spreads and manifests itself in strikes, wildcats, takeovers and other forms of political opposition, it becomes more and more intolerable. And, as we all know, these are not matters which affect only an isolated group of workers; the government sector as we shall see is immense, and major labour management disputes in it inevitably become political crises.

Because of the lack of an ongoing socialist critique of the State in capitalist society, a social democratic liberal view still prevails far too widely. This view associates the State as the tool of reform, the redistributor of wealth and services. The State is the path to the "just society"; so the further we are along this path the nearer we are to socialism. (Note that this is how the American Communist Party regarded the New Deal...). Liberals point to the growing bureaucracy, the expansion of an industrial "public sector", and other government initiatives as portents of the good society tomorrow. Because the Left lacks a profound empirically based understanding of the State in Canada and Québec, our critique has not overcome the left-liberal assumption that the resolution of the contradictions of capitalism lies in the gradual enlargement of the "public sector".

We set the term "public sector" in quotes on the basis of facts to be found in this book. Basically we learn that the role of the State is to serve private capital, and those segments of the economy that are owned by the State are nevertheless private in their fundamental purpose and thrust. Socialists know this; they know that an enlarged State under capitalism means only a strengthened capitalism — if they do not then they are blind to the developments in the industrialized world in this century.

To render this theoretical understanding critically useful to a movement whose goal is to negate the prevailing capitalist system, what is first required is concrete data of a particular sort. First, what is this public sector, what parts of the economy are involved in it, how has it grown, what is its relation with private capital? Second, what does it in fact do to serve the public as compared to what it claims to do? Third, who pays for the services provided by the government bureaucracy and through what mechanisms? Finally, how is all of this justified by the propaganda services of the capitalist state, i.e. the media?

The essays in this book we believe, go a long way toward answering these questions, and thus provide us with the analytical tools we need. While each author views the situation from a different vantage point, each faces up to one or more of these questions and answers them. Rick Deaton's article, deals with the early development of the Canadian State, of the sources for the tax money used to pay for it. It goes on to lay out the role of the "public sector" in the capitalist economy with particular reference to the fiscal crisis in government funds. Finally, it points to some of the conclusions the public employee might draw from these facts.

B. R. Lemoine writes mainly about Québec. Working with the results of some of the excellent research now being carried on at the Québec unions, he brings together a wealth of rather revealing statistics to expose the underlying reason for the growth of the Québec State in the Quiet Revolution : namely, to modernize the capitalist structure and infrastructure and thus increase its profits. Further, he shows how federal government economic initiatives in Québec such as DREE (Department of Regional Economic Expansion) especially in its newly revised form, contribute to stabilizing the domination of private (and foreign) capital in Québec.

Lorne Huston's article looks at another dimension of the same phenomenon. He investigates the purposes of the Federal government's OFY (Opportunity for Youth) and LIP (Local Initiatives Projects) projects, demonstrating how they are but a new and sophisticated way in which the State preserves the prevailing socio-economic system, only in this case it is by managing and deflecting discontent. The great poster of the LIP proclaimes 'Canada Works'. What Huston, Lemoine, and Deaton show through analysing LIP, DREE, the CDC, or others among the numerous state activities, is just whom Canada and Québec works for.

Graeme Nicholson examines the chain of authoritarian relationships that leads from the nature of the workplace all the way to the State. That it is in fact the basic structural cast of the State that shapes and influences most other relationships in society. Nicholson shows what the authority of the boss in the workplace is based on. This is followed by an examination of the stream of authority all the way up the ladder to the top — the State.

Margaret Ellinger and John Rowntree in their essay, *"On Revolution in the Metropolis"* concentrate on the social formations within the working class of the United States and on the State as economic actor. The essay empasizes that the economic contradictions of capitalism and imperialism have not been overcome by the system. In spite and because of State planning and Keynesian economic policies, the economy is still subject to major crises. The irrationality of profitability as a basis for the allocation of resources and the chaos of the market persist in the era of monopoly and State appropriation of the economic surplus. These economic contradictions underlie and interact with the social and political contradictions.

What Ellinger and Rowntree also demonstrate is that capitalism cannot by its nature be reformed into socialism. The political, economic, and social bureaucratic structures supporting the social order based on private property can only become more inflexible, intolerant, repressive, and disorderly ; they must be abolished in order to replace them by the democratic structures of the working class. The authors show how State power has grown during the century to meet the needs of continued monopoly centralisation and imperialist expansion. A decade of monopoly-bred depression was followed by the war from which the U.S.A. emerged as the economic and military center of the capitalist world. To meet its increased economic and military responsibilities, the State became a major participant in the web of social and economic relations of the country.

These relations were expressed by forms that pretended to be autonmous and independent of both labour and capital, the structure of the State institutions in fact bound the State to promote the interests of capital. Today, these ties to capital have become the cause of the State's economic problems. As State power has continued to grow, the State institutions have become enmeshed in the very contradictions they were set up to resolve. Established to prevent economic and social crisis, the State's economic policy has become part of the crisis.

The conclusions that emerge from these analyses combined are unmistakable. **First,** it is clear, if it was not before, that the growth of the State has been, liberal myths notwithstanding, to the benefit rather than the detriment of the corporate rich. While a few anachronistic businessmen object here and there, the State they fear has grown and expanded directly in response to their own corporate needs in such areas as transportation, education, resource development, communications, and scientific research to name just a few

The **second** point is that the growth of the "welfare state" which in theory redistributes services and wealth to those at the bottom of the capitalist order has been exaggerated and misrepresented. In relative terms, as compared to GNP or government expenditure, the social services of the State have more often than not remained constant. **Third,** the additional State revenues needed to pay for the growing State bureaucracy and increase activity has been disproportionately raised through increases in personal income taxes and sales taxes ; corporation income taxes now provide a less significant share of State revenues. Thus the great majority of salaried employees in Canada has paid for the creation of a vast State machinery the basic role of which is to serve the needs of the small class of corporate owners.

The **fourth** element is the growing importance of the State employee. The analysis presented in the essays herein shows that the very existence of the sector serves the economic needs of the private corporations. The general population, encouraged by the media, expects the public employee to show greater "responsibility". Furthermore, it assumes that the employer, i.e. the government, has the public interest at heart while the workers are pursuing selfish interests. (This is in large part a result of the failure of socialists to educate themselves and the public on the role inevitably played by the State under capitalism.) At the same time the State finds itself often in the most unproductive sectors of the production — those most subject to stress in periods of economic downturn. Added to this is the normal policy of capitalist governments to extend tax and other reliefs to corporations in times of economic difficulty so that government revenues are even further depleted.

At such times as now with high unemployment and lagging productivity — a situation, say some observers, which is likely to continue under present day capitalism long into the conceivable future, governments thus confront a political choice. They must either freeze wages, reduce fringe benefits, or reclassify in this already underprivileged sector or further raise personal income and sales taxes. In this political battle the public employee almost inevitably loses (except for the police, on whose

14

backs State power finally rests). At the same time it becomes the government rather than private corporations that crush the most militant labour insurgencies, thus enabling the corporate directors to discretely follow suit in their general attitudes to the demands of their workers out of "public duty". Of course, the most powerful corporate capitalists, because they have relegated low or no-return fields of the economy to government, can appear comparatively generous since they can transfer added costs to the public, through price increases. In this rather complex way the public sector provides a safety valve — channelling discontent among government employees against the public it is supposed to serve, turning public sentiment against unions, and allowing corporate executives to present themselves not as the exploiting privileged few but as unusually public-spirited citizens.

In sum, using public instruments to serve private ends in the complex ways outlined above, while at the same time laying claim to the liberal/social democratic ideology which associates the State with a socialist or just society has been very effective in maintaining and screening the basic inequality of wealth and power inherent under capitalism. It has led to the diffusion of popular discontent so that it could be defeated when necessary, but more often directed into harmless channels.

Yet that discontent is there, and has raised its head too often among certain groups and in certain areas for government as sophisticated as that in Ottawa not to devise schemes to meet this problem. So we get DREE's that promise economic recovery to depressed areas and OFY's and LIP's that hand out government money to young people and other citizens to solve their own and other people's problems. In fact what is provided is but the image of economic and social change ; in fact the programs serve to strengthen the system and confirm the power of the dominant class which is the real source of the problem.

LIP and OFY were designed to deal with a discontent that was unformed and unfocused, and to assure people that any suspicions they might have had that government was not really on their side were mistaken. Here was a government that was hip, that understood — even the employees were chosen to project that image, one they in fact too often believed. So an already unfocused protest loses its impetus. Such government programs then are innovative but not really new, merely the latest step in the pattern of the developing role of the capitalist State.

Two concrete examples might be briefly raised here, both in the field of housing. The first is the leaking of the CMHC's Dennis report. The events surrounding this report present an incredibly lucid illustration of what has been said. The task force hired young middle class intellectuals to assess low income housing. They submitted a report after the expenditure of a great deal of public funds exposing the role of the CMHC since World War II. This role consisted of aiding a few large developers to take over Canada's cities, to artificially raise property values through speculations, thereby earning extremely high profits while constructing a totally inadequate number of moderate and low income housing units. The report was shelved, 3000 copies it seems actually shredded and would have been completely forgotten were it not for a disgruntled re-

15

searcher spilling the beans to David Lewis.

The second example concerns the struggle of the Milton-Park Citizens Committee in Montréal against Concordia Development. Here was a concrete example of the kind of collusion the Dennis Report reveals, though in this case mainly at the provincial and municipal levels. Through legislation and financial aid the governments supported a private company to build a huge expensive development of elite housing and hotels, destroying the area against the will of residents and the advice of architects and town planners. In Milton-Park the citizens learned something in the process about the State and its relationship to the economic drives of a capitalist system — lessons they will apply in the future. The government, especially Federal, has been trying to keep these lessons unlearned. The goal is to make it appear that what is good for the State (and therefore for Genenral Motors) is good for Canada (and therefore you and me).

This we must not allow it to do. The facts revealed in the four essays provide the foundation for a criticism of the State under capitalism, out of which must come a more concrete programme for and vision of the achievement of socialism in Canada and Québec. Events have shown that the "public sector" has become the focus of working class radicalism and the essays explain why ; hence, a socialist strategy must concentrate on (rather than ignore it as has been the practice too often) this ever growing segment of society.

Specifically, we can conclude that when it comes to collective bargaining in the public and para-public sector, the State must as a rule be approached as one variation of a capitalist employer. As long as we are in a system where the primary function of the State machinery is to aid private capital rather then the government workers, this must be the case.

When confronted with the call to public responsibility the State employee must refuse to accept the prevailing definition of "public". His employer does not speak for the public. In fact the "general public" is a creation of the mass media. The only "public" that exists in reality is that public actually served in the work performed by the particular group of State employees. Thus hospital workers must seriously begin to work at involving the patients and others who use their services in the very definition of their role and in seeking them as allies in their demands for improved working conditions. Teachers must similarly regard students and parents ; bus drivers must work together with commuters . . .

The kinds of demands that must be raised must be more than those traditional ones of bread and butter — though these cannot be neglected. Forming coalitions with users and consumers necessitates that public employees organize around the quantitative aspects of their work, about exactly what they do, who sets the standards, whom they serve. The takeover by workers both non-professional and professional of the Albert Prévost Psychiatric Hospital in Montréal during the Québec Public Service Strike is an important precedent. It allied public employees of all categories directly with the needs of the patients against the government-appointed administration. The patients, it was evident to all, benefitted from the change to self-management. The reaction of the Castonguay social welfare ministry, the most progressive part of the Québec State, to the Prévost insurgency, should convince any remaining skeptics as to the primary function and ultimate loyalty of the State. The ministry unequivocally supported an obviously autocratic and unfit handful of bureaucrats against the desires of the entire staff, ignoring the effect this would have on the staff. It suspected, with good reason, that workers insurgency in support of self-management was a threat, not only to the hospital or even the ministry, but to the entire system.

While Prévost was defeated, as was inevitable, the possibilities it raises are indeed exciting. What if public service unions began increasingly to raise qualitative issues ? What if they demanded a new system of management of their institutions combining self-management by the workers with participation by that segment of the public affected by the service ? What if the workers of Hydro-Québec began to determine who got the contracts, and how much power was to cost consumers, and where new power installations would be created, and what kinds of institutions were to be given priority in the allocation power, all in consultation with the people directly affected ? What if ... ?

In sum what if the public employees began to ignore the State and directly serve the public ? Perhaps this is what "the withering away of the state" looks like ?

The kind of analysis and strategy outlined here is a personal challenge to those radicals who accept working for the government as a legitimate channel for bringing about real change. Whether employed by the State indirectly and temporarily with LIP, OFY, or a task force of some kind, or directly with CMHC, Hydro-Québec, or whatever, each government employee must rethink his position.

Can the State be used or is it not more likely that the State is in fact using us ? Of course none of this precludes organizing among State employees in the direction suggested above ; in fact we maintain this to be a very important area of activity.

The point is that an acceptance of such a strategy requires a total change in the attitudes that exist among most Canadians and (even) Québec radicals in relation to the State. The capitalist State is not a means of meaningful social change, it is a subtle and powerful means of preventing it. We must organize against it from without and within.

*by Henry Milner
and Dimitri Roussopoulos*

THE FISCAL CRISIS OF THE STATE

by Rick Deaton

> "The economists explain to us the process of production under given conditions; what they do not explain to us, however, is how these conditions themselves are produced, i.e., the historical movement that brings them into being."
>
> Marx, *The Poverty of Philosophy*

The increasing economic importance and accelerated growth of the public sector in Canada and other advanced industrialized economies has proceeded steadily without interruption. [1] In recent years the expansion of the public sector has been accompanied by dramatic and sweeping advances in unionization. [2] Yet, despite the rapid strides in unionization in the public sector little attention has been focused on why the public sector of the economy developed, what function the public sector fulfills and, most importantly, what is the role of the public employee in the economy.

An analysis of the growth, development and structure of the public sector and its interrelationship with the industrial sector and fiscal system is of key importance since in the long run this dynamic relationship will have pivotal importance with respect to the collective bargaining and wage determination process of public employees and may serve as a catalyst for a broader transformation of the existing political economy.

WHY A PUBLIC SECTOR ?

The growth and expansion of the public sector and government expenditures in Canada serve a number of different, although related economic and political ends which directly or indirectly serve corporate interests. The major determinants of government expenditures (all levels) stem from the general and specific interests of the corporate community as a whole or of specific industries. The Economic Council of Canada has said, " ... policy emphasis and ideological factors play an important role in ... government expenditure patterns." [3] Furthermore, the level of public expenditures, public finance expert R.M. Bird states is, " ... the result of an interlocking series of decisions and actions, past and present ... [and] are made by those who play the roles of 'politicians and the interests they represent." [4]

Thus the origins and development of the public sector are rooted in the past. Historically, the public sector in Canada developed to complement and meet the needs of the private profit-making sector of the economy. The public sector of the economy developed to build the necessary technical infrastructure (supportive services) for the corporate sector, to generate investment, to encourage profitable business activity and opportunities, to meet the social overhead costs of private profit-making production, and to "socialize" (make public) the private costs and risks of production thereby protecting and expanding profits. The public sector of the economy has developed in such a way as to directly or indirectly support and meet corporate needs so that there are *public costs and private benefits* of production in the private porfit-making corporate sector.

The public sector and government budgets continuously expand as a result of the increasingly complex, interdependent and interrelated nature of economic production which demands a greater quantity of public services which can only be funded through the government. The steady expansion of the State budget, expenditure and economic activities is a result of the increasing expenditure requirements of the corporate sector of the economy.

"The history of the industrialized economies", notes economist B.J. McCormick, "records the attempts ... of State intervention to provide a framework for stability and growth." [5] In North America and Canada this means, by definition, providing a "framework for stability and growth" for the private corporate sector of the economy by meeting its needs to expand production and profits.

The development of the public sector provides the framework for stability and growth of the corporate sector by absorbing the costs of social overhead and making public ("socializing") the costs of maintaining the technical infrastructure : railroads, highways, schools, universities, hydroelectric power, hospitals. The most expensive economic needs of corporations are the costs of research (R & D), development of new products, new production processes, and above all, the costs of maintaining the health and providing for the training and retraining of the labour force. No one corporation or industry can afford to educate, train and maintain the health of its labour force nor channel profits into the necessary amount of research and development.

The various levels of government engage in "complementary investment" : that is, investment which will stimulate private investment (and therefore profits) or aid the corporate sector. Such direct government investment to aid the private sector takes the form of harbour facilities, highways into depressed areas, Crown Corporations, regional expansion programs, airports. As one mayor of a major Ontario municipality put it, " . . . this [City] Council has a responsibility to provide facilities . . . which aid the further development of commerce and business." [6]

The various levels of the State absorb the social costs of production and minimize the private costs and risks of private production. George Steiner in a special work on the government's and public sector's role in economic life points out that one of the most important functions of government is the "socialization of risk"; that is, the assumption by government rather than individuals of risk associated with the operation of the economic system. [7] The government through the public sector absorbs the social costs of production by providing for pollution clean up, sanitation services, medicare, unemployment insurance, C.P.P. The private risks of production are absorbed socially, at public expense, through government subsides, grants, fast write-off depreciation allowances, "forgiveable loans", the underwriting of consumer credit and corporate research and development.

The needs of corporate interests are thus fulfilled through the public sector by having the direct or indirect costs of private production shifted to the government budgets, to taxpaying workers as a whole. Therefore there is a *public cost and a private benefit*. In this way, corporations have successfully defended their profits.

GROWTH OF THE PUBLIC SECTOR

The relationship between the state and the class interests it represents is an involved and complex subject. [8] In order to arrive at any understanding of the state, and the role of the state in the development of the public sector, it must be realized that there is a dynamic interaction and overlapping of economic and social interests between national, regional and local capital. [9] Only in the broadest sense can we speak of a homogeneous ruling class whose interests are defined in terms of the right to expropriate the economic surplus (profits), maintain private property (as opposed to personal property) and the sancity and enforceability of contract. The state serves a number of different, although related, economic and political functions which directly or indirectly serve corporate and finance interests of the ruling class. Any theory of the state which attempts to deal in any predictive fashion with the behaviour of the "agency of the ruling class" must take into account, as Paul Sweezy has argued, that : [10]

1. There are conflicts between the true long-run interests of the ruling class as a whole and the

20

short-run interests of particular segments of it ;

2. Under certain circumstances, other classes or segments of classes can force the state to make concessions to their interests.

However in the long-run :

" ... *it doubtless remains true that* in general *the state serves the interests of the ruling class. But in any given situation the range of alternatives is wide and the course to be followed by the state is far from mechanically predetermined".*

Only by understanding the implications of the trade-offs involved, in the above qualifications for the state, can we account for the national peculiarities of the role of the state in capitalist economic development be it the Junkers' Germany, Meiji's Japan or John A. MacDonald's Canada. [11]

The state in advanced capitalist economies has been the administrator of the public sector in the interests of the ruling class. Simultaneously, the state has been forced to make short-run concessions to the working class in order to protect the long-run survival of the existing social system in the interests of the ruling class.

The growth of the public sector has been a direct and indirect response to the various needs of the private profit-making corporate sector of the economy. One of the key functions of the State according to economist H. Patton is to, " ... take upon itself the function of compensating for the inadequacies of the private economy by such activities of its own ..." [12] Both in historical and contemporary terms, "compensating for the inadequacies of the private economy" in fact comple-

ments the needs of the corporate sector, lowers costs for corporations by absorbing social overhead costs, and socializies the costs and risks of the private sector.

The growth of the public sector has been a necessity for the expansion of the private profit-making sector because it compensated for the inadequacies of the private economy. Further growth of the public sector will be necessitated to meet corporate needs and will be paid for by workers through the taxation and budgetary mechanisms.

The state in Canadian economic history has played a major role in guiding and stimulating economic development. Given the interaction and over-lapping of economic and social interests between national, regional and local capital each level of government operated within its particular limitations to achieve its objectives. Within this framework Canadian governments have seen themselves as partners with business. Historian Kenneth McNaught writes that, "The duty of government, in the eyes of most businessmen, was to step in to provide a climate and facilities favourable to investment whenever private capital either failed or was unwilling to do the job." [13] In Canada the state has been used by a weak business class to undertake and protect activities which this class could not carry out itself. Therefore in the final analysis, "the creation of a national economy," economic historian H.G. Aitken can say, "was as much a political as an economic achievement." [14]

Historically, the Canadian government at various levels has served corporate interests through a variety of means. It was to make land grants and allow free homesteading. It was to aid building a national railway system by borrowing abroad and lending its credit through its guarantee. Tariff-protected industrialization was a systematic attempt to develop the corporate sector. "The assertion that the State," Aitken writes, "in the form of the federal government was merely acting as the agent . . . of private economic interests — the sale of the Hudson's Bay Company lands, and the chartering of a Pacific railroad — could probably be supported." [15]

The Provincial governments laid the infrastructure to support the corporate sector by heavy investments in education, highways, and the nationalization of hydroelectric power. For example in Ontario within two decades, many key sectors of the infrastructure were laid nearly simultaneously. In that period between 1900-1925, hydroelectric power was provincialized, important concessions by the provincial government were made to corporations like INCO, and highways were built into the mining regions of the northern interior. [16]. Thus under state guidance the infrastructure was laid which was necessary for a modernized economy.

More recently both the Federal and Provincial governments by sharing the overlapping fiscal responsibilities to national, regional, and local capital have aided the corporate sector by making steep investments in human capital (people) such as manpower retraining, health and welfare services, worker mobility, research and development, and exploration for natural resource development. And where private industry has been too timid to risk its own money, the Federal and Provincial governments have created Crown corporations in key areas of the economy.

The pattern of government expenditures in the public sector has also served to further re-enforce the "metropolis-hinterland" relationship between the U.S. and Canada. Especially on the Provincial level, the pattern of government expenditures has systematically balkanized the Canadian economy by rationalizing the development and exploitation of key sectors of the economy.

A brief analysis of key areas of the economy will show how the government at various levels through the development of the public sector has served corporate interests.

RAILROADS & AIRLINES

From the early 1850's building and operating railways was a major concern of Canadian businessmen. A number of Fathers of Confederation were solicitors for railways and attached a great deal of importance to their construction. Through transcontinental railway construction the Federal government took a prominent part in developing the corporate economy between 1867 and 1914. [17] The Railway Act of 1881 called for a subsidy of $25 million and 25 million acres to business interests which would provide the necessary transportation network and linkages to markets. The East-West linkage, it was hoped, would protect the interests of Canadian businessmen by preventing American corporate penetration and competition.

The railway lobby at the turn of the century was so powerful that Canada was not a country with a railway but a railway with a country. One politician of this period openly proclaimed, "Railroads are my politics." Sir Thomas White, minister of finance in 1917, put the case in the House:

" . . . the large financial assistance which we have been granting to these companies . . . is against public policy while the ownership of

*these roads is in private hands...
If the public does the financing,
the public should enjoy the re-
ward.*" [18]

The Canadian National, created in
1923 through mergers of bankrupt
trunk lines was publicly owned not
by design but by necessity. Much of
the vigor of the economy in the 1920's
would have been inhibited had not the
Government rationalized railway transportation.

The following table indicates that
the corporate community is the prime
user of rail services.

RAILWAY OPERATING REVENUE, 1969

SOURCES OF RAILWAY OPERATING REVENUE	% OF TOTAL REVENUE
Freight service	85.0%
Passenger service	6.8
Other	8.1

*Source: Railway Transport Financial Statistics,
1969. D.B.S., 1970, Table I.*

More recently the 1951 MacPherson
Royal Commission report was blunt on
the economics of the privately owned
CPR : "To the extent that... rail
pasenger services (are) operating at a
loss... it shall be the responsibility of
the nation to bear that loss." [19] Jean
Marchand, then president of the
CNTU, warned that, "... transportation policy... must be linked to the
common good and not the profitability
of private enterprise." [20]

Airlines too primarily serve corporate interests at public expense. Trans-
Canada Airlines, the precursor to
Air Canada, was formed under state
sponsorship because the necessary capital couldn't be mobilized in the private sector for this risky venture.

According to *The Financial Analyst
Journal* nearly 75% of all airline pas-
sengers are businessmen. [21] As with
railroads, airlines receive heavy government subsidies in the form of
such things as public airports, navi-
gation aids, meterological services, and
in part government operation. Airlines
have afforded Big Business a speedy
form of transportation in its relentless
search for fun and profits.

HYDROELECTRIC POWER

The Provincial governments laid the
ground work for the expansion of a
modernized economy by nationalizing
hydroelectric power. An integrated,
rationalized and co-ordinated energy
grid is a necessary prerequisite for
industrialization which is to be carried
on by the private sector. [22] In the
words of economist Ian Drummond,
"... private business has benefited
handsomely from cheap power..."
Hydroelectric power is the keystone
of industry and industrial expansion.
Hydroelectric power is fundamental to
economic expansion because all other
industries depend upon it. The general
planning, co-ordination of services and
equalization of rates was a necessity
for continued industrial and economic
expansion and could only be accom-
plished through the nationalization of
a large part of the private-owned sector
of the electric industry in the interests
of the business community as a whole.

The following table reveals who is
the primary consumer of electirc
power.

ELECTRIC UTILITIES IN CANADA, PUBLIC & PRIVATE, 1969

ELECTRIC ENERGY CONSUMED BY SECTOR	% OF TOTAL ELECTRIC ENERGY CONSUMED	% OF REVENUE FROM TOTAL ELECTRIC ENERGY SALES REVENUE
Industry, as ultimate consumer	42%	31.2%
Industry, with generating facilities	13	5.5
Commercial	15	23.1
Domestic	27	37.1
Street Lighting	1	2.3
Exported	3	.8

(% of total electric energy consumed: first three rows grouped = 70%. % of revenue: first three rows grouped = 60%.)

Source: "Disposal of Electric Energy, 1969," Electric Utilities, 1969, D.B.S., 1970.

What these data reveal are that industry consumes 70% of the total hydroelectric power generated. Yet it accounts for only 60% of the revenue from energy sales. The domestic consumption of electricity accounts for 27% but provides for a little over 37% of the revenue. Despite the fact that utility rates are established on the basis of different elasticities of demand for domestic and industrial consumption as well as peak-load pricing patterns, what is suggested is that the public (i.e. workers) have absorbed or "socialized" a private cost of production for the private sector (and could probably be shown through the use of "separation-formulas"). [32] In the broadest sense industry has used the nationalized electrical utilities industry and had it administrated so that there is a public expenditure and a private benefit in the form of support services and lower rates.

EDUCATION

The education industry fulfills two functions: an increasingly refined training and selection mechanism for the labour force to meet the needs of industry and the enculturation of young students (future young workers) with the norms and values of our corporate capitalist society. [24]

The primary social function of the educational system is to perpetuate, extend and re-enforce what has been termed an "ethico-cultural hegemony." This "ethico-cultural hegemony" is the ideological cement of society. According to Professor Gwyn Williams, hegemony is:

"... a socio-political situation... in which the philosophy and practice of a society fuse or are in equilibrium; an order in which a certain way of life and thought is dominant... [and] is diffused throughout society in all its institutional [forms] ... with its ... taste, morality, customs, religious and political principles, and all social relations... An element of direction and control, not necessarily conscious, is implied." [25]

The educational system is used to infuse the dominant values and ideological outlook of society, the right to profit and private property, among students and future young workers.

No one industry or corporation can afford to train its own labour force. The reason is that there is absolutely no guarantee that their "investments" will not seek employment in other areas. The cost of losing trained manpower is especially high in those industries which employ technical workers with skills which are specific to a particular industrial process.

Thus the costs of education and the maintenance of the educational system has been shifted to wage earners through the tax system. Free public education socialized the costs of educational training and created a labour force which could use new technology. "In order to cope with rapid technological change", economist B.A. McFarlane states, "Western societies have had to raise the level of education and skills of the population". [26]

Universities are no longer just producers of knowledge but are also producers of technical research and of trained labour. The social sciences developed, according to business historian Loren Baritz, because " ... management came to believe in the importance of understanding human behavior because it became convinced that this was one way of improving its ... profit margin." [27]

In general, the basic economic function of the education industry is to meet the manpower requirements of private profit-making industry. By supplying educated and trained workers, the educational system complements the needs of corporate production: hence the name "Industrial — Education Complex". A quick look at the *types* of degrees taken in post-secondary education substantiates the claim that the primary purpose of education is to supply the needs of the private sector of the economy.

As seen below nearly 44% of all post-secondary school students are trained to meet the needs of industry (broadly defined). This is even more apparent for community colleges and CEGEP's. The Economic Council of Canada has said : Community Colleges "can ... best be described as multipurpose institutions making ... education more readily applicable to manpower needs ... "

COURSES OF POST-SECONDARY SCHOOL STUDENTS, 1968-69

TYPE OF PROGRAM	% OF TOTAL ENROLLMENT IN POST-SECONDARY SCHOOLS	
Engineering and Architecture	7.2%	
Science	14.5	
Commerce	5.1	43.6%
Law	1.3	
Technical & Vocational (Community Colleges & C.E.G.E.P.'s)	15.5	
Liberal Arts	30.4	
Education and Teacher Training	12.1	
Health Fields (Medicine, Dentistry)	9.4	
Other	4.5	
TOTAL	100.0	

Source: Calculated from Post-Secondary School Student Population Survey, 1968-69, D.B.S., 1970, pp. 119-21.

FIELD OF SPECIALIZATION OF COMMUNITY COLLEGE GRADUATES, 1969

FIELD OF SPECIALIZATION	% OF GRADUATES IN FIELD OF SPECIALIZATION AS A % OF TOTAL
Technologies and Vocational Programs	60% ⎫
Business and Commercial	12 ⎬ 72%
Applied Arts	6 ⎭
University Transfer Programs	22
TOTAL	**100**

Source : Canadian Community Colleges and Related Institutions, 1969-70, D.B.S., Table 4.

With respect to Community Colleges the figures speak graphically for themselves : 72% of all community college graduates are trained for the industrial labour market.

The educational system also plays a key role in absorbing surplus manpower, especially in the 18-24 year old range. As can be seen in the following table nearly a quarter of those people in the 18-24 year category who might otherwise be out on the labour market have been removed from it and absorbed into the educational system. In a mature capitalist economy the education industry fulfills a dual function by being one of the primary employment and income generating sectors of the economy as well as absorbing surplus manpower. [28]

Thus, the Education Industry is Big Business whose primary purpose is to educate and train the labour force. Education which is a cost of production has been shifted from corporations, through the tax system, to workers. Working class families subsidize the cost of higher education for middle and upper class families. [29]. The "Industrial-Education Complex" reinforces itself. What better community of interests could there be ?

POST-SECONDARY ENROLLMENT AS A PERCENTAGE
OF THE 18-24 YEAR OLD POPULATION, CANADA

	CANADA	
	POST-SECONDARY	UNIVERSITY
1955–56..	6	5
1960–61..	9	7
1965–66..	13	11
1970–71..	20	16
1975–76..	24	20

Source : 4th Annual Review of The Economic Council of Canada, 1967. p. 69.

HIGHWAYS AND
TRANSPORTATION LINKS

A highly developed transportation system is a necessary prerequisite for a mature capitalist economy. A transportation system links resource, product and labour markets together resulting in what Commons termed the "nationalization of the market place" thereby enabling corporations to achieve optimal economies of scale.

Highway expenditures complement private investments in manufacturing and distribution facilities, encourage new private investments, link up the major metropolitan centers, facilitate the mobility of labour, and provide a kind of social consumption—or goods and services consumed in common. Outlays on other forms of transport, communications, water supplies pipelines, utilities, and the like also simultaneously provide inputs to private industry and services to workers.

The most important provincial investments serving the interests of specific industries are highway expenditures. [30] Domestic economic growth since World War II has been led in part by suburban residential construction, which requires an enormous network of complementary highways, roads, and ancillary facilities. Rejecting public transportation, on the one hand, and toll highways, on the other, the state has "socialized intercity highway systems paid for by the taxpayer— not without great encouragement for the rubber, petroleum, and auto industries." [31]

Road transport intensifies the fiscal crisis of the cities, owing to the removal of land from the tax rolls for freeways, access roads, and ancillary facilities. Simultaneously, the cities' commuting population places an extra burden on city expenditures in the form of traffic control, parking facilities, and the like.

On the provincial level the pattern of public expenditures in the public sector has re-enforced the "metropolis-hinterland" relationship between the US and Canada. The tremendous sums spent developing the transportation grid — railroads, highways, pipelines — have permitted a systematic, rationalized exploitation of the natural resource sector of the Canadian economy.

In various provinces such as the B.C. interior, the Prairies and northern Ontario and Quebec, the transportation system has served corporate interests, especially American, by linking the Canadian resource base to the American product market. One financial institution has said that :

> " . . . the economy of the Prairie provinces has been dominated by the fortunes of a few export products and by the vital importance of transportation links.
>
> Development of the oil and gas industry, like that of wheat, has been closely tied . . . to the building of transportation facilities." [32]

The economy of British Columbia is dependent upon resource-based industries. "In a province so vast," another financial institution reports, "good transportation facilities are vital."

> "In British Columbia lines of communication have been expanded into a well-developed system of highways, railways, internal airlines, and ferry and steamship services." [33]

This transportation grid is responsible for providing links as industry develops and has been responsible for much of the development in the central and northern regions of B.C. by opening up rich timber and mineral resources.

Since World War II, hundreds of millions of dollars have been spent in British Columbia to extend and improve the highway system. This has been especially true in the 1960's since industrial development began to shift to the interior regions of the province.

The transportation system is a key part of an economy's infrastructure in that it links the economy together. The state by underwriting the expenses of the transportation grid and "socializing" its costs has intensified the "urban crisis" in one instance, and has been responsible for re-enforcing the economic dependence of the Canadian hinterland upon the industrialized metropolis to the south in another.

RESEARCH AND DEVELOPMENT

The intervention of the state through government grants to finance research programs, to develop new technical processes, and to construct new facilities and mobilize resources has converted production to a more social process. The motivation for this research and development was to aid industry by advancing new production processes and lowering costs. This cost is in part borne as a public expenditure — to help corporations and corporate profits.

As indicated in the table below Government and Big Business are partners in R & D, government thereby complementing a basic need of the corporate community at the taxpayers expense. [34] During the decade of the 1960's government supplied somewhat over half of *all* funds for R & D in Canada while industry supplied roughly a third. While *direct* R & D subsidies from government to industry in Canada are considerably lower than in the U.S. or the U.K., representing a high proportion of dollars going to government "in-house" projects, these subsidies accounted for 14% of all corporate funds for R & D in 1967. When government-sponsored assistance to industry through the Industrial Research and Development Incentives Act is taken into account direct government subsidies accounted for 24% of all corporate R & D. [35]

The purpose of these programs is quite clear. The basic purpose of the Program for the Advancement of Industrial Technology (PAIT) is to, " . . . to help industry . . . to improve its technology capacity . . . by underwriting . . . projects which . . . offer good prospects for commercial exploitation." The Industrial Research Assistance Program is designed to " . . . create new research facilities

MAJOR SOURCES AND AGENCIES FUNDING AND PERFORMING
RESEARCH AND DEVELOPMENT IN CANADA,
1963, 1965 and 1967

Year	INDUSTRY		GOVERNMENT		HIGHER EDUCATION & PRIVATE NON-PROFIT	
	Source of Funds	Performing R & D	Source of Funds	Performing R & D	Source of Funds	Performing R & D
1963	33%	40%	54%	42%	10%	17%
1965	32	43	51	36	13	21
1967	31	38	53	35	13	27

*Source : Industrial Research and Development Expenditures in Canada, 1967. D.B.S. Table I, p. 61.
Figures are for the latest year available.*

28

within industrial companies and to expand existing facilities." The Industrial Research and Development Incentives Act was passed to " ... provide general incentives to industry for the expansion of scientific research and development ..." [36] As is also clear both industry and government are now less directly involved in performing R & D functions which have been increasingly shifted to and performed by universities.

According to a former editor of *Business Week,*

"Most research prognosticators today believe that, although the government's annual investment will probably not increase much in the decade ahead, it will probably not decrease much either. The reason lies in the role Federal spending has come to assume in basic research. Basic research, especially in some of the newer fields of physical science costs big money. Except for the very largest companies, few individual corporate budgets are big enough to support this highly risky research investment." [37]

Historically, the direct intervention of the government in R & D in Canada can be explained in terms of the influence of multinational corporations in this field. A recent study by Dr. Arthur Cordell of the Science Council of Canada showed that there is little spin-off done in this country by subsidiaries of foreign-owned multinational corporations. Most of their important work will be undertaken in the U.S.

A recent survey of the impact of multinational corporations in Canada on R & D reveals how distorted the situation has become and why the Federal government must supply this vital service to the business community as opposed to funding R & D through industry. In six selected programmes of R & D funds going directly to industry, 57.3% of the funds were going to multinational corporations.

It is quite evident that countries showing a high rate of patent filings by residents of that country are also those countries showing the strongest industrial development. Conversely, countries with a low rate of patent filings by residents are almost, with the exception of Canada, underdeveloped countries with a poorly developed manufacturing sector.

Patent Statistics for the Year 1968

Country	per 100,000 population Resident applications
Switzerland	100
Japan	75
Sweden	58
United Kingdom	50
Australia	40
United States	34
Argentina	12
Mexico	8
Canada	8

Source : Survey by G.A. Rolston, Patent and Trade Mark Agent, reported in *Canadian Dimension,* August, 1971.

Thus, R & D, a basic of industry, has been directly and indirectly funded by government grants, subsides, non-repayable loans, income tax deductions and expenditures on higher education to offset the distorted R & D pattern in Canada. All these costs are absorbed by tax paying wage earners through the tax system. Thus for corporations there is a public expenditure and a private benefit.

GOVERNMENT CORPORATIONS

The State (Government) at different levels complements the needs of the corporate community by its direct or indirect involvement and investment in the industrial and financial sectors of the economy. The government has intervened in these sectors, broadly speaking, either to supply goods and services for which the business community could not mobilize funds or because these enterprises entailed a high risk investment which private business did not wish to undertake or because the industry or enterprise had become unprofitable for the private sector.

The Economic Council of Canada has stated that :

"Government agencies in Canada ... engage in a number of commercial activities. These include the provision of transportation services (such as CNR, Air Canada, various federal and provincial ferries, and harbour and airport facilities), communications services (such as the telephone services provided by various provincial governments), and other public utilities such as hydro commissions and municipal waterworks. Two provinces—Ontario and Alberta—provide some ser-

vices similar to those of banks or trust companies. Other government-owned business enterprises produce products ranging from synthetic rubber and uranium to bricks and tiles.
Governments engage in a variety of financial activities. A number of government agencies act as financial intermediaries, often channeling funds into areas that might otherwise suffer from imperfections in capital markets. Examples in Canada include Central Mortgage and Housing Corporation, the Industrial Development Bank, the Farm Credit Corporation, the Ontario Housing Authority, Industrial Estates Limited (Nova Scotia), the Alberta Municipal Financing Corporation, La Caisse de dépôt et placement du Québec, to name only a few. Many of these organizations have appeared on the scene only since the Second War." (8th Annual Review, ECC, 1971).

According to Philip Mathias, assistant editor of the *Financial Times* :

"... few of Canada's Crown corporations are inspired by the need to create jobs for the unemployed or to help the unfortunate. ... Crown corporations have been set up for special historical reasons. Canadian National Railway Co. was formed by the merger of several private railroads in northern Canada that were unable to operate profitably but were needed for development of such places as Sudbury and Timmins. Air Canada was created because there was not sufficient private capital to

*set up a Canadian-owned airline.
Polymer Corp., the rubber producer in Sarnia, was formed during
World War II because Canada
needed a rubber producer in a
hurry.*

*At the federal level, the 1960s
brought many major assistance
programs such as the Agricultural
Rehabilitation and Development
Act (ARDA), the Fund for Re-
gional Economic Development
(FRED), the Area Development
Incentives Act (ADA) and the
Atlantic Development Board
(ADB) ..."* [88]

Mr. Anthony Hampson, the Chairman of the newly formed Canada Development Corporation has stated that
the purpose of the CDC is to, " ...
help develop ... strong Canadian-
managed corporations in the private
sector ..." Again according to Mathias :

*"Provincial ownership of Canada's
power generation and distribution
facilities is as much for the benefit
of free-enterprise industry which
needs a reliable power source as
it is for the domestic user.*

*At the provincial level, the new
lending agencies like the Manitoba
Development Fund and Nova Scotia's Industrial Estates Ltd. were
born, and endowed with the power
to borrow large sums of money for
assistance programs.*

*In the late 1950s and early 1960s,
many provincial agencies for at-
tracting industry were created. The
most controversial have been the
Manitoba Development Fund
(MDF) and Nova Scotia's Industrial Estates Ltd. (IEL). Both IEL*

*and MDF were made responsible
to a board of directors which,
though appointed by the Government, was not directly responsible
to the Government for the activities of the corporation. The directors were all members of the business establishment.*

*As Woodrow Lloyd, the former
leader of the NDP opposition in
the Saskatchewan legislature sum-
med up the matter, Saskatchewan
had assumed 80% of the risk of
the project in return for 30% of
the equity. Additional commissions
and fees for supplying the machinery and looking after the sales
of the product make the [private]
returns ... even greater".* [39]

Thus through the Government(s),
corporate interests have been able to
use the public sector as a way in which
to build the technical and supportive
services needed by industry, make
public the risk of new investment and
use the government to lay out "complementary" investment to stimulate
profitable business opportunities for
the private sector. These costs are
borne by tax paying workers, thus
resulting in a public expenditure and
a private benefit.

The increasing role of government
in the management of the economy
"to provide the frame work for stability and growth" of the corporate
sector has resulted in an increasingly
important role in public investment.
This investment has taken two forms :
complementary investment to stimulate
new and profitable business opportunities and discretionary investment,
such as contracyclical Keynesian policies, to maintain stability and growth.

RELATIVE IMPORTANCE OF GOVERNMENT INVESTMENT IN CANADA, 1926-1970

YEAR	% PUBLIC INVESTMENT	% TOTAL BUSINESS INVESTMENT
1926	13.1%	86.9%
1950	14.9	85.1
1955	16.6	83.4
1960	19.0	81.0
1965	17.2	82.8
1970	18.0	82.0

Source: D.B.S., National Accounts, Income & Expenditure 1926-1956 and for selected years

As can be seen above, the level of public investment as a long-run trend has *increased* from roughly 13% to 18% of all investment in Canada. This has been accompanied by a corresponding *decrease* in the level of business investment from nearly 87% to 82% of all investment.

Not only has the absolute volume of public investment increased to nearly a fifth of all investment in Canada, but investment flowing from the public sector has in the past five decades increased at a faster rate than investment coming from the private sector.

Between 1926 to 1970 the rate of public investment *increased* by 27.2% while the rate of investment from business *declined* by 6%. In the post war period, 1950 to 1970, the rate of public investment increased by nearly 21% while the rate of business investment dropped off by nearly 4%.

Thus, the State (government) through the public sector and public investment has in large part, directly and indirectly, become responsible for providing an environment of stability and growth for the corporate sector. The management of the public sector is basically for the interests of the business community at public expense with a private benefit.

The steady expansion of government expenditures and the increase in the number of economic functions has proceeded without interruption.

PERCENTAGE INCREASE IN BUSINESS AND PUBLIC INVESTMENT AS A PERCENTAGE OF TOTAL INVESTMENT, 1926-1970

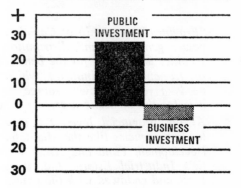

PERCENTAGE DISTRIBUTION IN CANADA OF VALUE ADDED OR NATIONAL INCOME ORIGINATING BY INDUSTRY, SELECTED YEARS 1870-1969

YEAR	PRIMARY INDUSTRIES (AGRICULTURE, FISHING, FORESTRY)	SECONDARY INDUSTRIES (MANUFACTURING, MINING, CONSTRUCTION)	TERTIARY INDUSTRIES (PUBLIC UTILITIES, GOV'T, SERVICE)
1870	44.9%	22.0%	20.9%
1890	36.6	28.1	26.7
1910	30.2	29.7	33.6
1929	18.3	31.0	56.6
1950	17.9	36.3	48.4
1960	.7.0	39.0	46.0
1969	5.0	37.0	58.0

Source: O. J. Firestone. Canada's Economic Development, 1867-1953, and "Gross Domestic Product at Factor Cost by Industry, 1926-1969."

Note: For 1870 to 1920 inclusive, the figures represent value added; for 1929 to 1969 data pertains to income. A "total industry" figure would not total 100 due to adjustments.

The above table indicates that over the past 100 years the level of national income originating in the tertiary (public service) sector of the economy has increased from nearly 21% in 1870 to 58% in 1969.

State expenditures in relation to Gross National Product have risen more or less steadily from the nineteenth century to the present. The level of government activity and economic functions, and the resulting increase in

GOVERNMENT EXPENDITURE AS A PERCENTAGE OF GROSS NATIONAL PRODUCT

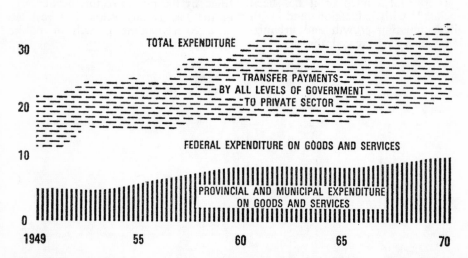

Note: Total Expenditure is not of intergovernmental transfers. Transfer payments by all levels of government to private sector include subsidies and debt interest charges.

Source: Based on data from Dominion Bureau of Statistics and estimates by Economic Council of Canada.

national income from this sector of the economy, has been a response to the increased expenditures required by the corporate sector.

In the post-war period government expenditures and purchases from the private sector have played an increasingly important role in the economy.

Government spending for all purposes in 1970 amounted to close to one third of Gross National Product. The direct use of resources by government—that is, the community's collective consumption of resources as measured by government purchases of goods and services—was just nearly one fifth of Gross National Product. This nevertheless represents a substantial increase in the proportion of the nation's resources which has gone to fill corporate and public needs since the end of the war. In 1949, government purchases of goods and services represented only 13.0 percent of Gross National Product. The greater part of this increase has taken place at the provincial-municipal level of government ; much of it has been associated with education and with swift population growth and urbanization which has created the need for a rapid extension of all types of services coming within the jurisdiction of these two levels of government. [40]

"Non-exhaustive" government expeditures in the past 20 years have increased as well. "Non-exhaustive" expeditures are essentially political expenses taking the form of income transfers, direct or indirect subsidies and debt charges. These political expenses undertaken by the Government in the form of non-exhaustive expeditures, and paid for by tax paying workers, are a necessary lubricant to maintain social peace and to preserve the existing social arrangements.

The heavy demands by the corporate sector on the government budgets is resulting in expeditures out-stripping revenues. It is the public employee who will be penalized the most.

GROWTH IN PUBLIC EMPLOYMENT

The rapid growth and expansion of the economic and social functions fulfilled by the public sector, particularly in the last twenty years, has resulted in a corresponding growth of public employment.

GROWTH OF GOVERNMENT EMPLOYMENT, BY LEVEL OF GOVERNMENT, AS A PERCENTAGE OF THE LABOUR FORCE AND GAINFULLY EMPLOYED, 1961-1970

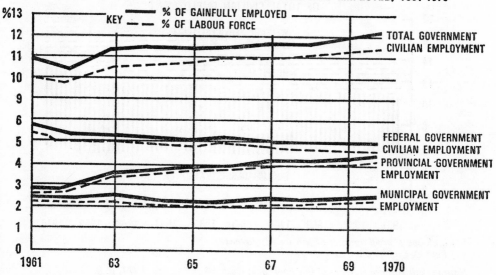

Sources: Federal Government Employment. December 1961 & 1970. D.B.S. Provincial Government Employment, 1961 and for selected years. D.B.S. Municipal Government Employment, 1961-1966. D.B.S., 1968. Local Government Employment, 1971. D.B.S. Also R. M. Bird, Growth of Government Spending in Canada, Canadian Tax Foundation, 1970.

Note: Municipal employment figures exclude transit systems, telephone companies, school boards and municipally owned hospitals. Federal Government employment includes staff agencies and corporations. The figures for "Public Administration" differ because of definitions.

As shown in the above graph, in Canada since 1961 the number of public employees as a percentage of the civilian labour force has steadily increased. Specifically, as of 1970, over 11% of the entire labour force was directly or indirectly employed by the various levels of Government. Of more importance is the trend which indicates that an increasing proportion of those EMPLOYED (as opposed to just being in the labour force) are dependent upon the State for their livelihood. Between 1961 and 1971 the percentage of those gainfully employed and who had jobs in the public sector increased from 10.8% to roughly 12.2%.

If we use a broad definition of the public sector and public employment an even larger proportion of the labour force is employed and is thus dependent upon the State.

By the decade of the 1970's, roughly 12% of the labour force was working directly for the State, while 18% of the labour force was directly or indirectly supported by Government payrolls. This becomes all the more important when we realize that between 1961 and 1970 the gross payroll of all public employees as a percentage of all wages, salaries and supplementary labour income increased from roughly 7% to 14.5%.

There are perhaps no better indicators than these to reveal the importance of Government as a Big Em-

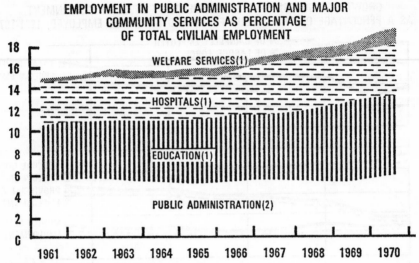

EMPLOYMENT IN PUBLIC ADMINISTRATION AND MAJOR
COMMUNITY SERVICES AS PERCENTAGE
OF TOTAL CIVILIAN EMPLOYMENT

WELFARE SERVICES(1)

HOSPITALS(1)

EDUCATION(1)

PUBLIC ADMINISTRATION(2)

1961 1962 1963 1964 1965 1966 1967 1968 1969 1970

(1) Includes a small number of private employees.
(2) Excludes military personnel.

Source: 8th Annual Review of the Economic Council of Canada, 1971, p. 9.
Note: The figure for "Public Administration" in this graph and the graph above differ
because of the definitions.

ployer which helps to stabilize the labour market, and to a lesser extent the overall economy. The government sector of the economy over the past decade has generated relatively more new employment than the economy as a whole.

It has been estimated in a number of studies, that for the U.S. between 1950 and 1970 nearly 66% of all new jobs generated in the economy were created in the state sector.[41] Unfortunately, because of incomplete statistical data for Canada, a full comparison of the two situations cannot be made. However, as indicated above, in the past 10 years in Canada total civilian employment increased by 38% while employment in the public sector expanded by nearly 47%.[42]

The tertiary sector of the economy seems likely to continue to play a key role in the overall employment situation. The fact that such a large proportion of people make their living in this way may contribute to less marked cycles in overall economic activity. In the recent slowdown, while goods production and inventory accumulation was moderated, it is signifiant that total wages and salaries have continued to rise. This in part is because of increasing wage rates which cover up for the lower employment in the goods-producing industries, but also reflects the fact that the public sector is affected later in economic downturns more than are other sectors of the economy.

In the North American economy, government (the State) is rapidly assuming the role of "employer of last resort." This is because as an advanced industrialized economy becomes increasingly capital-intensive, it creates

A COMPARISON OF THE RATE OF GROWTH IN TOTAL EMPLOYMENT VERSUS EMPLOYMENT IN THE PUBLIC SECTOR, 1961-1970

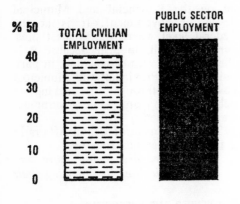

a stratum of workers who are unemployed, under-employed or are employed in low paying jobs in declining sectors of the private sector of the economy.

In the United States, for example, the Federal government has channeled emergency funds through the Public Service Employment Program to provide 200,000 new jobs mostly in the public sector : jobs in public agencies, police, sanitation, street maintenance, education and transportation. In Canada various levels of government have haphazardly become "employers of last resort." Devco in Nova Scotia, the new Opportunities for Youth program the Local Initiatives Program, winter works programs and the regional expansion programs all represent a trend in this direction.

The government's acting as employer of last resort is no longer a temporary policy but is rapidly becoming a permanent feature of the North American economy both in periods of recession as well as in periods of relative prosperity. In Canada all that is needed is a formal policy to give recognition to this reality. [43] Even Keynes was forced to cryptically suggest that : " ... a somewhat comprehensive socialization of investment will prove the only means of securing an approximation to full employment." [44]

The expansion of the role played by the State (government) in the economy and labour market has generated two sets of conflicting forces. The role of the Government in the economy has in one instance helped to stabilize employment and the income stream but, simultaneously this is increasing the financial burden on Government by exerting increased pressure on the expenditure side of the fiscal and budgetary processes. The increasing conflict between Government revenues and expenditures is rapidly assuming the proportions of a fiscal crisis.

• ● •

THE FISCAL CRISIS

What is the fiscal crisis ? What are its origins ? How is it related to the development of the public sector and how does it affect the public employee ?

The fiscal crisis consists of the contradiction between State (government) expenditures a n d revenues, which is one form of the general conflict between public costs and expenditures and private benefits such as profit. [45] In the last two decades the conflict between Government (all levels) expenditures and revenues has intensified. This is a result of Government's increasing its expenditures on social overhead, complementary investment expenditures, socializing (making public) the private costs of production and an increasing volume of public investment. The State budget contin

37

uously expands owing to the increased degree of economic integration and interdependence. This has led to a greater demand for revenues to meet corporate demands made on the budget, resulting in a situation where government expenditures are beginning to outstrip revenues. In the long run this will have profound social importance for all workers and, more immediately on the wages and wage determination process of public employees in particular.

As the data above suggest Government expenditures are beginning to outstrip revenues. Specifically, on the Provincial and Municipal levels of government and on a consolidated basis total accumulative expenditures between 1950 and 1970 have exceeded total accumulative revenues. Only on the Federal level do revenues exceed expenditures. This situation has resulted in all levels of government running a series of deficits, then going further in debt or raising the tax rate.

The fiscal crisis has become focused on the Provincial and Municipal levels of government. It is at the Federal level where the greatest pressure is brought to bear because it is the Federal government which, in part, bails out the Provincial and Municipal governments through its backing of debt creation and intergovernment transfer payments.

The Department of Urban Affairs in a positon paper has stated :

" ... cities are facing more and more difficulties in financing their

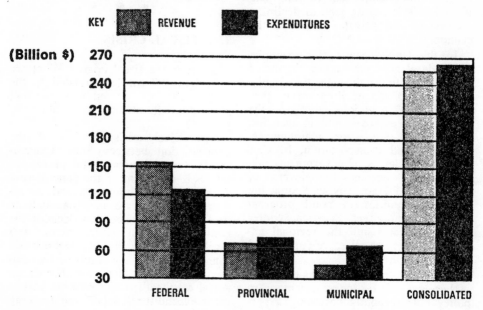

TOTAL ACCUMULATIVE GOVERNMENT REVENUES AND EXPENDITURES,
BY LEVEL OF GOVERNMENT,
EXCLUDING INTERGOVERNMENT TRANSFER PAYMENTS, 1950–1970

KEY   REVENUE   EXPENDITURES

Source : *Taxation Statistics, 1970,* D.B.S., and *National Income & Expenditure Accounts* and *Bank of Canada CANSIM series.*

growing expenditures ... most areas faced with expenditures greater than revenues respond by borrowing or cutting back on public services." [46]

The cities have found themselves in a vicious cycle. Each new hike in the property tax rate drives businessmen and middle-class homeowners into the suburbs. In order to continue providing municipal services with a sluggish tax base, cities must keep pushing the tax rate even higher. In the words of the Mayor of Ottawa, " ... the tax dollar on real estate can only provide so much revenue and we are coming dangerously close to the maximum." [47]

Governments, especially the Provincial and Municipal levels of government, have tried to cover their revenue needs through deficit spending and debt creation. Between 1950 and 1970 this has led to a deteriorating budgetary situation.

This has meant that between 1950 and 1970 total accumulative surpluses were $3.3 billion, while total accumulative deficits were $5.6 billion. This has resulted in a net total accumulative deficit in this time period of $2.3 billion.

The various levels of government by funding their expenditures through deficit financing have had to go to the money market and have incurred a heavy increase in their debt structure. Between 1950 and 1968 the Federal government increased its debt (direct and indirect) by 136%, the Provincial and Municipal governments by 505% and 511% respectively. [48] The Keynesian economists' cliché that the public debt does not hurt because "we owe it to ourselves" misses the point. Interest on debt devours badly needed tax dollars for other purposes. Debt service is now the third highest public expense; most of the money goes to banks which are the major buyers of bonds which governments at all levels sell to cover their deficits.

In order to understand the origins of the fiscal crisis and the conflict between revenues and expenditures it is necessary to understand the relationship between the tax structure and revenues, because *it is taxes which are the revenue.* It is axiomatic in the field of public finance and fiscal policy that revenues determine expenditures. The revenue or income of the government is dependent on the tax rate and tax base.

The level of government expenditures are limited by the level of incoming revenues which are based on the existent tax rates and share of income tax revenue paid by corporations and individuals.

The above graphs describe the corporate and individual share of Federal and Provincial income tax revenue. Between 1962 and 1970 the corporate share of all Federal income revenue *fell* by roughly 38% while the individual share of Federal income tax revenue *increased* by over 23%. With respect to all Provincial income tax revenue between 1962 and 1970 the corporate share *fell* by over 60% while the individual share *increased* by roughly 83%.

Thus it can be seen that corporations have been more than successful in shifting the burden of increased taxation and revenue generation to wage earners. It should be noted that on the Federal level the sharp decline in revenues from corporations in 1966 occurred two years before profit levels peaked in 1968 and therefore is not just a result of the economic slowdown, inflation, or demographic shifts. Given that the corporate share of income tax revenue has sharply declined in the U.S. and Britain over the past decade, despite some cyclical fluctua-

CORPORATE AND INDIVIDUAL SHARE OF FEDERAL INCOME TAX REVENUE, 1962—1970

TABLE 6

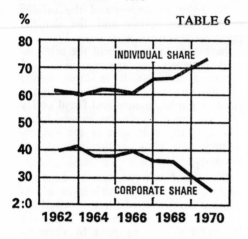

CORPORATE AND INDIVIDUAL SHARE OF ALL PROVINCIAL INCOME TAX REVENUE, 1962—1970

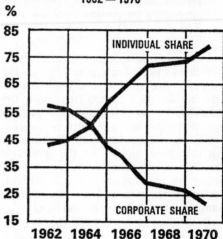

Source : Taxation Statistics, 1970. D.B.S., 1971, pp. 164-165. Calculated on a National Accounts accrual basis. Includes Ontario and Quebec.

tion, we may speak of a general tentency in mature capitalist economies for the corporate share of tax revenue to decline. Furthermore the optimistic predictions by economists that the new capital gains tax will generate about ten times as much revenue in 1985 as now is dependent on the state of the economy. When profits are high so are corporate tax revenues. With the economy beset by "stagflation" the situation is at best murky.

Corporations have not only shifted the burden of taxation to wage earners but the taxation system for individuals is inherently regressive. That is, people in the lower income brackets pay proportionately more of their income in taxes than do people in the higher income brackets.

TOTAL TAX INCIDENCE FOR THE TAX STRUCTURE, 1961

INCOME	TOTAL TAXES AS A PERCENTAGE OF INCOME	PERCENTAGE OF POPULATION
Less than $2,000	60.0%	20.6%
$2,000 — 2,999	32.9	11.7
$3,000 — 3,999	32.2	13.5
$4,000 — 4,999	30.5	14.9
$5,000 — 6,999	32.8	22.0
$7,000 — 9,999	34.2	12.1
$10,000 and up	38.4	5.3

Source : Poverty in Canada, A Report of the Special Senate Committee, Ottawa, 1971, p. 15. J. R. Podoluk, Incomes of Canadians, D.B.S., Ottawa, 1968, p. 247.

FISCAL DEFICIT OR SURPLUS, BY LEVEL OF GOVERNMENT, 1950—1970

LEVEL OF GOVERNMENT	NUMBER OF SURPLUSES	NUMBER OF DEFICITS
Federal	11	10
Provincial	8	13
Municipal	1	20
Consolidated	8	13

As is readily seen, the burden, or incidence, of taxation is unfairly distributed. Total taxes as a percentage of income for people falling in the $2 - 7,000 income range is virtually the same—that is the tax structure is neutral. The incidence of taxation in the higher income brackets is only slightly progressive despite the fact the upper income group has a greater ability to pay and receives a disproportionate share of income.

The ability of corporations to shift the burden of taxation to the public has been made possible not only through the income tax system but more important, through hidden and indirect taxation on the provincial and municipal levels. Nearly 50%-60% of a worker's total tax bill is a result of hidden taxes. According to the Economic Council of Canada indirect taxes rose more sharply than any other major cost component and indirect taxes now account for about 15% of G.N.P.. [49] There are, for example, over 150 hidden taxes in buying a loaf of bread. Most of the revenue generated by the Provinces and Municipalities is through a regressive personal income or property tax structure or through the use of regressive hidden or indirect taxes. By using hidden and indirect taxation which is inherently regressive in nature, the burden of taxation falls most heavily on those who can least afford it or escape it : the workers. That this situation has not changed over the past decade, and is perhaps worse, is indicated in the table below. The total tax bill paid by a worker is the same as some one in the $10,000 bracket indicating a high degree of regressivity in the tax structure.

Workers might have good reason to echo the sentiments of the Beatles' song "Taxman" :

"If you drive a car, I'll tax the street,
If you try to sit, I'll tax your seat,
If you get too cold, I'll tax the heat,
If you take a walk, I'll tax your feet."

ESTIMATE OF TAXES (INCOME TAXES AND HIDDEN TAXES) PAID BY A FAMILY OF FOUR IN TORONTO, 1970

Annual Income	$ 5,200	$10,400	$52,000
Weekly Income	100	200	1,000
Total Taxes	1,965	3,913	25,023
% of Annual Income	37.8%	37.6%	48.1%
After Income Tax	3,235	6,487	26,977

Source : Ontario Federation of Labour, Facts and Figures, February, 1971, p. 6

CORPORATE PROFITS IN RELATION TO OTHER MAGNITUDES

YEAR	CORPORATE SAVINGS (A) AS A % OF TOTAL VALUE ADDED BY CORPORATIONS	CORPORATE DEPRECIATION AS A % OF GROSS CORPORATE PROFITS (B)	CORPORATE DEPRECIATION AS A % OF TOTAL DOMESTIC INVESTMENTS (B)
1929	14.6%	36%	15%
1950	14.8	28	16
1955	17.6	45	22
1960	16.8	56	25
1968	16.3	51	22

(a) *Corporate savings is equal to the sum of "retained earnings" plus "corporate depreciation."* Dept. of National Revenue.

(b) *National Income & Expenditure Accounts, 1926-1968. D.B.S., 1970 Table 8, p. 22 and table A.*

Superficially, it would appear that the upper income group and corporations are taxed in a number of ways — corporation income taxes, property taxes, personal income taxes and now a capital gains tax. In fact corporate interests, for the most part, escape taxation altogether.

Corporate managers completely shift the corporate income tax to consumers and workers in the form of higher prices. Corporate taxes in the post-war years have tended to induce corporations to hide their real profit earnings by inflating depreciation allowances and other cost items as well as maintaining a higher level of retained earnings. [50]

When we take this into consideration we see that corporate saving (retained earnings and depreciation) as a percentage of total value added by corporations in the post World War II period is consistently higher than in the most prosperous pre-war year of 1929. Furthermore, corporate depreciation as a percentage of gross corporate profits has increased tremendously in the past 40 years. Since depreciation, charges have increased markedly, even when taking into account expansion and justified replacement costs, net profits have been

kept low resulting in lower corporate tax rates. It should also be noted that in the post-war period a higher proportion of total investment in the economy has been funded through depreciation as a result of fast write-offs.

These statistical indications support the contention that corporations today have as much profit under their control as they did in 1929, despite the fairly high rates of corporate income tax.

Another tax concession for corporations is unpaid corporate income taxes.

LIABILITY FOR FUTURE INCOME TAXES ALL CORPORATIONS (MILLIONS OF DOLLARS)

	1965	1966	1967	1968
Reserve for Future Inc. Taxes	1,472	1,864	2,301	2,778

Source: D.B.S. Corporation Financial Statistics.

In effect, taxes on corporation profits of approximately $5.5 billion remained unpaid as of December 31, 1968. The amount of $2,778 million represents government loans to business for one specific purpose, to invest in plant and equipment. The loans carry no interest charge, whatsoever.

RELATIONSHIP BETWEEN TAXABLE INCOME AS A
PERCENTAGE OF PROFIT AND FOREIGN OWNERSHIP, 1968

INDUSTRY	PERCENTAGE TAX TO PROFIT	NON-RESIDENT CONTROL
Metal Mining	9%	55%
Oil & Gas	12	69
Refineries	19	99
Other Mining	32	51
Manufacturing	63	59
Electrical Products	37	66
Transportation	33	27
Textile	47	25
Construction	65	15
Wholesale Trade	87	28
Retail Trade	90	21

Source : Calura, Report for 1968

It is tax relief extended principally to foreign owned capital-intensive industries such as mining, oil, and gas and in manufacturing to the larger, capital intensive firms. [51]

In certain key areas of the economy there is a close relationship between foreign ownership and the low corporate taxable income paid as a percentage of book profit.

The above table suggests that there is a close relationship between the high degree of foreign ownership and low percentage of tax paid to profit. This is especially true in the extractive resource sector of the economy. Multinational corporations have not only been able to gain control of vital sectors of the Canadian economy but have also been able to keep the level of taxes paid low thus depriving government of badly needed additional revenues.

Another area where the upper income group and business interests largely escape taxation is the property tax. The property tax falls mainly on workers not businessmen. Within the urban core residential properties assume the larger share, and commercial land and buildings the smaller share of the total property tax burden.

Many studies indicate that owners of tenant-occupied residential buildings usually shift the property tax to their tenants — most of whom are workers. It has been estimated that nearly 75% of property taxes on local industry and retail establishments is shifted to consumers. [52]

As has been seen the tax system is an economic instrument created and used by the State to promote, protect and strengthen the interests of corporations and the upper income group at the expense of working people. Taxes are a political issue, not merely an economic one, because every important change in the balance of socio-economic forces has been registered in the tax structure.

In its most basic sense, every dollar of taxes avoided or given away to business and industry is a dollar more that must be paid by someone else, or a dollar's worth of public facilities and services that are foregone. That "someone else" is the Canadian worker. He is now over burdened with high taxes and poor public services.

And Canadian workers are rapidly approaching the upper limit of their political tolerance.

INFLATION AND PLANNING

The expansion of the public sector has simultaneously built inflationary forces into the economy, and has led to a rigidity in the state's budget. As a result of the tendency towards "stagflation" in mature capitalist economies, short and medium term planning, to control the multitude of increasing contradictions, is increasingly being relied upon by the state.

State efforts to bolster a stagnating monopoly capitalism have led to chronic inflation.

According to the Rowntrees :

"Wages must increase enough so that taxes on those wages can support more workers for government or on government contract. Fewer workers in private production must experience enough increased productivity to support more workers in the government production of services to capital. Increased taxes have also had to finance welfare programs to support the vastly increased number of under-employed and under-paid workers who are victims of the stagnation in new jobs. Profits in the consumer economy have depended on this tax-spending redistribution of worker productivity among workers to maintain consumer demand for goods and services". [53]

Across-the-board increases in wages without increases in productivity and production are inflationary. They are especially inflationary to the degree that there is an expansion of employment and production in the competitive and state sectors, where productivity is relatively low, hence pulling down average productivity in the economy as a whole.

The entire inflationary mechanism is perpetuated because wage increases in the monopolistic-oligopolistic sector spread to the state sector, increasing unit labour cost in the state sector. If monopolistic industries protect their profit margins by becoming more capital intensive workers are "pushed" into the lower paying competitive sector. If capital depends on price increases to protect profit margins, inflation worsens. [54]

Inflationary forces are reinforced and built into the state budget as a result of "social inflation". Social inflation is a result of the budget's rigidity stemming from the increased state expenditures on the economy's infrastructure and reproduction costs and the absorption of the social costs of production.

The contradictions of the State's inflationary dilemma are revealed when : " . . . the government tries to curb inflation by cutting back on spending, as it is doing currently ; it must not only hold down the wages of government workers, but also constrain the size and growth of private profits. Even if the government could find new projects so that it could continue to create . . . new jobs, the mounting inflationary crisis would mean that its new projects would end up undermining the values of private debt and capital instead of enhancing them. Attempts to curb the inflation by holding down government employees' wages or raising taxes, meet public employee and taxpayer resistance ; if they succeed at all, it causes consumption to fall, which undermines the profits in the consumer goods of the economy. Consumers go deeper into debt to keep up their consumption level, which temporarily postpones the problem, but intensifies it in the long run as worker resistance to higher prices and increased indebtedness grows with each successive year. On the other hand, if the governments try to fight inflation by cutting purchases rather than or in addition to cutting payrolls, monopoly profits will fall in manufacturing and construction which will create a further lack-of-jobs crisis in the private sector. If the government slows its expansion relative to the private sector, ... the unemployment crisis of monopoly stagnation will reappear, and even more inflation will be created as unemployed people apply to the social welfare-transfer institutions. These considerations define the fiscal context in which the state finds itself in a stagnating monopoly capitalism." [55]

In order to deal with the problems of unemployment, balance of payments, inflation and government expenditures, many capitalist countries guided by social democratic parties, have out of necessity, turned to short or medium term planning.

The sources of capitalist planning have historically been Keynesian short term demand management, as well as war-time and early post-war wage and price control. "The fusion of these elements under the impact of high-employment inflationary capitalism has produced modern capitalist planning". [56] The national income budget represents an implicit recognition of the relationship between the budget and the private sector, and is a precondition for over-all planning. As it is, according to the Organization on Economic Co-operation and Development, "Most governments now frame plans for the major components of the public expenditure 3 to 5 years ahead."

The purpose of long or medium term formalized planning is to provide the :

" ... close co-ordination of government expenditures with those of the larger private firms plus various controls, including wage policy, over private consumption. This planning aims not only at influencing the over-all growth rate of the economy, but also at bringing about structural changes ... and specific social expenditures designed to strengthen the ... fabric of capitalism." [57]

The state is faced with three basic alternatives to solve the inflation-job crisis : managed recessions, wage and price controls, and increased productivity in the state and private sectors. Wage, price, and credit controls, as evidenced by the events of the last year, are becoming an increasingly viable and necessary policy. It is within this framework that the capitalist state is being forced to turn to economic planning in order to contain its own contradictions.

PUBLIC NEEDS AND PRIVATE WANTS

The social significance of the fiscal crisis is of immense proportions and goes well beyond short-run budgetary issues. The fiscal crisis appears in the form of *both* issues of public policy *and* personal problems. This is because there is an increasing disparity between the flow of private and public goods and services. There is a dangerously widening gulf between public needs and private wants. [58]

The delivery of public goods and services — the infrastructure which supports our economy and society is slowly, but steadily collapsing and falling apart as a result of financial starvation. The infrastructure is collapsing because there isn't enough revenue to support it. The well-known liberal economist John Kenneth Galbraith grimly describes this process of social disintegration resulting from the imbalance between the production of public and private goods and services :

" ... the papers of any major city ... told daily of the shortages and short comings in elementary municipal and metropolitan services. The schools were old and overcrowded. The police force was under strength and underpaid. The parks and playgrounds were insufficient. Streets and empty lots were filthy, and the sanitation staff was underequipped and in need of men. ... Internal transportation was overcrowded, unhealthy, and dirty. So was the air. ... The automobiles that could not be parked were being produced at an expanded rate. The children ... disposed to increasingly imaginative forms of delinquency, were admirably equipped with television sets ... Our colleges and universities were severely overcrowed and under provided, and the same was true of mental hospitals. The family which takes its ... air-conditioned, power-steered, and power-braked automobile out for a tour passes through cities that are badly paved, made hideous by litter, blighted buildings, billboards ... They picnic on packaged food from an icebox by a pol-luted stream and go on to spend the night at a park which is a menace to public health and morals. Just before dozing off ... amid the stench of decaying refuse, they may reflect on the curious unevenness of their blesisngs." [59]

This infrastructural breakdown in the delivery of social (public) services is but another form of the fiscal crisis. In the last analysis infrastructural collapse is inherently a part of the fiscal crisis. As corporations have been able to shift the private costs of production to the public, hide taxable profits through inflated cost items such as depreciation allowances and decrease their share of Federal and Provincial income tax revenue there is less revenue to be channeled into public services and social investment. Since management and advertising operates in Galbraith's words, "to produce a profit ... on behalf of privately produced goods and services, public services will have an inherent tendency to lag behind." This imbalance and misallocation of public expeditures between the public and private sectors results in grave social problems and personal problems taking social forms.

Social breakdown and disorganization, inherent in the development of monopoly capitalism, and whose solution is made impossible because of the fiscal crisis, also takes a highly personalized form. [60] Dr. Daniel Cappon, a social psychiatrist, has constructed what he terms an "index of social malaise and health." [61] This index attempts to measure the degree of social and personal stability, and conversely anomie and alienation, by taking into account social, economic, psychiatric, criminological, and educational factors. When we realize that the incidence of suicide, alcoholism, psychosis and drug usage are increasing : that family breakdowns, child neglect, runaway children and divorces are rising; that juvenile delinquency and the crime rate are soaring and that there is a disturbing increase in veneral disease, illegitimate pregnancies and high school drop outs, it is painfully obvious that the fiscal crisis and anomie compounded on top of one another, result in social collapse and the tragedy of broken or wasted lives.

As a result of financial starvation stemming from the imbalance between the production of public and private goods and services it is clear that social and personal problems are being created, and compounded on top of one another, at a faster rate than are the solutions, incoming revenues and social planning that is necessary to deal effectively with these problems.

Given the present economic and social arrangements, social problems and personal problems taking social forms are never solved, only postponed.

THE DIRTY WORKERS

Workers in the public sector of the economy have become the "invisible man." Many types of public employees have also become "dirty workers." As social problems multiply, society indifferently leaves in the hands of others a sort of mandate to deal with these problems without wanting to know how. The people who are used to clean up or control our social problems have been called "dirty workers" by sociologists Hughes and Rainwater. [62]

The public employee who is a dirty worker has become a zoo keeper and is engaged in a social control function. Social workers, prison guards, garbagemen, teachers and employees in Homes for the Aged are employed to keep our social misfits, inconveniences and undesireables off the streets and out of sight. We have created an en-

tirely new type of worker — one whose job it is to hide and control our society's failures.

Many public services and institutions officially intended to further well-being have become perverted into institutions of custody and constraint. Social welfare workers find that their profession, designed to help, has been turned into one designed to spy and punish. Schools have become custodial institutions in which less and less learning takes place and where conformity-producing classrooms serve a prison-like function. Prisons which are intended to rehabilitate, not punish, people to lead useful lives, only breed more crime. Nursing homes intended to provide our old with care and dignity after a life-time of work have become waiting places to die. Low-cost public housing with its demeaning and rigid regulations and high-rise architecture has produced a high incidence of mental illness, anxiety and frustration.

The public employee who is employed as a dirty worker faces a conflict between the formal and informal requirement of his job. Teachers who view themselves as educators are required to patrol school halls and cafeterias as policemen. Probation officers are faced with more red tape and control from above. Nursing home employees are told to work quickly and not bother socializing with patients; sanitation workers fight to remain "garbagemen, not garbage." [63] Public employees faced with the conflict between the formal and informal requirements of the job have often had to redefine their job and its social purpose.

Society's indifference which created dirty workers and the fiscal crisis which increases the quantity of dirty work has also hindered the drive of public service workers for more equitable wages. In the context of a fiscal

47

crisis which increasingly inhibits meaningful wage and salary increases, all people in the public service sector are becoming more unified in their identity of interests.

Public employees and dirty workers are increasingly caught between the silent middle class which wants them to do the dirty work and keep quiet about it, fiscal strangulation, and the objects of that dirty work who refuse any longer to tolerate mistreatment. Both the public employee and his counter part, the client of public services are dependent upon the State budget to meet their own needs. Expanded and reallocated economic resources, between the public and private sectors are necessary so there is no longer a need for dirty workers.

WAGES AND THE FISCAL CRISIS

The deepening of the fiscal crisis will have important implications for collective bargaining and the wages of public employees.

A number of long run trends will become more severe. First, historically because the government is either directly or indirectly assuming greater responsibility for the functioning of the private profit-making corporate sector and the increased social costs of maintaining the economic infrastructure which primarily benefits corporate interests, government expenditures are outstriping incoming revenues. This conflict between expenditures and revenues is grounded in the development of the public sector. Corporations through the fiscal and tax structure have been able to socialize the costs of production and shift the burden of taxation for the maintenance of the technical infrastructure to workers so that there is a public expenditure and a private benefit. Second, because on both the Federal and Provincial level the corporate share of income tax re-

venue has been declining and the major sources of revenue are derived from a regressive tax system this means that with the continued pressure for public goods and services (expenditures) new sources of revenue must be found in order to meet this demand and to raise wages in the public sector.

The increased pressure for equitable wages for public employees and for increased public goods and services, to promote the quality of life and halt infrastructural collapse, focuses on the central issue : the reallocation of the economic surplus between the public and private sectors. [64] There is only one remaining source of revenue left : profits. The real issue, as it historically always has been, is which class will use the economic surplus, benefit from it and allocate it. In order to expand and reallocate the economic surplus between the public and private sectors, radical institutional changes must occur in the existing political economy accompanied by the socialization of profit.

Corporations in the private sector, in the short run are able to pass on wage increases won by workers in the form of higher prices. Government administrators do not have any such indirect "taxing" mechanism. Wage and salary increases in the public sector given the present fiscal arrangements must be absorbed by wage earners. In the long run, corporations have responded to the militancy of workers in the private sector by introducing laboursaving technology, lowering costs and increasing productivity. Government administrators have been hard pressed to squeeze out increases in productivity in the public sector. [65] There is no way for wage increases in the public sector to pay for themselves except through increased taxation.

In the field of public finance, revenues determine expenditures. The revenue or income of Government is dependent on the tax rate and tax base. Therefore, the wages and salaries of public workers which are government expenditures are LIMITED or RESTRAINED by the level of incoming revenues. The recent work by labour economists Carlson, Robinson, Craft and Owen assumes that, " ... salary budgets (are) fixed" and wages therefore are " ... subject to a salary budget constraint" which suggests that wages in the public sector are determined according to a wage fund theory. [66] The point to be emphasized is that in-coming government revenues or the lack of them as well as political forces, determine the level of wages in the public sector. Thus given the present situation where the corporate demand for Government revenues is increasing and the corporate share of tax revenue is declining means that wage increases in the public sector are a function of the "margin of political tolerance" [67] of ALL workers who will have to bear the brunt of increased taxes in order to fund wage increases in the public sector. With increased unionization and militancy in the public sector, the pressure for increased wages may bring the public employee into conflict with his counterpart in private industry because :

"... the wages of public employees are tax-financed, so that the demands of public employees for wage increases are demands on the real wages of other workers. Public employment is almost entirely service employment, much of it the provision of a personal service—such as teachers, social workers, hospital personnel—and the rest a kind of service that depends more on labor than capital. Only where an increase in capital investment can greatly increase productivity can an increase in workers' wages be granted without decreasing the real wages of other workers (through the increased prices of the good or service produced) or reducing profits. Public employment is non-profit ; so, in effect, the only wage gains the public employees can make either decrease the number of jobs in the public sector or reduce the real wages of workers in the private sector. (For instance, if an office installs an automatic typewriter to answer form letters, it can afford to pay the operator more than a regular typist because the machine reduces the number of typists needed.) But since the public sector has the responsibility to capitalism of absorbing the surplus labor that cannot find work in the private economy, public employment tends not to be automated, since that would eliminate jobs. Therefore increased wages for public employees brings them into conflict with workers in the private economy who must pay higher taxes if public employees are to get higher wages." [68]

GOVERNMENT CRACKDOWN

This poses an explosive problem for the state and divisive pressures within the working class. The growth of the public sector and the state has been for the benefit of the corporate ruling class. Public employees, as workers, are called upon to perform services to capital under the rhetoric of providing public services. Although wage demands may bring public employees into conflict with workers in the private sector, demands to make the state serve the interests of workers, not the corporate community, could bring public and private workers together.

The fiscal crisis has led to tightened government budgets or budget freezes and rising taxes which cut into the real income of workers. If Provincial and Municipal governments fail to get a tax hike, they stop giving public services and start laying off public workers. The day of the secure public service job is over. The public employee is not immune to cutbacks and hiring freezes in education, health care, police, fire and public works.

Because of the dynamics of the fiscal crisis, in the long run, there will be a concerted massive effort to hold down the wages of workers in the public sector. The counter-attack has already begun and for public employees it is a crunch situation.

The various levels of Government, to cope with the situation where expenditures are exceeding revenues, are taking an increasingly hard stand on wage issues. In Ontario, for example, the President of the Ontario Municipal Personnel Association has said that " . . . municipalities are moving towards a more firm position . . . and are ready to stand by it ;" furthermore "the decision to let a wage dispute go to a strike is . . . one which may have to be taken more often." [69] As one Mayor of a large Ontario city put it : " . . . we cannot face increasing costs which bear little relationship to the . . . ability to pay." In British Columbia the Provincial government has imposed a 6.5% ceiling on annual increases for teachers and school board employees. The B.C. government is seeking to impose broader wage controls over a large sector of the province's labour force by imposing this 6.5% ceiling on civil servants, hospital employees and other workers. In Saskatchewan, the now deposed Liberal government used the Prices and Income Commis-

sions guidelines as an excuse to clamp down on wages, particularly in the public sector. In Nova Scotia, the Provincial government is attempting to impose a wage increase ceiling or guideline on teachers and school board employees.

The prolonged major municipal strikes in Vancouver, Toronto and Montreal are indicative of the breakdown of traditional labour-management relations under the pressure of the fiscal crisis. [70] Municipal employers are for the first time using a rigorous costing approach, as in the private sector, in negotiations. Throughout Canada municipalities are using contracting out and layoffs as a way of dealing with the mounting pressure from expenditures. Some of the most bitter strikes, for example the 1971 Ottawa garbage strike, have been against private contractors.

In the health care field where wages and salaries account for 70% of all costs there is increasing pressure to introduce change in the number and type of personnel and better use of personnel to produce greater efficiency and productivity in order to cope with the fiscal crisis. In Ontario the Hospital Service Commission has attempted to impose a 7.2% ceiling on wage increases. The two recent illegal strikes in Toronto hospitals indicate that the system of mandatory and binding arbitration in the health care field in Ontario is losing its legitimacy and is crumbling under the weight of the fiscal crisis. [71]

There can be little doubt that in all of the advanced capitalist societies the most dramatic reawakening and revitalization of the working class has occurred in France and Quebec. Both in France and Quebec the hegemony, legitimacy and power of the state was directly challenged and severely tested. In both situations public employees helped to trigger the labour unrest.

In Quebec a fiscal crisis, aggravated by the accelerated rate of public expenditures for technical infrastructure, begun during the Quiet Revolution in order to telescope modernization because of that province's historical underdevelopment, propelled the recent labour upheaval in the public sector. The coalition bargaining and the stand of the three public service unions in the Common Front representing some 210,000 workers caused the Provincial Finance Minister to state that the cost of the demands would, " . . . cancel all new projects . . . as well as require a tax raise." Editorialists screamed that, "Wage increases must roughly coincide with the province's growth if taxes are not to get further out of line." Premier Bourassa indicated that he may deal with the situation by limiting the right to strike in the public sector.

More recently a Gallup Poll (April 26, 1972) showed that 57% of all Canadians favoured eliminating the right to strike in the public sector. More ominously 48% of all "union homes" and 47% of all NDP'ers favoured taking the right to strike away from public employees. This stiffening attitude, even among those who purport to be Labour's friends is indicative of the political explosiveness of the fiscal crisis. Tax revolts, a political form of the fiscal crisis, are becoming more common. The rejection of new bond issues in B.C. school districts is but one recent example. Reactionary politicians have turned the fiscal crisis on its head and have made public employees the target of public resentment.

The state is being forced to rationalize and centralize the industrial relations system in the public sector. Under the pressure of the fiscal crisis and mounting expenditures, public employers are attempting to impose more direct control over their payrolls. This rationalization is manifesting itself in formal and informal centralized bargaining arrangements. This is particularly true on a provincial and regional basis. In New Brunswick there is already centralized province-wide bargaining in hospitals and school boards. There is movement in Ontario and Saskatchewan hospitals towards regional coalition and/or Provincial bargaining. In Vancouver and the Metro-Toronto area, regional bargaining (as distinct from the already existent pattern bargaining) for municipalities and school boards is a possibility in the future. In all instances the trend towards formal and informal centralized bargaining arrangements represents an attempt by the state to deal with the fiscal crisis by exerting more direct control over labour costs and payrolls. The state by attempting to more firmly control expenditures through centralized bargaining is forcing workers into direct confrontation with the state in its capacity as an employer. This is a path frought with political and social volatility. Yet the state in order to grapple with the fiscal crisis, has little alternative.

The fact is, even compulsory arbitration of wage disputes has failed to keep wage settlements in line with the financial capabilities of the various levels of government. To keep wage demands and settlements "in line" would ultimately require "no strike" pledges and wage controls resulting in the abolition of free collective bargaining as we know it. This raises a whole series of explosive political issues.

THE POLITICS OF THE FISCAL CRISIS

As the fiscal crisis deepens and broadens the public employee like Alice in Wonderland is apt to ask, "would you tell me, please, which way I ought to go from here?" But that said the Cat, "depends a good deal on where you want to get to."

"Political action," Louis-Marie Tremblay Professor of Industrial Relations at the University of Montreal has written, "is complementary to economic action ... it is a supplement to weaknesses of union's bargaining power." [72] What does this mean for the public employee ? In a study session with the Canadian Union of Postal Workers, community organizer and activist Saul Alinsky suggested that, "governments, whether they are municipal, provincial or federal see public service strikes as a loss of votes ..." This means, "with a political employer, the union should be constantly in action, seeking allies and getting people involved and committed."

The burden of the fiscal crisis, in terms of social and economic effects, falls most heavily on State dependents, i.e., workers who depend on their livelihood from the government, and state clients, i.e., consumers of social services such as welfare recipients, and hospital patients. Both the public employee and the client of public services are dependent upon the State budget. This suggests that in the long run, because the fiscal crisis effects both workers in the public sector and consumers of public services that a POLITICAL alliance between public employees and consumers of public services is increasingly necessary to strengthen and complement traditional trade union economic action.

Today, there are few sectors of the State economy which remain unorganized. Welfare recipients have organized welfare rights groups ; student organizations have fought for control of the budget for student activities ; minority groups and the poor are forcing the Government to intervene on their behalf ; public health workers, doctors, women, probation officers, prisoners, even patients in mental hospitals are beginning to organize themselves. All seek better work facilities or better social services, more finances and resources for themselves. This at the same time increases and aggravates the financial burden on the government.

Unions in the public sector, unlike unions in the private sector do not justify wage demands on the basis of rising profits, but rather in terms of the need for better "public services," "maintenance of essential services," or "quality education". It is impossible for people to work in essentially social-public-jobs without their considering their counterpart, the person who uses the services. The economic and social interests of state workers and clients are linked through the state's budget.

The fiscal crisis of the state (the tendency for expenditures to outstrip revenues) is at root a crisis in the form of economic, social and political antagonisms that divide not only labour and capital but the labour force as a whole. [73] The fiscal crisis mirrors and enlarges the social crisis ; the bitterness and conflicts between English and French speaking Quebecois workers, the tension and suspicion between old and young workers, women's liberation and welfare rights struggles. The fiscal crisis, with its contradictions, coupled with the social composition of the public sector, make the public employee as a stratum within the working class, potentially explosive. Young workers, women, new workers and some national minority groups are concentrated in the public sector. Women constitute over 30% of all workers in the public sector ; the proportion of young workers between the ages of 20-24 has increased by 38% in the public sector in the past decade ; women and the French speaking Quebecois are discriminated against. The social contradictions within the public sector are aggravated by the fiscal crisis. The taxes of husbands pay the low wages of wives; the taxes of older workers keep the young out of the labour market, and the taxes flowing from a sub-colony like Quebec support a predominantly English speaking Federal bureaucracy. The existence of open intra-working class conflicts can be interpreted as a sign that the ruling classes' ideological hegemony is breaking down. [74] The increasing social unrest in Canada is not only a crisis over language, sex or generation; it is fundamentally a job crisis, and a crisis over the quality of life for all workers. [75] Central to this crisis, and linking the different manifestations of the crisis, is the State.

Alliances and unity among those who are directly or indirectly dependent upon the government (state) is an increasing necessity in order to struggle against the fiscal crisis. Alliances between school board and university employees (academic and non-academic) and students, between welfare workers and clients, alliances between hydro and telephone workers and the overcharged consumers of public utilities, between hospital and nursing home workers and those who use public medical facilities and alliances between transit workers and commuters are necessary. Simply, alliances between those who supply public services and those who use them must be built in order to fight financial starvation, low wages, deteriorating social services and the fiscal crisis.

The dynamics of the fiscal crisis are such that it inevitably results in widespread social infrastructural collapse, alienation and the worsening of the socio-economic position of those dependent on the state and the public sector of the economy. Increasingly in mature capitalist economics, because of the fiscal crisis, a situation is developing where in Marx's words, the bourgeoisie:

"... is unfit to rule because it is incompetent to assure an existence to its slave within his slavery because ... it has to feed him instead of being fed by him. Society can no longer live under this bourgeoisie ... its existence is no longer compatible with society." [76]

The dynamics of the fiscal crisis in a mature capitalist economy adds a new qualitative dimension to the "laws of motion" of monopoly capitalism and casts serious doubt on the Apocalyptic formulation of social change resulting from the alleged "declining rate of profit." The fiscal crisis of the state is further indication that Keynesian social democracy, with its fiscal and monetary policies, under the aegis of the capitalist class and state is rapidly playing out its last historical option.

These alliances are important as a jumping off point. Employers are not neutral. The different levels of government acting as Employers are not neutral. In the public sector where the Employer is the government there is no neutral agency to act as a "mediator" between the public employee, their unions and the government. For the public employee the logic and necessity for political action is clear: because the government is the Employer and is thus fulfilling both an economic and a political function, in order to have the demands of public employees met as the fiscal crisis intensifies necessitates that the Employer — the State — must be changed so that economic priorities can be reordered so as to deal with the fiscal crisis. In an advanced capitalist society, with the expansion of state functions, there has been a tighter integration — fusion — between the base and super-structure. There has been a greater fusion of state structures with the economic, political, social and cultural systems of society. This increased integration between the base and super-structure increasingly means that the public employee is being forced to directly confront the state.

Because of the fiscal crisis in mature capitalist economies the strength of the state is in fact its weakness. "As state power has continued to grow, the state institutions have become enmeshed in the contradictions they were set up to resolve. Established to prevent economic and social crisis, the state's economic policy has become part of the crisis." [77] The fiscal crisis has undermined the strength of the state. It has rendered it vulnerable to some forms of attack, and may offer a new strategy for social change. As a result of the dynamics of the fiscal crisis there may well be, under certain historical conditions, a qualitative shift in the political center of gravity *within* the working class *from* the industrial sector *to* the public sector which maximizes the pressure against the state apparatus ; with political leadership and a vehicle, this pressure could break the State.

In advanced capitalist economies, as a result of the tighter fusion-integration — between the base and super-structure and because of the dynamics of the fiscal crisis, the public employee is being forced to directly confront the state in the same way in which a hammer is poised to come smashing down upon the anvil. The state, erected and expanded to protect the interests of the ruling class has been rendered vulnerable by the fiscal crisis. What is at issue is power (and more importantly the exercise of state power), not the question of which segment of the labour force generates surplus value. The fiscal crisis has explicitly transferred onto the political plane matters which had previously been

viewed as being decided on the economic plane. The dynamic dimension of the fiscal crisis will make it impossible, in the long-run, for unionized public employees to be locked into the corporatist industrial relations characteristic of the unionized monopolistic sectors of the private, profit-making economy. The dynamic dimension of the fiscal crisis, given political leadership and a political vehicle, will make it impossible for public employees to become "angels in marble." As a result of the fusion of the base and super-structure, and because of the deepening of the fiscal crisis which is simultaneously rendering the state vulnerable and forcing the public employee to confront the state, the bourgeoisie, to paraphrase Marx, may well have produced its own grave-diggers.

As the fiscal crisis broadens and deepens affecting the social conditions of the entire working class and the immediate position of public employees, workers in the public sector will be increasingly forced into action, not because they want to but because they will have to. Building POLITICAL alliances between workers in the public sector and users of public services is a necessary step towards a broader transformation of society. Putting forward QUALITATIVE collective bargaining demands which affect both groups — workers and clients — is a necessary prerequisite to building these alliances. These alliances are necessary to strengthen trade union action in the immediate future in the public sector, as well as serving as a springboard for later politicization. In the short run the fiscal crisis can only be fought by militant struggle and action on the picket line or "dans les rues". In the long run, as Marx suggested, "Philosophers have only interpreted the world in various ways ; the point . . . is to change it." Change it !

FOOTNOTES:

1. The first serious effort to deal with the public sector is Colin Clark, *Conditions of Economic Progress,* London, **1954.** Standard references to the Canadian situation are the annual reports of the Economic Council of Canada, in particular the 1st, 6th, 7th and 8th annual reviews. Other standard references are the *National Income and Expenditure Accounts* and *Taxation statistics* (Statistics Canada). An interesting volume is R.M. Bird, *Growth of Government Spending in Canada,* Canadian Tax Foundation, 1970 ; standard in the field of public finance and fiscal policy are *Public Finance* and *Fiscal Systems,* by Richard Musgrave. Classic works are James O'Connor, "The Fiscal Crisis of the State", *Socialist Revolution* parts I and II, January-February and April-May, 1970 and Margaret and John Rowntree, *On Revolution in the Metropolis,* unpublished, 1970. The author is deeply indebted to both Prof. O'Connor and the Rowntrees. It is interesting to note that working independently, all these parties by using the same methodology, have arrived at nearly identical conclusions.
2. For example the Canadian Union of Public Employees has increased its membership from 106,000 in 1967 to 163,000 in 1971, an increase of about 54%. The Public Service Alliance has increased its membership from 92,000 in 1967 to 120,000 in 1971, an increase of about 30%. Independent provincial Civil Service Associations have also experienced similar growth. Unlike the U.S., public sector unions in Canada are far more structurally rationalized and concentrated in membership. See. J. K. Eaton and K. Ashagrie, *Union Growth in Canada 1921-1967,* Queens Printer, 1970.
3. E.C.C., *8th Annual Review,* p. 11.
4. Bird, *op. cit.,* p. 123.
5. B.J. McCormick, "The State and the Labour Market," *Wages,* London, 1969, p. 166.
6. Interviews with Mayor Kenneth Fogarty of Ottawa in *The Usually Reliable Source,* vol. 1, #2, January 18, 1972.
7. G.A. Steiner, *Government's Role in Economic Life,* New York, 1953, p. 137.
8. The best contemporary work is Ralph Miliband, *The State in Capitalist Society,* New York, 1970. Two interesting articles are Alan Stone, "Modern Capitalism and the State" and Isaac Balbus, "Ruling Elite Theory vs. Marxist Class Analysis" *Monthly Review,* May, 1971.
9. For a general discussion see O'Oconnor, op. cit., part I, pp. 17-22.
10. Paul M. Sweezy, "Has Capitalism Changed ?", in Shigeto Tsuru (ed.), *Has Capitalism Changed ?,* Tokyo, 1961, pp. 87-90.
11. For a brilliant comparative analysis of the role played by the state in modernization in capitalist economies see, Barrington Moore, *Social Origins of Dictatorship and Democracy ; Lord and Peasant in the Making of the Modern World,* Boston, 1966.
12. H. Patton, *The American Economy,* New York, 1953, p. 365.
13. Kenneth McNaught, *The Pelican History of Canada,* London, 1969, p. 222. The standard Canadian economic histories are W.T. Easterbrook and H.G.J. Aitken, *Canadian Economic History,* Toronto, 1956 ; Alexander Brady, "The State and Economic Life In Canada", in G.W. Brown (ed.) *Canada,* Los Angeles, 1950 ; Maurice Lamontagne, "The Role of Government", in E.P. Gilmour (ed.) *Canada's Tomorrow,* Toronto, 1954.
14. H.G.J. Aitken, "Defensive Expansion : The State and Economic Growth in Canada", in W.T. Easterbrook and M.H. Watkins (ed.), *Approaches to Canadian Economic History,* Toronto, 1969, p. 184.
15. Aitken, op. cit., p. 209.
16. For example see Main's *History of the Nickel Industry in Canada.*
17. For the standard histories of the railways are G.P. de T. Glazebrock, *A History of Transportation in Canada,* Toronto, 1964, 2 vols. ; and Harold Innis, *History of the Canadian Pacific Railway,* London, 1923. A popularized and informative history is Robert Chodos, *Right of Way,* Ottawa, 1971.
18. McNaught, op. cit., p. 221.
19. Chodos, op. cit., p. 26.
20. Ibid., p. 28.
21. Robert Brooks Deaton, "Airline Profits under Recession Conditions", *The Financial Analyst Journal,* October, 1966.
22. Paul Sauriol, *The Nationalization of Electric Power,* Montreal, 1962 ; and

Ian Drummond, *The Canadian Economy*, Toronto, 1969.
23. The standard textbooks in the public utilities field are W.F. Lovejoy and P.T. Garfield, *Public Utility Economics*, New York, 1964 ; and E.W. Clemens, *Economics and Public Utilities*, New York, 1950.
24. D.K. Cohen and M. Lazerson, "Education and the Corporate Order", and J. H. Spring, "Education and the Rise of the Corporate State", *Socialist Revolution*, March-April, 1972.
25. Gwynn Williams, "Gramsci's Concept of Egemonia", *Journal of the History of Ideas*, XXI, 4, October-December, 1960 ; and Eugene Genovese, "On Gramsci", *Studies on the Left*, Vol. 7 #2, March-April, 1967.
26. B.A. McFarlane, "Education and Manpower : Some Sociological Aspects of Growth, T.N. Brewis (ed.), *Growth and the Canadian Economy*, Toronto, 1969, p. 76. Also the 7th and 8th Annual Reviews of the E.C.C.
27. Loren Baritz, *The Servants of Power*, New York, 1965 ; for an interesting study tracing the curriculum changes in Canadian universities to meet the needs of a changing corporate capitalism see, Canadian Union of Students (CUS), "Trends in the Development of Curriculum and Governing of Canadian Universities", n.d.
28. John and Margaret Rowntree, "Youth as a Class", *Our Generation*, Vol. 6, #1-2, pp. 160-7.
29. A recent study of the subject is "Commission on Post-Secondary Education in Ontario", *Cost and Benefit Study*, Toronto, 1972. The standard treatment dealing with the class selectivity of the Canadian educational system is John Porter, *The Vertical Mosaic*, Toronto, 1965, Ch. 6.
30. O'Connor, op. cit., part I, p. 37 and pp. 40-41.
31. Ibid.
32. Bank of Nova Scotia, "The Prairie Provinces — Strengthening Resources and Markets", *Monthly Review*, Toronto, January, 1967, p. 1.
33. Canadian Imperial Bank of Commerce, "British Columbia : Centennial, 1871-1971" *Commercial Letter*, (Toronto, May 1971), pp. 2, 7, 8, 11, 12.
34. The standard work is A.E. Safarin, *The Performance of Foreign-Owned Firms in Canada* (Montreal, 1969), chapter 5 ; A.H. Wilson, *Science Technology and Innovation* (E.C.C., Ottawa,

1968) ; H.E. English, Research and Development in Canada," in T.N. Brewis (ed.), *Growth and the Canadian Economy* (Toronto, 1965).
36. Ibid, pp. 11-13.
37. L.S. Silk, The Research Revolution, (New York, 1963), p. 173.
38. Philip Mathias, *Forced Growth* (Toronto, 1971), p. 12.
39. Ibid, pp. 1-7.
40. ECC, *8th Annual Report*, Chapter 2.
41. Rowntrees, *op. cit.* and *On Revolution in the Metropolis*, p. 35-36.
42. Bird, *op. cit.*, Table 49 and 50.
43. This policy is rapidly taking form, "Make-work programs here to stay — Munro", *Ottawa Journal*, March 20, 1972 ; "It's LIP forever if Mackasey Wins Way," *Financial Post*, June 10, 1972 ; "Govts. must provide youth jobs," *Ottawa Citizen*, June 5, 1972. "Ascramble for New Public Jobs," *Business Week*, July 24, 1971.
44. J.M. Keynes, *General Theory of Employment, Interest and Money* (London, 1936), p. 378.
45. O'Connor, *op. cit.*, part II, p. 73-74. That the fiscal crisis is a universal phenomenon of capitalist economies and is viewed with alarm even by Liberal commentators is evidenced by, "Is the U.S. Going Broke ?" *Time* Magazine, March 13, 1972 and Jack McLeod, "How We Favor the Rich at the Poor's Expense," *Saturday Night*, May 1971 ; Canadian Economic Policy Committee, *The Government Sector in the 1970's — Economic Context for a Tax System*, 1971 ; "The Budget Quandry," *Fortune*, June 1972 ; *Economic Review : A General Review of Recent Economic Developments*, Department of Finance, Ottawa, Apr. 1972 ; The Bank of Nova Scotia, "A Look at the Government Sector of the Economy," *Monthly Review*, April 1972.
46. Position paper by Irwin Gillespie, for the Federal Department of Urban Affairs, cited in the Toronto *Globe and Mail*, August 24, 1971.
47. *The Usually Reliable Source, op. cit.*
48. Figures prepared by Governments Division, Statistics Canada ; also Bird, *op. cit.*, table 48, p. 294.
49. E.C.C. 3rd Annual Review, p. 103.
50. For this general methodological approach see Shigeto Tsuru ; "Has Capitalism Changed ?" in Shigeto Tsuru, (ed.) *op. cit.* pp. 51-53.
51. Eric Kierans, "Contribution of the Tax System to Canada's Unemployment and

Ownership Problems," address to the Canadian Economics Association, June 3, 1971 and Cy Gonick, "Taxes" *Canadian Dimensions*, 1971.

52. O'Connor, *op. cit.*, part II, p. 67.

53. Rowntrees, *On Revolution in the Metropolis*, p. 41-42.

54. For a thorough analysis of inflation in modern capitalist economics, the reader is referred to James O'Connor, "Inflation, Fiscal Crisis, and the American Working Class," *Socialist Revolution*, March-April, 1972. Also, Paul Sweezy and Harry Magdoff, *The Dynamics of U.S. Capitalism*, New York, 1972. Especially "Notes on Inflation and the Dollar" and "The Long Run Decline in Liquidity."

55. Rowntrees, *op. cit.*, p. 42. A provocative treatment of trade union action under inflationary conditions is V.L. Allen, *Militant Trade Unionism* London, 1966.

56. An excellent review of planning in capitalist economics is Bill Warren "Capitalist Planning and the State," *New Left Review*, March-April 1972 ; also "Public Expenditure Trends in OECD countries," *OECD Economic Outlook*, Occasional Papers, July 1970.

57. Warren, *op. cit.*, p. 8.

58. The classic works are, Francis Bator, *The Question of Government Spending* New York, 1962 and J.K. Galbraith, *The Affluent Society* New York, 1958.

59. Galbraith, *op. cit.*, chapter 18. A key issue, far too complex to be undertaken in this paper, is why the rate of infrastructural collapse is different between Canada and the U.S. Suffice it to say that the U.S. industrial-military complex and the corollary long run budgetary committments lends a rigidity to the state budget. Conversely in Canada, with its neo-colonial status, not having to allocate the economic surplus in this way affords the state budget additional flexibility for investment in social overhead. See for example, Alexander Crosby, "The Price of Utopia," *Monthly Review*, May 1968.

60. For a fascinating and sensitive analysis the reader might want to refer to Paul A. Baran and Paul M. Sweezy, *Monopoly Capital*, chapter 10 and pp. 345-362 ; for the role of woman in a disintegrating social order see the Rowntree's, *op. cit.*, pp. 11-12.

61. Dr. Daniel Cappon, "Canadian Cities : Their Health, Malaise and Promise," *Habitat*, Vol. 12, #13, 1970 and "Men-tal Health in the High-Rise" *Housing and People*, vol. 2, #4, December 1971.

62. E.C. Hughes, *Good People and Dirty Work* and Lee Rainwater, "The Revolt of the Dirty-Workers," *Transaction*, Vol. 5, #1, November 1967.

63. "We're garbagemen, not garbage" was the slogan of the 1971 Ottawa garbagemen's strike.

64. The classic volume is Paul Baran, *The Political Economy of Growth*, especially chapters 2-4 ; and Paul Baran and Paul Sweezy, *Monopoly Capitalism*, chapters 3-6.

65. E.C.C., 7th Annual Review, table A-1 ; "Federal Output Hard to Increase," *Financial Post*, n.d. ; "City Hall Discovers Productivity," *Fortune*, October 1971 ; "The Push to Boost government Productivity," *Businessweek*, May 13, 1972 ; "A New Productivity Yardstick," *Businessweek*, May 13, 1972 ; A.W. Johnson, "People, Prodctivity and the Public Service," *Optimum*, vol. 2, #1, 1971.

66. R.J. Carlsson and J.W. Robinson, "Toward a Public Employment Wage Theory," *Industrial and Labor Relations Review* (ILRR), Vol. 22, #2, January 1969 ; J.D. Owen, "Toward a Public Employment Wage Theory," *ILRR*, vol. 23, #1, October 1969. These labour economists by assuming that "Salary budgets are fixed" in their models have neatly circumvented the key issue for political economists, which is what are the parameters which establish the salary budgets.

67. The term is used by the late Paul Baran.

68. Rowntree's, *op. cit.*, pp. 18-19.

69. "Prepare for Tougher Stand on on Pay, Municipalities are Told," Toronto *Globe and Mail*, August 25, 1971. During the three major Municipal strikes in the first quarter of 1972 in Vancouver, Montréal and Toronto, Managements' offers ranged from 5% - 7% per year average annual increase while throughout Canada all settlements were 10% per year average annual increase.

70. "More Strikes Simmering in Public Service," *Financial Post*, March 18, 1972 ; "Labour Bitterness Spreads" *Financial Times*, March, 1972. For the U.S. see, Jerry Wurf, "Revolt of the Public Worker," *The Progressive*, December 1970 and "When Cities Collide with Unions," *Business Week*, January 2, 1971.

71. "Hospital Disputes Catch Both Sides

in Dollar Squeeze," *Toronto Star*, July 13, 1972.

72. Louis Marie Tremblay, "Organized Labour and Political Action," *Relations Industrielles*, Vol. 21, #1, January 1966 ; also T.M. Love and G.T. Sulzner, "Political Implications of Public Employee Bargaining," *Industrial Relations*, Feb. 1972.

73. O'Connor, "Inflation . . .", *op. cit.*, p. 38. See for example Kathleen Archibald, *Sex and the Public Service*, Ottawa, 1970 and Gilbert Levine, "The Coming Youth Revolt in Labour," *The Labour Gazette*, November 1971.

74. The concept of hegemony is central to Antonio Gramsci's analysis of the cultural super structure in a capitalist social order. See for example, John M. Cammett, *Antonio Gramsci and the Origins of Italian Communism*, Stanford, 1967, Chapter 10 and Giuseppe Fiori, *Antonio Gramsci : Life of a Revolutionary* (Translation, London, 1970).

75. Rowntrees, *op. cit.*, chapter 2.

76. Karl Marx, *The Communist Manifesto*, p. 78.
Rowntrees, *op. cit.*, p. 38.

77. For the dialectical relationship between the States' strength and weakness and political repression see Alan Wolfe, "Political Repression," *Monthly Review*, December 1971.
Rowntrees, op. cit., p. 38.

THE GROWTH OF THE STATE IN QUÉBEC

by B. Roy Lemoine

The study of the evolution and role of the state in the transformation and maintenance of the system of monopoly capital in both its state and private forms is of crucial importance to the development of the libertarian movement in North America. The contradictions of capitalism in the other industrial nation states, including both east and west Europe as well as Japan, have been brought under control by a "reasonably successful integration of the workers" through varying degrees of state capitalism which were established over a relatively long period of time. The mature industrial states of Europe — West Germany, France, Sweden, and to a certain extent Italy — are able to control unemployment levels partly because the presence of a state-owned sector of the economy allows a certain degree of directive planning. The advanced stage of economic development, the resulting rapidity of social and economic change, the development of the consumer society, the persistence of economic and social inequality, and the relative underdevelopment of social and

health services have led to the rapid development of particular forms of state intervention in the economy to regulate and/or eliminate some of the structural contradictions found in the North America economy.

CANADA AND QUÉBEC — SPECIAL CASES IN NORTH AMERICA

Canada has differed in some respects from the United States in the role assigned to the state in the management and control of the economy. These differences are due to both historical and economic reasons. The generation gap between the two economies, i.e. the fact that the American economy has been at a higher stage of capitalist development, required the introduction by the U.S. of distinctive forms of state intervention including the development of the military-industrial complex, an imperialist foreign policy accompanied by "give away" foreign aid programs, and a reorientation of the civilian sector of the American economy to harmonize with these new developments. The degree to which the American economy is now dependent upon this type of economy was illustrated in a rather dramatic fashion by the reaction to the McGovern proposal to cut the defence budget by 30 billion dollars. Many of the traditional supporters of the Democratic party including the labour bureaucracy are strongly opposed to any reduction in the military-industrial complex.

The desire of the English settlers and the empire loyalists to build an economy independent of the United States, the presence of a social democratic movement in Canada with a state socialist ideology and finally government itself through a form of federalism have encouraged greater state intervention in the Canadian economy. The United States does not have any equivalent to the C.B.C., the C.N.R., AIR CANADA or the Polymer Corporation ; the first three were required for the purpose of maintaining adequate communications across Canada while the fourth was created for the purpose of manufacturing synthetic rubber during the Second World War. It should be noted that only the constant intervention of nationalist, labour and socialist pressure groups has prevented the government from selling Air Canada and Polymer to private interests ; of course these private interests are not interested in purchasing either the C.B.C. or C.N.R. There are signs, however, that social forces are now at work in the Canadian economy favouring new forms of state intervention in the economy. The Lamontagne Royal Commission on scientific research has recommended a massive shift of government funds from the support of fundamental research and the National Research Council to the funding of private industrial research

for the purpose of promoting economic growth through the development of new products. Another indication is the creation of the long-awaited Canadian Development Corporation. The organization formula, the role of the Corporation as defined by the legislation, and the management officials selected certainly do not indicate any movement in the direction of libertarian socialism or even state socialism. Results of similar experiments in Québec suggest that the state capitalist formula will not achieve the desired results — it will not lead to Canadian economic independence, nor will it lead to a socialist Canada.

THE GROWTH OF QUÉBEC STATE CAPITALISM

We have chosen to concentrate on the development of the Québec state and its evolving role in the economy for purposes of research as well as for political reasons. The "quiet revolution" in Québec, begun in 1960 with the election of Jean Lesage's Liberal government has given us the unique opportunity to study the growth dynamics of a state apparatus and bureaucracy, its organization, its class orientation as well as the organs of state power and economic management that have been created — all within a relatively short period of time. The relatively short time available to the different factions of the nationalist bourgeoisie who are attempting to carry out the task of consolidating state power in a Québec whose economy is already functioning as an advanced consumer society has generated tremendous social and political conflict. The failure of the "quiet revolution" to solve the most important problems of "La Nation" including high unemployment and regional under-development as well as those of cultural innovation has already led to the emergence of a critical analysis of the state. All of these must now be solved within a period of rapid economic and social change characterized by the growing influence of the multinational corporation and the consumer society with its planned waste and obsolesence.

It is significant that this critique has led to a growing divergence between traditional social democrats, bourgeois nationalists and technocrats on the one hand and state socialists, marxists and libertarians on the other. The lines have been drawn for or against the "quiet revolution" ; Claude Ryan, editor of **Le Devoir** has strongly opposed the CNTU document "Ne Comptons que sur Nos Propres Moyens" because of its supposed doctrinaire Marxist, non-scientific analysis and for its complete rejection of the achievements of the "quiet revolution". The Parti Québécois program involves the continuation, refinement and completion of the "quiet revolution" which its technocratic faction feels has been betrayed by the Liberal party.

The cleavage that now exists between the nationalist social democratic forces including Claude Ryan and the Parti Québécois and a faction of the Liberal government in Québec, and the main thrust of the trade union movement can be seen by the following references to the "quiet revolution" taken from the main documents produced by the Q.F.L., C.N.T.U. and C.E.Q.* for study and analysis by their membership. In part 2 of "Ne Comptons que sur Nos Propres Moyens", appropriately called "The Mistaken Paths of Economic Independence or the Mistakes of the Quiet Revolution", the C.N.T.U. gives

us its impressions of the origin and results of the quiet revolution :

> How does the French Canadian bourgeoisie see the problem ? ... For these people the problem is not capitalism but the fact that the capitalists are Americans or English Canadians. These people think this way : let us act so that these decisions can be taken in Québec, let us take control of our economy. [1]

But French Canadian capitalists lack a solid base ; everybody knows that. They have not the means to buy back a large enough part of the economy to assure their control. The conclusion : The Québec State must come to their aid.

These ideas, were and still are, very popular. At the beginning of the sixties many people thought this way. This was the era of "Maîtres Chez Nous" ; we thought big, the state and the French Canadian bourgeoisie were going to acquire the means to take control of electricity, forests, mines, oil and the manufacturing sector. It was in this period that the "great government enterprises" Hydro Québec, the General Investment Corporation, Sidbec, SOQUEM, SOQUIP, REXFOR, Caisse de Dépôt, and others were conceived. [2]

Furthermore the Québec 'collectivity' becomes aware that its industrial structure is out of date, and that every substructure (education, highways, health, public service,) is archaic.

Of course the French Canadian bourgeoisie fears intervention by the state ; having no other choice though, 'enlightened' Québec capitalists accept this intervention all the more readily assum-

---

* The initials, respectively, refer to the Québec Federation of Labour, the Confederation of National Trade Unions and the Corporation des Enseignants du Québec. Because the first two have English members their names are used in French and English (in French they are respectively the FTQ and the CSN) ; the Teachers Corporation uses only French and has no English equivalent. The QFL is a member of the Canadian Labour Congress ; the CNTU is largely Québec based (see **Québec Labour,** Black Rose Books, Montréal, 1972, for a history).

61

ing they have sufficient control over the politician and the state.

These latter have easily found allies among the emerging group of technocrats ; these technocrats are, first of all products of a rationalist ideology which posits a more direct role for the state in the economy ; but they are also the leftover from a local bourgeoisie who couldn't fit into an industrial structure dominated by the Americans and the Anglo-Saxons. These technocrats hope that the state will allow them this minimum of power which had been refused them by the external monopolies. The technocrats and indigenous capitalists could thus lean on the old nationalist ideologies. For these 'nationalists' the power to be gained by the Québec government appeared as the means to realize the old dream of being set free from Ottawa's tutelage. The alliance between the capitalists, technocrats and the nationalists thus was made. On the bases of interests and ideologies which often diverged, it was agreed that the state was to become the major means of development, the 'protector of the Québécois'. Henceforth political power was to be based on the idea that the state must be "the engine of development". [3]

The C.N.T.U. feels that these objectives were not achieved. In fact, it refers to the whole effort as a "flop".

"But the concerted drive did not produce the hoped for results for the simple reason that its base didn't exist : there was no single Québécois 'rationality' because each social class had its own rationality founded on its own class interests. It is evident that the Iron Ore Co., Jean Louis Lévesque and the workers of Québec could not agree on a definition of the 'common good'. This fact is even more evident when one understands that the workers have never been fairly represented at the centers of state decision-making. In sum, it is the rationality of the strongest,

that is, capitalist rationality, which triumphed." [4]

At their 21st. congress (1971) the Québec Teachers Corporation included the following evaluation of the Quiet Revolution in its manifesto :

During Québec's Quiet Revolution, change brought about struggle and struggle brought about change. In the course of these interactions, the teacher became a part of the proletariat. Here, as elsewhere, every change in the production sector made itself felt in the educational system. Already under the Duplessis regime, technical schools had been set up to provide for the needs of business and the labour market, both of which required more skilled manpower. ... All this came about through politics controlled by capitalists and had nothing to do with what the people wanted. The capitalists wanted to modernize and consolidate 'their' means of production ; to do that they needed an adequate supply of manpower. As a result a new educational system came into being and worker-teachers had to make do with it whether they wanted to or not! [5]

Although contradictions in the Q.F.L. critique of the liberal state are more substantial than that of either the C.N.T.U. or the C.E.Q. in that it seems to be suspended somewhere between state capitalism and state socialism, its critique of the liberal state is nonetheless exhaustive and penerating.

It is important that this exploitive structure be understood before the documents on the economy are read. Then, the problems described can be better understood. This process will lead to an important discovery about the role of the state. We will see the truth which politicians hide behind slogans. For example, we will see that contrary to what you are led to believe, the state's intervention in the economy does not lead to socialism but instead reinforces capitalist domination. Stripped of its cover, the state is seen for what it is: the exploiter of the working class. [6] The liberal bourgeois state shows its true colours: it is the essential element which supports the capitalist system. Neither the Federal government, with its theoretical powers of economic control, nor the government of Québec, that truncated political entity, is an impartial arbiter in conflicts between the working class and capitalists. Both Québec and Ottawa are agents of economic power which is primarily American, English-Canadian to a lesser degree, and only minimally Québécois. Thus, we must no longer regard the bourgeois state as the defender of the public interest. [7]

The above re-evaluation of the role of the liberal state emerged very rapidly within the Québec trade union movement because of a particular convergence of historical circumstances. These would include a comparatively weak national bourgeoisie, and an organized working class which has played a significant role in development of the French-Canadian national consciousness, particularly with respect to the domination of foreign capital. In most of the countries of the third world the progressive, educated faction of the bourgeoisie which usually led the struggle for national independence has been able to consolidate its state power before the workers and peasant organizations were in a position to establish their own power. The national bourgeoisie of these newly independent nations usually govern through a one party system with a state capitalist type of economy. The Québec union movement and citizens action movements may succeed in pre-empting this type of "self-determination" by proceeding to a radical critique of the state at this time. The critique of the state was also re-cognized as an integral part of the educational and politicization effort by the trade unions in preparation for the major confrontation between the Common Front of all public and para-public state employees and the Québec government.

Of particular interest in this view is a document prepared by Kemal Wassef of the research department of C.N.T.U. for the Common Front, "La Situation du Gouvernement du Québec dans les Affaires Economiques de la Province." Mr. Wassef defined the purpose of his analysis in the following way :

We will try to establish the true role the government is playing in the economic and social life of Québec in the present context. To achieve this, we will study the fiscal policies and budget expenses of the government, being conscious of the fact that we would only be examining a few of the fundamental aspects of the influence of government in the economic life of the province. We will try to establish : who profits from the redistribution of public expenditures throughout the province and who finances these expenditures through their taxes. [8]

An attempt will be made to use Wassef's material to illustrate the growth of state power in Québec as the result of the "quiet revolution," and to develop some insights into the functioning of the liberal state.

THE SCOPE OF THE FINANCIAL AND ECONOMIC ACTIVITIES OF THE QUÉBEC GOVERNMENT

The details in Tables I-V give us a wealth of information about the growth of the Québec state during the period covered by the "quiet revolution" ; if the contribution of the Federal govern-

TABLE I

A Comparison of the Gross National Product of Québec With the Total Revenues Reported By The Three Levels of Government, Public Enterprises and Public Services for The Period 1961-70

Year	Gross National Product	Provincial Government Revenue	Revenue of Public Enterprises	Revenue of Hospital Services (in millions)	Revenue of Educational Services	Federal Government Revenue (1)	Revenue of Municipalities	Total Revenue of the Public Sector
1961	10,226	939	148	32	163	1,576	288	3,147
1962	10,664	1,095	160	38	180	1,626	274	3,375
1963	11,331	1,198	256	40	193	1,701	302	3,692
1964	12,784	1,545	327	39	248	1,709	286	4,156
1965	14,233	1,752	357	40	290	1,783	51	4,276
1966	15,832	1,992	586	40	364	2,057	349	5,391
1967	17,025	2,491	691	41	392	2,198	613	6,428
1968	18,314	2,884 (2)	762	43	442	2,400	650	7,182
1969	20,221	3,114	870	44	457	2,700	727	7,913
1970	21,535	3,785	1,054	44	473	3,000	789	9,146

(1) Total financing of the Federal Government in Québec minus transfers to the Québec Government. The figures, in brackets, are to ensure that the revenue yield of the Federal Government will be similar to Québec's.

(2) Québec, Public Accounts.

TABLE II

A Comparison of the Gross National Product of Québec With the Total Revenues Reported by the Three Levels of Government, Public Enterprises and Public Services for the Period 1961-70 (Data is presented in both simple and accumulated percent)

Year	Revenue Reported by the Constituents of the Québec Public Sector						Revenue of the Public Sector (Provincial Government)	Total Revenue of the Public Sector (Provincial plus Federal)
	Provincial Government	Enterprises	Hospitals	Education	Municipalities	Federal Government		
1961	9.18	1.44	.31	1.59	2.82	15.41	15.34	30.75
1962	10.27	1.50	.36	1.69	2.57	15.26	15.39	31.65
1963	10.57	2.26	.36	1.71	2.67	15.02	17.57	32.59
1964	12.08	2.56	.31	1.94	2.24	13.38	19.13	32.51
1965	12.31	2.51	.28	2.04	.36	12.54	17.51	30.05
1966	12.58	3.71	.26	2.30	2.21	13.00	21.06	34.06
1967	14.63	3.98	.24	2.30	3.60	12.91	24.75	37.66
1968	14.54	4.02	.23	2.41	3.55	13.10	24.75	37.85
1969	15.40	4.03	.22	2.26	3.60	13.35	25.51	38.86
1970	17.58	5.83	.21	2.20	3.66	13.93	29.47	43.40

ment is considered, we see the emergence of a new type of economy characterized by massive state intervention.

In fact in 1970 the revenues and expenditures of the Québec government represented, respectively, 29.47 and 31.82 percent of the gross national product of Québec. These had grown from 15.34 and 17.99 percent in 1961 (Table II-IV). These figures are clear indications of the dramatic growth of the French-Canadian (Québécois) bureaucracy. This is further supported by the decrease in the percentage of the Québec GNP collected and spent by the Federal government : from 15.41 percent in 1961 to 13.93 percent in 1970 (Table II) ; obviously the nationalist demands of the 60's succeeded in transferring some of the power from the Ottawa-based technocracy to a French-speaking Québec-based group. Tables II and IV indicate the nature of this bureaucratic expansion. Whereas the revenues and expenses of the Québec government as a percent of GNP increased respectively from 9.18 to 17.58 percent and 10.13 to 18.80 percent from 1961 to 1970, the revenues of government enterprises grew from 1.44 to 5.84 percent of the GNP (Table II) and the expenses of these same state enterprises went from 2.44 to 5.53 percent of the GNP in the same period (Table IV). The above changes constitute a clear indication of the growth of state capitalist enterprises in the period studied, 1961-1970.

To get a complete picture of the extent to which the Québec economy is now dominated by the public sector we should add the revenues and expenditures of the Federal government in Québec to those of the provincial government. In 1970 the total revenue of all governments and their enterprises in

Québec was 43.4 percent of Québec's GNP, while expenditures of these public and para-public bodies were 45.85 percent of the GNP. According to Wassef, "if we had based our calculations on the net national income instead of the GNP used by the capitalists, the conclusions would have been overwhelming."

A word should be said about the originality of Wassef's approach to the analysis of the public sector in the Québec economy.

Such an approach is unconventional in that it does not look only at the expenditures and revenues of the Québec government but also at the autonomous revenues and expenditures of the state corporations such as the Québec Hydro-Electric Commission and other areas where the state assumes some of the expenses ; these include school commissions, public hospitals and Québec municipalities. We have also indicated the scope of the expenditures and revenues of the Federal government in Québec.

The originality of this approach is that it is not restricted to the expenditures and receipts of the Québec government ; it includes the fiscal and para-fiscal government revenues, the annual increase in the public debt as a percentage of the GNP, the total flux of revenues and expenditures which circulates around or are generated by the different levels of government or whose use by the public administration, public services and specialized administrations which attempt to render minimum services to the Québec community. [9]

Wassef does not accept the legal objections to this analysis raised by bourgeois economists who consider the different types of institutions to be autonomous units.

In fact these objections would be valid on a legal basis. However, on a practical level, following the elaboration of strict budget controls which regulate

TABLE III

A Comparison of the Gross National Product of Québec With the Expenditures of the Three Levels of Government, Public Enterprises and Public Services for the Period 1961-70
(in millions of dollars)

Year	Gross National Product	Provincial Government Expenditures	Expenditures of Public Enterprises	Expenditures by Hospital Services	Expenditures by Educational Services	Federal Expenditures for Québec (1)	Expenditures by Municipalities	Total Expenditures of the Public Sector
1961	10,226	1,036	250	72	206	(1576)	275	(3415)
1962	10,664	1,200	309	56	231	(1627)	299	(3722)
1963	11,331	1,367	513	40	238	1632	381	4171
1964	12,784	1,761	645	48	306	1688	412	4860
1965	14,233	2,025	584	55	417	1774	449	5304
1966	15,832	2,312	852	41	420	1978	547	6150
1967	17,025	2,661	985	41	449	2284	831	7261
1968	18,314	2,995 (2)	974	123	503	(2400)	872	(7867)
1969	20,221	3,348	1,145	94	518	(2700)	959	(8756)
1970	21,535	4,049	1,192	104	534	(3000)	995 (3)	(9874)

(1) Total Federal Government expenditures for Québec minus transfers to the Québec Government. For those years which were not available (in brackets) the estimated figures assume that the funds spent by the Federal Government for Québec will not exceed its receipts in Québec.

(2) Québec Public Accounts 1968-69.   (3) Order of importance.

TABLE IV

A Comparison of the Gross National Product of Québec With the Total Expenditures of the Three Levels of Government, Public Enterprises and Public Services for the Period 1961-70
(Data is presented in both simple and accumulated percent)

Year	Provincial Government	Enterprises	Hospitals	Education	Municipalities	Federal Government	Expenditures of the Québec Public Sector (Provincial Government)	Expenditures of the Québec Public Sector (Provincial plus Federal)
1961	10.13	2.44	.70	2.01	2.68	15.41	17.99	33.40
1962	11.25	2.89	.52	2.16	2.80	15.25	19.64	34.90
1963	12.06	4.52	.35	2.10	3.36	14.40	22.41	36.81
1964	13.77	5.04	.37	2.39	3.22	13.20	24.82	38.02
1965	14.22	4.10	.38	2.92	3.15	12.46	24.81	37.27
1966	14.60	5.38	.25	2.65	3.45	12.49	26.36	38.85
1967	15.62	5.78	.24	2.63	4.88	13.47	29.12	42.65
1968	16.35	5.31	.67	2.74	4.76	13.10	29.85	42.95
1969	16.55	5.66	.46	2.56	4.74	13.55	29.99	43.34
1970	16.80	5.53	.48	2.47	4.62	13.93	31.82	45.85

the subsidies given these different institutions by the Québec government, one can clearly see the scope of government control and influence in these institutions. This control is exerted mainly through the expenses of these different institutions. It is also done via the legislature as with Hydro-Québec and other state corporations. [10]

THE ROLE OF THE PUBLIC SECTOR

If the scope of the public sector of the economy has now taken on such significant proportions, has this accelerating shift from a free enterprise economy to a form of state capitalism been accompanied by a shift in the priorities of the state ? Have these massive amounts of public capital been used to generate community wealth or corporate wealth ? What role is public capital playing at this higher stage consumerism-capitalism ?

After consulting the data presented by Wassef, which in many ways complement those of Rick Deaton (in this book) in the sense that the federal and provincial roles in the economy are complementary, one must conclude that :

> to the extent that we feel that in a society which is divided into social classes, the state constitutes a superstructure above the economic base, built according to the relationship between the different social forces involved in production and exchange, we suggest that most of its activities are only elements of this superstructure and have only been created to allow the state to assume its role in the service of the dominant class. [11]

DISTRIBUTION OF EXPENSES

One of the myths constantly placed before the public by the free enterprisers is that expenditures for welfare, education and health have gotten out of hand, that they are exceeding the capacity of the system to pay for them. Implicit in this claim by capitalists and many liberal economists is that the advanced capitalist states have actually redistributed their spending priorities in favour of social objectives. This was one of the myths spread during the period of the "quiet revolution" in Québec. In fact if we examine Table VI it is apparent that in fact no shift in government spending priorities has occurred ; the percentage of the budget given to education has dropped from 25.9 percent in 1961 to 24.0 percent in 1970, the portion spent on health and welfare had decreased from 28.8 to 25.4 percent in the same period. If we look at the statistics in another way (Table VI) we see that the percent of GNP spent on hospitals dropped from 0.7 percent in 1961 to 0.48 percent in 1970, while in the same interval the amount spent on education has risen from 2 to 2.47 percent of the GNP. In other words the percentage of the GNP spent on health and education, in Québec, did not change significantly since the beginning of the "quiet revolution".

THE QUÉBEC BUDGET, WHO PAYS ?

Before proceeding to an analysis of the advantages derived from the growing state apparatus by the different classes in Québec society, we should establish the sources of revenue of the Québec government.

Québec enjoys a privileged position within the Canadian federal system in that it shares the collection of personal income tax field with the Federal government in addition to collecting

TABLE V

Public and Private Investments In Québec — 1965 to 1970

(in millions)

Year	Public Sector		Private Sector	
1965	1,802.5	(43.5%)	2,336.9	(56.5%)
1966	1,842.3	(40.7%)	2,678.4	(59.3%)
1967	1,813.6	(41.7%)	2,532.3	(58.3%)
1968	1,818.4	(41.6%)	2,554.0	(58.4%)
1969	1,954.0	(42)0%)	2,691.4	(58.0%)
1970 (2)	1,977.5	(42.8%)	2,646.4	(57.2%)

(1) Includes public utilities, institutions and government ministries.
(2) Provisionary real expenditures.
Source: Dominion Bureau of Statistics — Private and Public Investments in Canada.

TABLE VI

Classification of Public Sector Expenses
According to the Different Functions

	Expenditures of Public Sector		
	1961	1967	1970
General Administration	4.79	3.77	4.91
Protection of People and Property	5.05	4.22	4.28
Transportation and Communications	10.90	7.75	7.27
Health and Welfare	28.86	25.46	25.42
Recreation and Culture	.96	1.30	1.44
Education	25.93	24.17	24.04
Natural Resources	15.51	15.63	12.13
Commerce and Development	.23	.27	1.03
Planning and Municipal Development	.05	.07	.40
Public Debt	5.76	5.51	5.93
Unconditional Transfers to Municipaities by the Québec Government	—	2.43	2.06
Others	1.99	9.45	11.00
Public Sector	100.00	100.00	100.00

various indirect taxes on goods and services. The other provinces allow the Federal government to collect their share of personal income tax on their behalf. Québec and Ontario are the only provinces which tax corporation income.

The statistics in Table VII clearly indicate that the salaried population has financed the "quiet revolution" and the growth of the new bourgeoisie.

The fiscal receipts of the Québec government have increased more than fourfold during the ten year period ; the income derived from personal income tax, however, has gone up by a factor of eleven, while the sales taxes returns increased four times. In global terms, corporations paid 118.8 million dollars in taxes in 1961 to the Québec state, while individuals contributed 85 millions ; these were respectively 23 and 16.4 percent of total tax revenues of Québec. In 1970 the corporations contributed 175 million or 10.8 percent of the tax revenues while individuals paid 940 millions, which represented 41.7 percent. In the ten year period corporation taxes increased by 47 percent, **taxes paid by individuals increased 905 percent.**

If we consider the fact that most of the sales tax is paid by the salaried population either directly or indirectly as consumers, we find that the corporation's contribution to total Qubec tax revenues has decreased from 23 to 10.8 percent while that of the individual taxpayers has gone from 68 to 86 percent in the same period (1961-1970).

Because of the special arrangements between the Québec and Federal governments, mainly reflected in opting-out privileges negociated by the Québec government with respect to federal programs, it has been difficult to in-

tegrate the tax yields of the two systems. We therefore refer directly to Wassef for an accurate estimate of what the Québec worker actually pays.

First, on the level of the Québec government revenue : in 1961 the taxes collected by the Québec government represented 56.01 percent of government revenue, revenue from institutions and interest was 18.33 percent, conditional contributions from other governments represented 18.53 percent and the fiscal arrangements or unconditional Federal government contributions to Québec represented 7.08 percent. However, in 1970, Québec government revenue from taxes was now 59.52 percent of the total, parafiscal * revenues were down to 11.3 percent, conditional contributions from the Federal government were 8.95 percent and the total of unconditional transfer payments from the Federal government came to 20.21 percent.

If we consider the total of federal transfer payments in the same category as tax revenue, (most of it is collected as such) paid to the Québec government, we can then conclude that the revenue of the Québec state is all collected through a system of double taxation which yields respectively 81.6 and 88.7 percent of its revenues in 1961 and 1970. [21]

As we have seen, the main source of government revenue in the liberal state is the salaried workers and not the capitalist, as apologists would have us believe. **Moreover, even if the taxation rates appear to be progressive, they are not in fact.** These taxes have a much greater effect on low-paid workers and retired people with fixed incomes. Even if the progressive taxation rates have been lowered since 1959, the taxation ranges and exemptions have remained

---

* "Parafiscal" is a literal translation from the French, and means revenue from such government owned, but legally separate, corporations as the Québec Pension Fund and Hydro-Québec.

unchanged. As salaries increased, mainly due to inflation, more workers who were previously exempt, are now paying income tax. Others who were paying taxes are now paying more. Taxes on consumer goods affect everybody without reference to their income. Since consumption is relatively more important in the case of people with low incomes, taxes on consumer goods have a much greater effect on low-paid workers and retired people with fixed incomes.

> We should also note that corporation profits have never been taxed at progressive rates, that their fiscal charge is a function of their position in the financial oligarchy. In fact, not only do the financial circles benefit from tax deduction privileges, and are not taxed at progressive rates, but, with the concentration of capital and the formation of giant capitalist corporations, it is virtually impossible to talk seriously in terms of controlling their profits or the incomes of their owners ; whereas for small and medium enterprises it is valid and for workers' salaries, it is real. [13]

EXPENSES OF THE QUÉBEC GOVERNMENT : WHO BENEFITS ?

We have previously traced the rapid growth of the public sector in the Québec economy as the natural consequence of the evolution of the Canadian and North American economies and the attempt of the new French-Canadian industrialist and technocratic bourgeoisie to expand its role in this process. We have clearly shown that the salaried workers of Québec have financed the greatest part of this economic leap forward. Inevitably there has been a growth in public wealth or public capital. It has been difficult, however, to determine whether there has been a significant shift in real income distribu-

tion between the various classes in Québec society. We must emphasize real income because shifts in income distribution patterns are sometimes more apparent than real in that the tax structure may shift the balance back in the direction of the upper income brackets as has been recently shown in the United States. We do have some indication, in the resistance offered by all elements of the Québec bourgeoisie (nationalist or otherwise), as well as some social democrats, of the attempts by the trade union movement to effect a moderate shift in income distribution pattern in recent collective bargaining with the Québec government ; this struggle suggests that there had not before been much of a shift in this area. In fact, only the police forces, who have a potentially repressive role, have been given generous wage raises in Québec.

Because of the absence of the necessary data in Québec and Canada, one cannot really determine the complete economic effect of the different elements of the expenditures of the liberal Québec or Canadian state apparatus. However, Tables V and VIII give us some idea of the key position that the public sector constitutes in the financial superstructure of Québec ; Table V shows that in the period 1965 to 1970 between 40-43.5 percent of the investments in Québec have been in the public sector ; there are indications that public investment has now exceeded that of the private sector in Québec. The role of capital investments of this size throughout the economy is obvious.

Evaluation of the data in Table VIII contradicts the myth spread by bourgeois liberal governments about their role in redistributing income. The following points should be noted :

TABLE VII

Fiscal Revenues of the Québec Government — 1961 to 1970

Annual Revenue (in millions)

Source of Tax Revenue	1961	1962	1963	1964	1965	1966	1967	1968	1969 [1]	1970 [1]
CORPORATIONS	20.7	29.2	33.3	33.0	38.7	37.0	45.8	61.2	71.0	67.4
REVENUES: a) Corporations	118.8	119.7	121.4	130.0	144.4	149.8	153.7	182.3	172.0	175.0
b) Individuals	85.1	98.3	106.0	170.2	335.7	470.0	527.6	678.4	825.0	940.0
SALES TAXES a) Alcoholic Beverages	—	—	—	—	—	—	—	—	—	—
b) Amusements	7.8	8.9	9.1	11.6	9.1	10.3	13.5	23.7	16.5	29.0
c) Fuel	107.8	120.5	150.8	167.2	192.3	202.3	217.7	272.0	285.0	298.3
d) Tobacco	24.3	25.9	25.0	27.6	35.3	38.3	38.8	67.7	63.0	68.4
e) General	115.9	153.1	167.8	288.8	327.6	343.1	465.9	513.7	519.8	562.9
f) Other Commodities and services	9.1	10.8	12.0	14.0	24.6	30.2	52.6	39.8	52.2	48.0
INHERITANCE TAXES	25.5	27.8	36.4	35.4	36.0	37.8	35.9	46.0	42.0	46.0
RAMQ										15.0
OTHERS	2.1	1.8	2.3	2.3	2.4	2.0	2.8	2.7	4.2	3.0
TOTAL FISCAL REVENUES	517.2	596.0	664.1	880.1	1146.1	1320.8	1554.3	1885.5	2050.7	2253.0
NET GENERAL REVENUES	758	865	948	1240	1600	1817	2288	2697	2962	3383

(1) Preliminary estimate.

Source: DBS — Provincial Government Finance.

TABLE VIII

An Economic Classification of the Total Expenditures of the Public Sector in Québec — 1967 to 1970

Public Sector	Salaries (1)	Purchase of Goods & Services (2)	Transfers			Others
			Individuals (3)	Business (4)	Public (5)	
Québec Government						
1967-68	316.0	458.5	333.9	116.5	1,385.5	74.1
1968-69	350.7	437.0	343.8	143.5	1,598.7	86.9
1969-70	387.9	470.6	359.3	179.9	1,965.1	81.7
Public Enterprises (6)						
1967	85.0	343.0	53.0	363.4	.08 (7)	124.7
1968	97.5	327.0	64.4	367.8	.08 (8)	110.9
1969	108.2	309.2	73.1	462.4	.06 (9)	186.0
Provincial Public Services						
Health and Welfare						
1967	382.8	336.3	—	—	(637.8)	—
1968	436.6	362.0	—	—	(716.0)	—
1969	538.9	441.6	—	—	(886.4)	—
Education						
1967	490.5	490.5	—	—	(531.9)	—
1968	595.0	595.0	—	—	(687.4)	—
1969	687.3	687.3	—	—	(856.9)	—
Municipalities						
1967	—	706.6	3.6	162.8	(164.4)	6.5
1968	—	—	—	—	(149.3)	—
1969	—	—	—	—	(159.4)	—
Federal Government to Québec						
1967	484.0	853.6	—	—	—	845.9
1968	—	—	—	—	—	—
1969	—	—	—	—	—	—
Québec Public Sestor						
1967	1758.3	31.97.3	390.5	642.7	52.2	1051.2
1968	—	—	—	—	—	—
1969	—	—	—	—	—	—

Economic Classification

—the salaries paid to people employed in the public sector constitute 24.8 percent of the total expenses.

—consumption in the public sector represents 45 percent.

—transfers to individuals are in the order of 11.2 percent.

—transfers to private companies and business equals 9.1 percent.

—the remaining transfers from the public sector which could not be completely explained were 9.9 percent.

In more general terms the data presented in Tables V and VIII support Wassef's definition of the role of the public sector in the economy of a liberal state. This role includes the following :

1) To provide consumption (investments and purchases) which insures a large volume of business for corporations and the profits that go with it ; as an illustration of this we should again refer to Tables V and VIII which compare levels of public and private investment.

2) To provide certain goods and services to private corporations at low prices : we should recall that the purpose of the nationalization of electric power and the subsequent formation of Hydro-Québec which was largely financed through the public sector was to provide electricity at reduced cost. This leads directly to increased profits for corporations. (See Deaton)

3) To intervene in the economy, depending on the particular phase of the business cycle ; guided by the needs of the economy, government may slow or increase the rate of investment, participate directly in projects through subsidization, use its taxation power and encourage either inflation or recession.

4) To moderate contradictions inherent in the system by controlling and regulating relations between classes ; the use of police power, the labour code, government intervention in labour conflicts would be included in this category.

5) To manage the education and public

health systems to increase the potential and productivity of the work force, both of which are indispensable to the survival of capitalism.

6) To provide studies (statistics, economic and market) to large corporations which permit them to retain their control over the economy and over their employees. [14]

In subsequent sections we shall examine (a) some of the links that have been forged between the state structure and the most powerful elements of the financial and industrial establishment in Québec, and (b) the new role assumed by the federal state in supporting the free enterprise system in Canada by direct subsidization of industry, a role which the Québec state has neither the means nor the constitutional powers to play effectively, but which the French-Canadian bourgeoisie aspires to play.

THE LINKS BETWEEN THE STATE, THE FINANCIAL COMMUNITY AND PRIVATE INDUSTRY

We have examined the evolution of the Québec economy and, to a lesser extent, that of Canada, into the state capitalist stage. We have seen how the Québec state is being used as a massive service industry for both the parent Federal government and for private industry (education, health, welfare and roads are the responsibility of provincial states). These service functions provide a large transfer of fiscal resources from the salaried population to all types of industries in the form of billions of dollars of lucrative contracts every year. Even though the real pork-barrelling, that is, defense and industrial expansion, are within federal jurisdiction, the total expenditures of provincial governments are of the same order. What then, if any, are the means by which the business community exerts its influence?

We have always suspected the existence of direct links between the economic and political communities. Unfortunately the debate in Canada has concentrated largely on the direct involvement of big business in the financing of political parties. The intensive research applied to the questions of foreign ownership and poverty has not been applied to the investigation of the relationship between state power and the financial community. Porter's important work THE CANADIAN MOSAIC on the Canadian elite and Myers' book THE HISTORY OF CANADIAN WEALTH on the origins of Canadian wealth have not been updated or expanded. Porter has told us that there is a community of social origin, education and interest between the higher civil servants and the directors of Canadian corporations, but we have no analysis of the mechanisms through which they co-operate. We are aware that many of the large Canadian fortunes and industrial empires have been built through levels of governmental corruption and collusion between government and private industry. There has never been adequate analysis of the manipulation behind such schemes as the Alberta pipeline construction, the St. Lawrence Seaway, the Arrow project, the Peace River Dam, and now James Bay. Individually none of these are as spectacular as the military-industrial complex in the United States but when considered as parts of an emerging pattern they are perhaps just as significant to the evolution and survival of liberal corporate capital.

The "quiet revolution" in Québec, because of the presence of specific cultural, political and economic factors, has created conditions which allow some insight into the development of state capitalist economic institutions. Under the influence of the French Canadian nationalists, Québec established a series of state-owned public corporations in the key economic sectors of forestry, steel, and electric power, in order to promote the "liberation" of Québec. These have failed to effect any decisive changes in the ownership pattern or management of the Québec economy. Foreign control of the economy has probably increased during the "quiet revolution". At best, the infrastructure has been modernized and new French Canadian technocracy has been partially coopted by the system — the progressive elements into the newly expanded state bureaucracy, the more conservative technocrats into the middle levels of industry. By what techniques has the Québec power structure managed to retain "control" over the main elements of the Québec economy in the face of the powerful nationalist pressures unleashed by the "quiet revolution" ? The traditional methods of controlling the press, manipulating political parties and integrating the labour movement can only be partially successful in the Québec situation. The preliminary research efforts into this area suggest that the power structure has (a) successfully opposed all attempts by the Québec government to free itself from control of the "financial syndicate" which has financed virtually all credit required by the Québec government, and (b) influenced directly and indirectly all government bodies created to "liberate" or "modernize" Québec's economy, the definition being determined by whether it was in the initial or latter phase of the "quiet revolution".

In the latest issue (no 23) of SO-CIALISME QUÉBÉCOIS [15] which is mainly concerned with imperialism and regional development as these affect the economic structure of Québec, the editors have published results of preliminary research into the workings of the different elements of the Québec industrial and financial elite. A great deal of this material is particularly useful in illustrating the links between the state and the different elements of the power structure.

ORGANIZED ECONOMIC TERRORISM

The blackmail waged by the financial community and the federalist establishment after each escalation of the Québec people in their collective movement toward self-determination is analogous to the economic terrorism practiced by the imperialist powers against countries of the Third World who have attempted to achieve their economic as well as political independence. France succeeded in retaining control of its former African colonies by organizing them into a special trade block with the French franc as the common currency and credit controlled by France. The organized blackmail campaign by the French government which preceded the formation of this bloc was resisted only by Guinea. American attempts to prevent Chile from carrying out a social revolution by an organized campaign of economic terrorism including the restrictions placed on all attempts to obtain credits through the International Monetary Fund, which is of course dominated by the USA, is the most immediate example of this type of imperialist activity. Peru, Bolivia and Argentina under Peron have been victims of econ-omic terrorism. In Africa we can add Ghana and the former Belgian Congo to the list of victims.

In Québec, the campaign of economic terrorism peaked during the period of attempted stabilization which followed the visit of Charles de Gaulle in 1967 and the temporary unification of all the political parties promoting Québec independence. The highlights of this concerted campaign have been summarized by Brunelle and Papineau in an article called "Le Gouvernement du Capital", written for **SOCIALISME QUÉBÉ-COIS,** no. 23.

—An influential member of the Montreal financial elite, also a former official of the Royal Bank, who also happens to be the president of both the Montreal and Canadian stock exchanges, is discreetly appointed to the Board of Directors of the Québec Deposit and Investment Fund. It is now the 28th of July ; rumors are already circulating as to flight of capital from Québec.

—October 14th. A group of bankers (whom we can presume to be linked to the Ames-Bank of Montreal financial syndicate of which the Royal Bank is a leading member) issue anonymous threats, through the newspapers, to the Québec government with respect to its future bond issues. There is also a statement by M. Neapole.

—October 31st. In the face of this, the government backs down. In exchange for the emission of a 50 million dollar government bond issue by the syndicate under normal conditions, the government promises to establish an economic development plan which would include the creation of a "taskforce" (read : a General Industrial Council) and appoints Marcel Faribault as the leading coordinator of "all economic affairs" to this council, as an additional guarantee.

—The following day, Charles Neapole gives the all-clear signal to Daniel Johnson, the Québec Premier, by issuing a statement to the effect that the "flight" of capital has reached "its peak and is beginning to drop off."

—November 2nd, the government bonds are issued on the market where they are rapidly snapped up. [16]

According to the authors,

We simply witnessed a political hatchet job whose significance is still not completely understood, but whose sequence of events is clear. The pretext was the "desire by the business community to make its voice heard, at a time when the political and social situation was becoming more and more confused," through the establishment of a para-governmental body : this was the General Industry Council.

Two groups, whose differences are more apparent than real, participated in the operation : on the one hand, the manufacturers' group, represented by Paul Ouimet, on the other, the financial sector to which Charles Neapole is connected. The actions of the two groups were concerted, the second (probably the financial syndicate) promoted the idea of the flight of capital, the first group proposed the creation of the General Industry Council. The whole operation was apparently directed by the financial group through whom the government was obliged to issue all government bonds.

The operation was a complete success: the decision to establish the General Industry Countil is announced ; in the interval Faribault is appointed as advisor to the Québec cabinet and Neapole to the Québec Deposit and Investment Fund. [17]

The objectives and composition of this General Industry Council established in February 1969 by Premier Jean-Jacques Bertrand provide some additional insight into the links between the state and monopoly capital. The Council was to "tighten the bonds between the Industry and Commerce Ministry and the Québec business community with their colleagues from the other provinces and foreign countries ; to inform the ministry about any changes in the opinions of business about Québec and to suggest means of orienting and modifying these opinions ; to suggest economic policies and if necessary help direct these policies." The second objective of the council was of a public relations nature.

Brunelle and Papineau affirm that "on the 13th of March, 1967, at perhaps its first statutory meeting, the Council invited the following government ministers : M. Masse, J. N. Tremblay, J. J. Cardinal and M. Beaulieu, to 'appear' before members of the Council to answer questions about their personal opinions on French unilingualism and the future of Québec." [18] Could this have influenced the positions adopted by these nationalist ministers during the debate on Bill 63 ? It was later established that pressures from international finance were concerted with those originating inside Québec to ensure passage of this bill which in effect ensured the use of English as the language of business.

When one examines the composition of the General Industry Council it is difficult to conclude that the above objectives will not be interpreted in favour of using the state fiscal power and public capital in favour of the private sector of the economy. Besides the members of the Industrial Credit Bank (3 civil servants, 5 small businessmen), the 48 members of the General Industry Council include 4 members of the Desmarais-Lévesque (Power Corporation) group, 4 people coming from banks and financial institutions connected to the Desmarais-Lévesque group including the Bank of Montreal, the Royal Bank, the Banque Canadienne Nationale and the Banque Provinciale, 4 people from "holdings" (Power Corporation, C.P.R., Fonds F-I-C Inc.). But by far the largest

76

number (24) comes from the manufacturing sector. Most significant is that no representatives of either SIDBEC, the government-owned steel complex, or of the General Investment Corporation, a "holding" of the Québec government, were appointed to this General Industry Council.

REGIONAL DEVELOPMENT AND THE LIBERAL STATE

In the consolidation of the national market through the formation of the Canadian federal state the Fathers of Confederation left behind them a series of problems which we have come to know through the euphemism, "regional inequalities". As Canadian capitalism expanded along the tracks laid out by the Canadian Pacific Railway the regions left behind became relatively stagnant and underdeveloped while industrial development and expansion concentrated in parts of Ontario and in the Montréal area. It is rarely mentioned by those who complain about handouts to Québec and the Maritimes that their own wealth is largely based on surplus value earned from the Maritimes and Québec. The present crisis in Confederation is due in part to the relative underdevelopment of most of Québec and the maritime provinces in relation to Ontario. It is of interest that most of these underdeveloped areas have voted in opposition to the Liberal party of Canada, which has been the architect of continentalist economic policies.

To meet the problems raised by such persistant regional inequalities most liberal states have attempted various types of regional development schemes. Perhaps the most interesting regional development programs attempted by liberal states were by Britain and Italy.

Even Yugoslavia has not been able to correct the problem of regional inequalities between the different nations and republics after a concerted effort.

Our purpose here is to analyse the results of the first serious attempt by those who control the Canadian state to solve the problems of unemployment and poverty in the underdeveloped regions of Canada through a program of giving incentive grants to private industry to locate in these areas. Our critique will be built from the base, i.e. from the experiences of one of these "designated areas", at the level of the community. It is at this level that the failure of these programs becomes apparent ; that no structural or socio-economic changes in St. Jérôme, Québec have resulted from the program of handouts to private industry ; and finally that the local elites and the Canadian power structure have integrated these subsidies into the regular pattern of capital and profit accumulation.

L'Agence de Presse Libre du Québec in its Bulletin no. 69, 13 to 20 July, published the text of an interesting study carried out by a group of St. Jérôme militants of the effects of the Federal government's policy of subsidizing private industry in St. Jérôme. Incidentally, this text had been prepared for an audio-visual presentation to groups of St. Jérôme workers. It is significant that this type of community action project oriented towards the working class was conceived in St. Jérôme, a city which has been the centre of considerable newleft and labour contestation in recent years.

The following quotations from the document indicate the reason why St. Jérôme became a "designated area" under the Regional Development Incentives Act.

It is really the working class of St. Jérôme, particularly the workers of Dominion Rubber Co. and the activists of the Christian Workers Movement, who were the first to sound the alarm about the disastrous economic situation faced by the workers of St. Jérôme in 1966. The strike by 1,200 workers at Dominion Rubber in September of that year as well as the strikes at Rolland Paper and Regent Knitting and the study completed by the Christian Workers Movement which showed that the salaries paid in St. Jérôme were inadequate (weekly average of $69.59), were the factors which finally convinced the working class of the state of under-development of their city.

The layoff of more than 725 workers at the Dominion Rubber Co. and 250 at Regent between June and December 1966 did not leave any doubts as to the future awaiting them if there was no economic recovery forthcoming. The fact that only three companies: Dominion Rubber, Regent Knitting, and Rolland Paper employed more than one-half of the active work force of St. Jérôme was clearly an indication of the particular type of problem caused by industrial concentration. This high degree of industrial concentration had a direct effect on the economic instability of the region : in effect the economic dynamism of St. Jérôme was dependent upon a very limited number of companies and decision making centres. Moreover, the products manufactured by these 3 enterprises were competing in a highly competitive market.

Between November 1965 and November of 1966, the rate of unemployment varied between 11.5 and 18.0% which was more than twice the national average, the basis for qualifying for the regional development program. It was subsequently learned that between January 1967 to April of the same year almost one out of every 4 workers was unemployed in St. Jérôme.

The problems of unemployment, low salaries and industrial concentration were linked to the low educational level of the St. Jérôme work force. A study completed in 1961 showed that 16% of the work force had not gone beyond the 4th grade and 53%, the 7th grade. It was also learned that those who had completed secondary schooling could not find jobs nor could they aspire to a higher education. Another major factor contributing to the deteriorating situation revealed by the study was the lack of overall planning of the city's industrial promoton program.

Faced with this drastic situation, the local trade union leaders unequivocally demanded that St. Jérôme become a designated area, that is, that the industries be given subsidies paid for by our taxes, to expand existing plant or build new industries. In May of 1967 St. Jérôme was integrated into the designated areas program. [19]

The different citizens groups proposed the following long-term objectives for the regional development program to the Federal government :

1) Take inventory of the human and material resources of the region.
2) Evaluate job openings in the manufacturing and service industries within the framework of employment possibilities, educational requirements and incomes of the population.
3) Study the possibility of the fusion of municipalities.
4) Encourage the organization of employers in support of socio-economic improvements.
5) Intensify trade union education.
6) Promote large scale community projects as a means of encouraging identification with and growth of a community consciousness.
7) Integrate the adult population into the planned educational reforms.[20]

These proposed objectives can hardly be described as revolutionary ; they constitute a coherent plan for modernizing and updating the social and economic structures of the St. Jérôme area through a combination of reformist and technocratic measures which were in apparent harmony with the objectives of the Federal Department of Regional Economic Expansion. Between 1967 and 1969 the Regional Development Incentives Act offered the following : (a) development incentives in cash or tax credits of up to one-third of capital costs, (b) accelerated depreciation of up to 50 percent per year, and (c) a special capital cost allowance of up to 20 percent per year.

THE SOCIO-ECONOMIC EFFECTS ON ST. JÉRÔME

In spite of the very moderate demands and expectations raised by the community action groups of St. Jérôme and the rather large injections of public funds the results have been mainly negative.

A total of 25 new industries were subsidized by the Federal government during the period 67-69 at a cost of 5.7 millions. These industries created approximately 1,100 jobs compared to a projected 1,914 promised by the companies in their original applications for subsidies. These new jobs may have decreased social tensions but they did not increase the number of available jobs in the industrial sector. Only 10 of these new St. Jérôme industries can be classified as offering employment of a technical nature (electricity, communications, chemicals : Price, York, Transom Electronic). These plants employ a total of 448 workers whose salaries are just above the poverty level which the Senate Report on Poverty established as $5,400 per year, after tax deductions, for a family of 4, in 1970. An additional 381 jobs were created in factories where manufactured products are assembled (trailers, neon boxes, cigarette paper. toboggans, steel tubing : Boisé-Cascades, Mundet, Phillips and Secor). Working conditions in these latter plants are unacceptable.

In spite of an already imposing overconcentration in the textile and shoe industries, 4 more in this category were opened in St. Jérôme between 1967 and 1969. These industries pay low wages,

are technically backward and face strong foreign competition. Because of this strong competition, employment levels in these industries are constantly being threatened.

In additon to the textile and shoe industries, the government subsidized several plants without having done the necessary market studies. This was so in the case of several plants in St. Jérôme, particularly Sicma and Alfex. We know that the airplane seats built by Sicma are of such poor quality, according to one of the workers, that the company has managed to obtain only one contract, with Air India. Alfex, which produces thermo-alumina, has not been able to complete any sales while St. Jérôme Bandag and Duprex have recently ceased operations.

We should add that when we referred to 1,100 new jobs we should have added that these figures are only a part of the overall picture, because many of these jobs already existed in other cities : ITT already operated with 100 employees in Pointe Claire. Lange Canada employed 50 workers in its Montreal plant. Price operated in Montreal and Rayonese left Ste. Rose to establish in St. Jérôme. The original figure of 1,100 should be reduced by 100 to 200 if we consider those workers who already worked for these same companies elsewhere before moving to St. Jérôme with them.

The most reprehensible of these tactics is that the companies used the government subsidies to renew their machinery ; the tactic is very simple : they sell their plant and machinery, build new plants in St. Jérôme and equip them with new machinery while getting government subsidies. Profits increase because of the use of new machinery and the lower wage level in St. Jérôme compared with Montreal. [21]

Not to be outdone by the largesse of the Federal government, Québec has also decided to contribute its share of public capital to finance the development of private industry. The document affirms that the Québec law applied most frequently to St. Jérôme was the

79

legislation creating the Industrial Development Company which was given the following powers :

—to provide loans at below market rates.
—to absorb some of the borrowing costs.
—to provide exemptions on the repayment of part of the loans depending on the condition of the company.
—to purchase up to 30% of the stock issued and paid by the company or 10% of the total working assets.
—to build plants for sale or rental.
—to issue bonds whose interest would not be subject to provincial income tax.

To further help private industry, in April 1972, the Québec government even removed the 8 percent tax on the purchase of industrial machinery.

"Secor Industries, a company that produces aluminum chairs and toboggans, was given a Québec government assured loan of $190,000 ; Federal subsidies were $118,581. We have learned from official sources that the plant cost $381,000 while the company itself issued shares for $125,000" :[22] a perfect example of promoting private enterprise with public funds.

Only underdeveloped areas such as St. Jérôme were entitled to subsidies between 1967 and 1970. Amendments to the Regional Development Incentives Act which became effective as of January, 1971 specified that :

a) The ceiling of 12 million dollars per grant is removed.
b) All of southwestern Québec, including Montréal and Hull become a designated area entitled to special development subsidies.
c) In this newly designated area, the subsidy may be up to 10% of estimated capital costs of expansion and modernization. An additional $2,000 may be given for each job created where either a new industry or a new product is involved.
d) New commercial enterprises such as hotels and shopping centres, in certain cases, may benefit from government guaranteed loans of up to 30% of total capital costs.

Since the above amendments went into effect in 1971, the research document refers to data for that year only. Four additional enterprises received federal subsidies ; these include another textile plant, a shoe factory, a pottery manufacturer and a printing company. The first two are in a category which requires extremely high productivity and low wages to meet the international competition ; the pottery manufacturer could hire only artisans. None of the four industries have any significant cumulative effects in creating new jobs.

ST. JÉRÔME AFTER FIVE YEARS OF "REGIONAL DEVELOPMENT"

After five years of federal subsidization of private industry in the St. Jérôme area, in which a total of almost six million in public capital was invested (the total of Québec government aid given in the St. Jérôme area is not available) we must conclude that none of the major socio-economic problems faced by the population of this area have been solved.

1. UNEMPLOYMENT NOT DECREASED

In spite of the presence of new industries, industry in St. Jérôme is still very weak.

— Regent Knitting mills and Uniroyal, who employ a total of 1,000 workers between them, have signified their intention to close their doors in three years.

— Collective bargaining at Rolland Paper is always accompanied by company threats to move to Ontario.

— 16 of the 27 companies subsidized between 1967 and 1969 have ceased operations or function at less than one-half of capacity.

— In 1971, industrial production increased by 1% in St. Jérôme while the cost of living increased by 4%.

It is difficult to know the exact level of unemployment in St. Jérôme. It appears, however, that overall employment has decreased. Approximately 1,100 jobs were created through government grants. Dominion Rubber has reduced its work force by 800, Regent Knitting by 200, Diva Shore has closed — another 200 jobs. A total of 1,200 jobs have been lost since 1966 ; in spite of the regional development program there are now 100 less jobs in the industrial sector. To this we must add the hundreds of workers who have come from the outside as well as local young people coming into the labour market. [23]

II. INCOME DISTRIBUTION NOT AFFECTED

"According to the bureau of statistics, 4,987 wage earners in St. Jérôme earned less than $4,000 in 1969 while 536 people earned more than $10,000." Also, "if we compare St. Jérôme in 1969 with 1966, there has not been any significant change for the workers ; in 1966 the average salary was $69.59 per week (approximately $3,600 per year) in 1969 the average salary increased to $82.50 per week ($4,290 per year). If one allows for inflation, the average wage in St. Jérôme did not increase in the three year period." [24] It is obvious that the new industries brought into St. Jérôme due to regional development grants did not alter the basic wage or income structure of the area.

III. INDUSTRIAL STRUCTURE OF ST. JÉRÔME NOT FUNDAMENTALLY ALTERED

In its incisive critique of the DREE program the Q.F.L. document, "L'Etat, le Rouage de Notre Exploitation", had pointed out that :

> its general effect is to maintain and perpetuate every flaw or deficiency in Québec's economic structures. To see this, all one has to do is to compare the percentage of the labour force employed in each of the twenty industrial manufacturing categories to which the grants apply, with the percentage of jobs created by DREE in each of these industrial sectors. [25]

While the statistical data supplied by the St. Jérôme animators is incomplete, no doubt due to the limited means available to them, their document does indicate that the Québec-wide experience was repeated on a smaller scale in St. Jérôme. The dominant position of unstable, low-paying, light industry was not changed by the new, subsidized industry. In fact, 60 percent of the new industries were in the light industry category, i.e., textiles, shoes, foods. When based on the number of jobs, the light industry sector created 37 percent of the new jobs, while the more productive heavy industry category created approximately 44 percent of the new jobs. The relative improvement here was too small to affect the overall industrial structure of St. Jérôme which is basically built around light industry.

IV. THE SUBSIDIES PERPETUATED FOREIGN CONTROL

The research document gives the following order of investments in St. Jérôme for the period 1967-1971 : [26]

Source	Investment	Percent of Total
Foreign Capital	$12,013,000	58%
Anglo-Canadian Capital	7,700,000	37%
French-Canadian Capital	949,000	5%
Total Capital Invested	$20,662,000	100%
Total Government Subsidies	$ 6,000,000	

Only 10 percent of American capital invested in manufacturing was actually brought in from the United States during the 1963-68 period ; the remaining 90 percent was raised in Canada. [27] If this was the case in St. Jérôme, only approximately 1.2 million dollars of the 12 million was actually brought in by the foreign investors compared to approximately 3.7 million dollars of subsidies given to them in the form of DREE grants. The 3.7 million dollars is obtained by multiplying the total amount of DREE grants, 6 millions, by the percentage of the grants given to foreign investors, 63.2 percent, during the same period. The above figures strongly suggest that the policies followed by the Department of Regional Economic Expansion not only perpetuate regional inequalities through the use of public funds to subsidize private enterprise, but that these same policies tend to strengthen the control of the Québec economy by both the Anglo-Canadian and foreign capitalists.

The failure to effect any signifiant changes in the socio-economic structures of the St. Jérôme area through the application of federal aid programs to "designated areas" and the frustration of aspirations raised by these programs is illustrated in the following comment by the St. Jérôme militants.

Five years of government investments and handouts have only created a situation where the worker is exploited by machines working at an ever faster rate, by an even more modern machinery, by bosses who must be enjoying the fact that they now exploit the workers both through their work and through their subsidies paid for by the workers and without which they could not build their factories where they exploit us. Today, we are still completely out of the decision-making process and, today, we should feel the urgency of organizing the workers of St. Jérôme to halt this contempt for the workers shown by the bosses and their friends in the Federal government. [28]

REGIONAL ECONOMIC DEVELOPMENT PROGRAMS

The initial attempt to eliminate regional disparities in Canada by promoting industrial expansion in "designated areas" through grants given directly to private industry by the Federal Department of Regional Expansion (DREE) under the Regional Development Act has been a dramatic failure. The failure has been very well researched and documented with respect to the Maritime provinces in Robert Chodos' article "The Business of Jean Marchand is Business" (**LAST POST,** July 1972). An even stronger critique of regional development programs is made in the Québec Federation of Labor document. ""L'Etat, le Rouage de Notre Exploitation" ("The State, The Source of Our Exploitation"). This document, written within the context of a class analysis of the state, traces the evolution of the regional incentives programs in Québec from their conception in 1963 through the first two phases where the DREE grants were directed to "designated areas", into the present phase which began January 1, 1971.

A major turning point in the history of DREE occurred on January 1, 1971, when amendments to the map of designated areas went into effect. Added were all previously undesignated parts of Québec, along with the eastern tip of Ontario. To cushion the effect this would have on the Atlantic provinces, maximum grants for capital costs in the Atlantic region were raised to 35 from 25 percent (a gain that was largely illusory, since almost all DREE grants are below the maximum).

Before the changes, 38.3 percent of the money given in grants had gone to firms establishing in the province of Québec and 34.1 percent had gone to the Atlantic provinces. After the changes, Québec got 54.4 percent, the Atlantic provinces 17.3.

$34,752,000 in RDIA grants had gone to Québec up until December 1970; from January 1971 to March 1972 it got $82,637,000. The Atlantic provinces got $30,913,000 up to December 1970, and $26,357,000 from January, 1971 to March 1972.

Québec's share has increased steadily: it got 39.3 percent in the first 6 months of 1971, 53.6 percent in the last 6 months of that year, and fully 74.8 percent in the first 3 months of 1972. [29]

This significant increase in grants to Québec is a direct consequence of a report, "The Orientation of Regional Economic Development in the Province of Québec," presented by B. Higgins, F. Martin, and A. Raynauld to the Federal Minister of Regional Economic Expansion, February 1970. The report was apparently prepared partly in response to the economic and political problems created by the October (1970) "crisis" and, secondly, because of the clear failure of previous regional aid programs to solve the problems of unemployment and inequalities between different regions. In the report the authors proposed a complete reversal of federal aid programs ; large urban centres such as Montréal which have already displayed economic growth potential will be given priority in government subsidies ; the previous policy of favouring underdeveloped areas was to be abandoned.

Given the importance of economic development in this model, the authors define a certain number of preconditions which favour innovation and conclude that only the large urban centres offer a favourable framework for economic development. [30]

Of all the urban centres in Québec, Montréal is the 'only autonomous dynamic entity' using the expression of the authors. Moreover, Montréal is open to the exterior ; Québec is integrated commercially and financially into the North American economic complex through Montréal, which is done along the natural Montréal-New York axis. Among the assets of Montréal, we should mention the head offices of 187 American subsidiaries. The Montréal region, then, constitutes the only development pole in Québec, and in this perspective, it becomes imperative that all Québec favour the priority of Montréal development ... Finally, the industrial structure of Montréal is aging and must be renewed. Considering all of these elements, the authors concluded that the growth of the Montréal region must be promoted. To accomplish this, we must adopt policies which would favour greater economic concentration in Montréal and in the satellite cities (Sorel, Joliette, Saint-Jérôme, Granby, Saint-Hyacinthe, Saint-Jean and Valleyfield). Montréal being a development pole, the investments placed in that area, would of necessity have a stimulating effect on the rest of Québec. Eventually other cities such as Saint-Agathe, Drummondville, Trois-Rivières and Sherbrooke will become satellite cities. The mechanisms by which this diffusion of economic growth would occur is not described here. We would mention only that each development pole has a corresponding 'zone of peripheral influence' which becomes a growth zone through stimulation by the development pole which dominates. The pole drains the periphery of its resources and offers it a market for its products.

Within this general perspective of development, the other regions of Québec 'must integrate themselves progressively into the circuits coming out of Montréal,' otherwise they will gradually disappear. This slow death will unavoidably be accompanied by the migration of people from peripheral regions to the large centres, in other words to the Montréal area. [31]

The new DREE policies have already come into effect. In fact, "between October 1970 and April 1972 (18 months) the 4 most highly developed regions in Québec (Montréal, Trois-Rivières, Québec City and the Eastern Townships) have received 81% of the grants given by the Ministry of Economic Expansion, which created 88 percent of the new jobs." Most of these grants were given out in the Montréal area ; "Québec had 2074 applications 63.3 percent of the Canadian total ; of those, 1,300 were for the newly named region around Montréal."

Our analysis of the St. Jérôme situation, which according to the Higgins, Martin and Raynauld proposal is in the first ring of satellite cities of Montréal, and the persistence of high levels of unemployment in Québec, including Montréal, suggest that this latest example of Trudeau's functional politics will fail as did the earlier attempts to eliminate regional underdevelopment. Aside from the inherent contradictions present in a policy of getting capitalism to invest in areas where it is not in its interest to do so, the subsidies given to them out of taxes which in turn must be raised to pay for them, have the

effect of reducing profits ; this contradiction will ensure that bourgeois governments will only pursue these policies in an incomplete manner. There is enough evidence to suggest that regional underdevelopment is inherent to the structure of the capitalist system, that it is necessary for its expansion and survival. In a penetrating analysis of "Growth and Development" Louis Gill quotes from an article by Ernest Mandel, "Capitalism and Regional Economy," where Mandel suggests that regional underdevelopment is a direct product of capitalism with the implication that it cannot be solved within a capitalist framework.

> Liberal apologists for capitalism naively thought that the creation of a national market would automatically lead to a harmonious development of a given country and that the development of international trade will eventually eliminate the differences in economic development between nations. An empirical study of the capitalist countries at the end of the 19th century and the early part of the 20th allows us to refute this optimism. In each case, without exception, the national capitalist market brings together overdeveloped and underdeveloped regions, the existence of one group determining that of the others. Whether it is Ireland in Britain, the South in the USA and Italy, Flanders in Belgium, the south and eastern parts of Holland, the centre and southwest of France, or Bavaria and large sections of the centre, north and east of Germany, regional underdevelopment appears to be a universal phenomenon in a capitalist economy. [32]

Gill goes on to suggest reasons for the failure of the various federal government subsidization programs.

> In a capitalist economy, regional underdevelopment plays an essential role ; in effect it assures a supply of reserve manpower always ready to join the proletariat in the concentrated industrial

areas (especially urban ones); the underdeveloped regions also offer markets for the products of the developed areas. The drainage of resources from the underdeveloped regions also takes other forms. In the commercial sector, trade in products which are of unequal value; i.e. unequal trade, lead to a transfer of wealth from the poorer to the richer zones. On the financial level the poor zones are also stripped of their savings by financial institutions and banks which reinvest them where they find the highest rate of earnings is to be found, that is, in the highly developed regions. This finally leads to the blockage of development in the poorer regions which can only profit the developed regions. [33]

In conclusion, what was started by Alvin Hamilton, the progressive Minister of Agriculture in the Diefenbaker government, as a program to redevelop depressed rural areas, to improve useage of rural land and retrain people, has gradually evolved in the ten year period, through a pork barrel type of applied solution to the problems of regional inequalities, to the present phase where the Department of Regional Expansion grants have been integrated into the whole fabric of Canadian capitalism. Capitalism in Québec, a province which with Ontario forms the heartland of Canadian capitalism, has achieved the enviable situation of having its position "stabilized" through the massive infusion of public funds by the state. Profits are more assured through the renewal of machinery financed with public funds and depreciation allowances, the amount of risk capital necessary has been reduced and the development of natural resource extractive industries required to ensure the supply of raw materials for industry is being partly financed through DREE grants. The missing link in the chain, industrial renewal and expansion in

the relatively developed areas such as Montréal, which previously had to finance the DREE grants to the "designated areas" through taxes (taxes on corporations reduce profits) has now been provided through the latest amendments to the Regional Development Incentives Act; DREE grants are now available to promote capitalist renewal and expansion in high-growth areas such as Montréal. The liberal state has now come full circle.

Some of the consequences which may result from this use of state power and public funds to reinforce the present socio-economic status quo through "rational" and "functional" economic policies have been suggested in the following reflections by Louis Gill:

> Far from suggesting a strategy designed to combat regional underdevelopment, the "diffusionist" thesis contained in the Higgins, Martin and Raynaud report proposes to the people of the underdeveloped areas that they wait passively for the diffusion of prosperity to reach them from Montréal, the growth pole. In the interval these regions must integrate themselves into the economic activity of which Montréal is the centre, or depopulate their communities by migrating to the cities of which Montréal is the largest. Moreover, the integration of peripheral regions around the growth and development poles will develop on the basis of the domination of the periphery by the growth pole. The frankness and casualness with which Higgins. Martin and Raynauld proposed this thesis should be noted. Whereas most of the proponents of the capitalist ideology, both theoreticians and practicians, at least attempt to hide the most undesirable effects and characteristics of the capitalist system, they coldly, and apparently with some satisfaction, vaunt the logical consequences of their thesis, in all that it implies in the way of an unconditional surrender to the domination of capital.
>
> The allusions to regional underdevel-

opment in the article by Mandel had shown previously that capitalist growth is based on regional underdevelopment and that the role of these regions is to furnish a market and raw materials for the highly developed regions. It is interesting to note that the economic policies advocated in the Higgins, Martin and Raynauld report (ed. note : and which have been adopted by the Federal government) are designed to reinforce the patterns which happen spontaneously in a regular capitalist economy. Far from being reformist, the bourgeois state which is guided by this thesis, plays the only role possible for it without risking any contradictions. [34]

SUMMARY

Within the last three years, because of historical factors particular to Canada and tensions created by the nationalist crisis in Québec, the Federal government has implemented a series of economic policies designed to "control", if not eliminate, the main causes of these social and political tensions, i.e. high unemployment and regional inequalities. The main thrust of this economic policy has been the direct subsidization of industries which either expand existing facilities or build new plants in these underdeveloped regions or "designated areas" of Canada. Because of the enormous sums of public capital committed to the program (more than one billion has been spent since 1969) and the shocking failure of the program to achieve its objectives, the role of the state in economic development is very rapidly becoming the most important topic of political debate in Canada. This is all to the good ; all issues related to the economic question, Canadian economic independence, class exploitation, cultural and social inequality are relevant to the question of regional inequality. David Lewis of the

N.D.P. and some newspapers have been particularly effective in bringing this crucial issue before the public. Walter Stewart, in a series of articles written for the Toronto STAR, has succeeded in bringing out the new forms of economic exploitation the DREE grants have introduced into Canadian society — his research into the Michelin pork barrel is of particular interest.

The editors of OUR GENERATION feel, however, that the issues of DREE grants to private enterprise and regional inequalities are much more fundamental ; we feel that these interventionist policies are the inevitable consequence of the crisis of the liberal state and of the failure of continentalist economic policies. We have attempted to show that the role of the public sector has expanded in direct proportion to the needs of monopoly capital and that the salaried population has financed most of this growth of public investments and services. We have shown that high unemployment and regional inequalities are a direct result of a capitalist exploitation and cannot be solved by the liberal state complementing the exploitation by the private sector of the economy. Certainly, social, health and educational services have been expanded, but the rationale has been the upgrading of the factors of production while not fundamentally shifting budget priorities away from providing contracts and services to the private sector.

We have presented our analysis mainly through a study of the development of the role of the public sector in the Québec economy during the "quiet revolution". We attempted to correlate the growth of state power with the development of nationalist or independentist technocratic bureaucracies in

Québec, and we referred to some of the links between the Québec state and the industrial elite.

Inevitably, the critique of the liberal state is most advanced in Québec, particularly by the trade union movement which is presently engaged in a complex social, economic and political confrontation with the Québec state through the "Common Front" of unions in the public sector. The contradictions are most sharply drawn in Québec ; Québec is the "designated area" for the confrontation between the forms of integration state capitalism being used in the attempt to solve Québec's economic problems and the type of alternatives proposed by the Common Front and the citizens of Cabano (Gaspé) and Mont Laurier (Laurentians). The people of Cabano have formed a "Peoples' Pulp and Paper Co." to build and operate a community-owned pulp mill and corrugated box plant, both to be run by a state socialist form of management. In Mont Laurier, the plant workers and wood suppliers have been successfully managing the operations of a plywood factory presently owned by a Québec Government crown corporation. Both of these community projects require some capital investment, both have been attempting to get DREE grants or other forms of government assistance, and both have been singularly unsuccessful in these attempts. One billion dollars of DREE grants have been handed out to private industry in the last few years, none of this has gone to the Cabano or Mont Laurier projects even though they are both relatively sound from a "free enterprise" point of view, certainly more so than the dozens of companies which have gone bankrupt after receiving sizable amounts of public funds. The collusion between the state (high-level civil servants in this case) and the large corporations has effectively blocked government help to these projects.

The liberal state, liberator or exploiter ?

To the people of Cabano and Mont Laurier, the answer is now self-evident — even if the state does eventually decide to give Department of Regional Economic Expansion subsidies to these communities.

FOOTNOTES :
1. QUÉBEC LABOUR, (Montréal : Black Rose Books, 1972), p. 147.
2. IBID.
3. IBID., p. 148.
4. IBID., p. 149.
5. QUÉBEC — ONLY THE BEGINNING, (Toronto : New Press, 1972), p. 112.
6. IBID., p. 151.
7. IBID., p. 156.
8. "La Situation Du Gouvernement du Québec Dans Les Affaires Economiques De La Province," Kemal Wassef, (ed), (Montréal : Research Department, Confederation of National Trade Unions, October, 1971), p. 2.
9. IBID., p. 5.
10. IBID., pp. 5-6.
11. IBID., p. 43.
12. IBID., p. 36.
13. IBID., p. 19.
14. IBID., pp. 44-45.
15. "Socialisme Québécois," UN MAILLON DE LA CHAÎNE, No. 23, 1972.
16. Brunelle, Richard and Pierre Papineau, "Le Gouvernement du Capital," SOCIALISME QUÉBÉCOIS, No. 23, 1972, p. 89. After completing this article, the authors, together with others, formed a research group for the purpose of exploring various aspects of capitalist exploitation in Québec.
17. IBID., pp. 90-91.
18. IBID., p. 96.
19. "Bulletin," L'Agence de Presse Libre du Québec, No. 69 (July 13-20, 1972), p. 14.
20. IBID., pp. 14-15.
21. IBID., pp. 15-16.
22. IBID., p. 19.
23. IBID., p. 20.
24. IBID., p. 18.
25. QUÉBEC — ONLY THE BEGINNING, (Toronto : New Press, 1972), p. 179.
26. "Bulletin," L'Agence de Presse Libre du Québec, No. 69 (July 13-20, 1972), p. 18.
27. QUÉBEC LABOUR, (Montréal : Black Rose Books, 1972). On p. 120 is noted a reference from CANADIAN DIMENSION, Vol. 7, No. 8, (April, 1971) in which the U.S. funds as a percentage of total investment averaged 10.4 percent between 1963 and 1968, with a high of 20.8 percent in 1965 and a low of 4.9 percent in 1968.
28. "Bulletin," L'Agence de Presse Libre du Québec, No. 69 (July 13-20, 1972). p. 22.
29. Robert Chados, "The Business of Jean Marchand is Business," LAST POST, Vol. 2, No. 6 (July, 1972), p. 43.
30. Louis Gill, "Croissance et Asservissement," SOCIALISME QUÉBÉCOIS, No. 23 (1972). p. 13.
31. IBID., pp. 14-15.
32. IBID., pp. 19-20.
33. IBID., p. 20.
34. IBID., pp. 21-23.

AUTHORITY AND THE STATE

by Graeme Nicholson

The Problem of Authority

For all but a few people today, working means working for somebody. For most people today, that is an institution, not an individual employer. In most of the institutions where people work, there is a pattern of authority. Anyone who works in an industrial plant, a hospital or a department store, is well acquainted with the authority of his or her boss. The boss gives the orders.

In most places nowadays, the boss has been ordered to give the orders, he has been told what he must expect of the men and women in his unit. Nowadays, one's immediate boss - foreman, manager or head nurse - is usually an employee too. He also has a boss. If he can't get performance out of the employees, then usually he must fire them or transfer them. If he doesn't do it, a higher boss will. And if he fails too often to get results, the boss knows that he will be fired or transferred himself. This is the setting in which most of us work.

There has been a great deal of discussion in recent years about the psychology of authority—in fact, altogether too much. Studies have been made on the "authoritarian personality" and on his opposite number, the rebel or dissenter. Adorno argues that authoritarian personalities are deeply anxious ; on the other side, Feuer argues that childhood malaise is at the roots of rebellion. They have all tended to obscure the basic point : that authority actually exists. No matter what personality types are involved, workers and bosses on the job are unequal in fact. Bosses have authority.

Authority is a social thing. It must be seen first and foremost as a social structure not as a personality structure. One person's authority lies in his relationship to others, so the main thing to describe is the relationship, not the personalities. This can be done by looking at the institutions where these relationships exist, the places where people work.

The guideline we can follow in clarifying the authority relationship is how the institutions are organized. In particular what interests me is the formal organization of these institutions, their official organization.

Sociologists today often distinguish the formal organization of, say, a business firm from its informal organization. The formal organization is the official constitution of the outfit, which is often visualized as a scheme of boxes and connecting lines, running from the chairman of the board down to the hourly wage workers. Sociologists tell us, and experience bears it out, that these schemes do not give an accurate picture of how things work in most institutions. Decisions do not get made in the orderly manner this suggests. There are loose informal alliances, power groups, in the institutions. They consult by telephone or in the corridor, disregarding the official chain of command. They see to it that official conferences are called of course, but only to give the rubber stamp. Real power to influence the outfit's course of action is distributed through this informal organization more than the formal one. The informal organization is also the locus of "company politics". Individuals in the company achieve their own self— interested aims by working the informal organization : knowing who to know and pulling strings behind the scenes is the way they advance their careers. And self— interested groups in a company, the backers of a new product, for example, work the informal organization in the same way.

None of this can be denied. Nevertheless, fascination with informal power structures can blind one to several important things. For one thing, the informal organization of a company is only a sort of shadow of its formal organization. How could climbers use backroom deals to get promoted if there could not be promotions, or positions arranged in a hierarchy ? But there is a more important point. The informal organization is confined to the managerial group. In looking at it, we do not grasp this group's relationship to the working class.

In the most general terms, our society is divided into a ruling class and a working class. The crucial point about the former is its possession of authority—or rather, what I want to argue at length, its possession of a particular type of authority. This type is what I have been calling the authority of the boss. The crucial point about the working class is precisely its lack of this authority. It is on the receiving end. The power struggles in informal one ; it is a relation of au- the authority group. They occur only on one side of the general antithesis between this group and the working class. The relationship between these two major classes is not at all an informal one, it is a relation of authority, a formal difference between them. Struggles among self—interested parties in the ruling class do not alter the authority relationship which each member of that class bears towards workers.

Most of the people who work in institutions have no hand in shaping policies. Their daily work consists in carrying out decisions, or in performing routine tasks which go on from day to day, like sweeping floors. They are the working class. The difference between them and the policy—forming group is not a matter of the informal organization. It is a difference of authority, a formal difference. If an ineffectual vice—president offers an opinion at the board meeting, people listen to him, though impatiently, perhaps gazing off at the ceiling, or drumming their fingers in irritation.

But if a cleaning woman does the same thing, she is told to shut up.

I have been identifying the ruling class as an authority group. This might seem to be an innocuous point, even on semantic grounds—after all, what is ruling if not a sort of authority? In fact, the point is not innocuous. In particular, what I want to bring out here runs afoul of a central claim of Marxism. For Marxists, there is a definite ruling class in capitalist society, namely, the capitalist class. They own capital and the means of production. But the authority group I am speaking of is more extensive than the capitalist class in two ways. First, the authority group within a capitalist corporation is more extensive than the owners. Managers have authority even if they do not own a single share. Second, the authority group is also found in institutions other than capitalist corporations. It is in full view whenever you visit a hospital, school or university. The claim I want to make, then, is that non—capitalist managers in corporations, on the one hand, and on the other hand, hospital personnel, for example, in positions of authority within a hospital, also belong to the ruling class of our society, not just capitalists. There is lack of an analysis of authority in Marxism. It is not only a question bearing on the spectrum of classes. There is a certain vagueness in Marxism as to what constitutes the 'ruling' of the ruling class. The authority of managers is something that can be analyzed and understood and that is what I want to attempt here. The analysis of authority, taken by itself, is neither Marxist nor non-Marxist. For all I know, it could make a contribution towards Marxist theory, offering an analysis of the "rule" of the ruling class.

The principal point in the present analysis of authority is a distinction that must be made in types of authority. The authority exercised by managers, administrators and so on is an *unspecific authority*. I shall seek to distinguish this sharply from another type of authority which I call *specific*.

What is non—Marxist here is the second main point I want to make. It is that the unspecific authority of managers is linked to the *State*. It is not enough to offer a mere distinction in concepts, between two types of authority, nor can one confine one's attention to the interior of the institutions where relations of authority prevail. Rather one must ask: how come they have their pattern of authority? And one must look at the overall framework in which they are situated. My argument is that when we look back in history to the origins of the authority relation, we find them in the State. And when we look at the present day, we find again that the framework of each and every institution is formed by the State. In the State lies both the prototype and the continuing support for the authority of our bosses. The State has put its mark on all institutions: business corporations, industrial plants, hospitals, schools, and transportation systems. To grasp this feature clearly, we need a new concept. From this viewpoint, these institutions should all be regarded as *micro-states*.

It is also necessary to think about the future. The pattern of authority in our places of work is so well established that it is often hard to imagine how things could be otherwise. Often it seems that the pattern is fixed for good. But it came into being, and it can pass. To break it entirely is no easy task, for it is sustained by powerful forces, especially the State. In order to break the pattern of authority in places of work, we must adopt the program of anarchism to abolish the

State. I shall have more to say on this at the end of the essay.

Institutional Authority

The institutions we are speaking of work on the principle of *authorization,* and usually this takes the form of the chain of command. For any particular type of action to be done, there is a specific level in the system from which it must be authorized. The one who can authorize an activity (let us call him the relevant authority) makes two kinds of interruptions : (a) he has the power to intervene between the worker and his work. He can tell him to make this rather than that ; to start working, to stop, and so on. Even though the worker himself initiated the activity in the form of a request sent up the channels, he must still wait for authorization. The authority must initiate the activity a second time. The nullifying force of his *refusal* to authorize is the very mark of his authority.

(b) The authority intervenes between worker and worker. When one worker must wait for authorization from above, there cannot be an uninhibited joint activity on the part of two or more. Proportional to the strength of the authority relationship, thinking and deciding become the activity of one small class, while the work of the large class of workers consists in carrying out decisions. This class division of labour gives social existence to an abstraction. In the lives of individuals, decisions are not separate things by themselves, they are only abstract aspects of our activity. Occasionally, perhaps, we decide, then act. From time to time, everyone has the experience of coming to a crossroads. But in the normal case, what we call a decision is not separated in this way from an ongoing activity. It

is just one element in our activity, like motions of the eyes. We probably identify our decisions most often in retrospect. But when activity is deprived of decision, as in institutions of the authority pattern, this abstraction has become a vicious reality.

The main reason given for the system of authorization is that, just as a human being needs a nerve centre, so an organization needs a decision centre. It must be unified. There are other reasons offered, of course, which bear on this or that feature of such organizations. For example, the need for career incentives is often said to justify the hierarchy of positions.

I want to argue that the system of hierarchy is not justified on these grounds—it does not spring up directly owing to the need for concerted activity in production, but has come from another source. I should like to claim, in fact, that it is in *conflict* with the social relationships which production requires and which productive work promotes.

For one thing and principally, the micro-states are incapable of satisfying the interests of workers. The central social fact of our time is the conflict between chain of command authorities and the working class, a conflict about the content of the decisions made by the ruling class, above all, over the distribution of the product and profits. This conflict has been documented in a hundred places, and we must never lose sight of it in a too formalistic analysis. Along with the conflict over the content of decisions, however, there exists a conflict over authoritarian procedures per se. Both on grounds of the content of decisions, and on grounds of the formal organization, critics of authoritarianism advocate a system of workers' control : all will decide and all will execute. The two motives are not separable. All through history questions of authority have been linked with questions of property. In the next section, I shall look a little further into the question of authority itself.

Specific and Unspecific Authority

Anarchists have always been suspicious of authority, and they have made a more complete and principled critique of authoritarian institutions than anyone else. Moreover, they have always linked authority and the State —this is the central issue in their long history of debates with Marxists. Nevertheless, there is a nagging doubt that always comes through when one reads anarchists like Godwin and Bakunin. They aim to abolish authority and the State, but, they hasten to add, they do want to decree that doctors shall be no longer "authorities" in matters of health, and so on. Bakunin declared : "respect the authority of the physician." What is the difference between the sort of authority Bakunin respected and the sort he did not respect ?

His answer was that he submitted to the authority of the doctor voluntarily, whereas the authority of the State was coercive. But, I do not think that distinction does the job. The distinction stated by Bakunin can justify democratic government just as well as anarchism. Even if there is no evidence that people have given their free consent to government, one could still reply that government would be justified in the case of a small country where consent could be checked. But such a position is not anarchist at all ; the trouble with authority is not merely that consent has not been given.

Godwin said that anarchists accepted the authority of *reason,* and rejected authority based on force. The doctor's authority was the authority of science

and reason, whereas the State's authority was not. The reference to reason is beside the point, because a government regulation could have been framed only after the most exhaustive and rational debate. The government proclaims a regulation rather than rationally convincing each person to obey, but neither does the physician who prescribes a drug give the patient a lesson in internal medicine, in science. He expects the patient to trust his competence.

There seems to be a distinction which neither Bakunin nor Godwin stated very exactly.

Skill : The very heart of human labour is the effort to control some object which offers resistance. Whether that be a lump of steel or a dislocated shoulder, or something not quite so material, such as a software problem in a computer, makes no difference here. Mastery is usually attained with a type of tool, and in the present condition of things, it is usually a joint achievement on the part of a number of workers.

In the joint performance of tasks, there are two main possibilities. (1) The task is broken down into subtasks which are different from each other, but dovetailed or interlinked. One worker cuts potatoes, another operates the deep-frier. The two subtasks are often done at different places in the plant. (2) The two do the same operation, together or separately. Where one is learning from the other by imitation, that is one case of doing the same thing together. In both cases (1) and (2) each subtask has a specific nature : cutting potatoes is not like operating the frier, neither is it just cutting apples. The specific character of tasks is a condition for their coordination as well as for learning.

Work performed in this setting is skilled labour. People often speak of unskilled labour, but this expression is misleading. They mean such activities as sweeping a floor or digging a ditch, but if these activities were lacking in all element or skill, then it would be impossible for them to be well or badly done ; a novice would produce as good a result as an experienced worker ; he would do it as quickly, with as little wear and tear on his instruments of labour and his own body (the skin on his hands or his shoulder joints) ; he would expend no more of his energy in doing the task, and would leave no more mess in the environment. But none of this is true ; no piece of work is lacking altogether in skill. When people speak of unskilled labour, they mean either that no particular schooling is necessary to do the job, or they have in mind the idea of routine tasks. But in the first case, there is a confusion between skill and the social recognition of skill. A mechanic is said to be a skilled worker because he is certified, but certification is not what makes anyone skilled ; it only guarantees that someone is recognized as skilled. People without papers still have skills. And as for the notion of routine labour, this again is not unskilled, for tasks are routine only after the skills they require have been learned. No tasks are routine from the very start.

Traditional forms of skilled craftsmanship, the carpenter in his workshop for example, have been surpassed and outmoded in many areas of production today, as a consequence of the industrial revolution. But there is a danger of obscuring elements which present day industry shares with the past, in particular the element of skill itself. The assumption can be made, and Marxists state it explicitly, that industry has developed to the point that the basic unit of work is merely labour time, or labour power. Some workers, of course, employ certain skills in their work, and, therefore claim a higher wage on account of the time and power that has gone into their education. But most do not ; they expend time and power, units which are undifferentiated in themselves. But the error which lies close at hand here is to insist too much on the undifferentiated time and power. Every encounter with a specific task demands a differentiated skill. This is not necessarily relevant to the worker's wage, or to the exchange value of the commodity produced, but it does exist, and it is highly relevant in another connection.

The exercise of a skill can generally be seen by others. This allows them to participate in the task alongside the skilled worker. In this joint labour, the second man can come to acquire the skill. All skills have a social character, and are educative in their very nature, because their exercise occurs out in the open. When a skill is mastered, its inherent tendency is to communicate itself to another. This is the relevance of the specificity of skills : they allow joint activity in two ways : workers can share in the *same* action, and they can link, or dovetail, *different* ones. While the social setting of most work now is vastly different from the old craftsman's shop, there is an analogue of the ancient practice of skills : joint specific activity, the joint mastery on the part of workers of a type of material with a type of tool in an ongoing social, dovetailed activity. Voluntary association of workers in a joint project is the social form which skilled activities of their own nature promote.

Here we come to the main point. We have spoken of mastering a skill, but this is a metaphor. Mastery or control is actually exercised upon the materials, the objects, the things, whatever it is that a specific skill (hammering, cooking, etc.) is exercised upon. The skill *is* the mastery over tools, raw materials and the like.

No skill is any more general than the particular type of tools and materials with which they can cope. The very possibility of a skill is tied up with a certain material it is exercised upon, wood, stone, steel, etc. The skill of a builder, for example, could simply not exist were it not for wood, or something sufficiently like it, and by the same token it cannot find application upon vegetables, the human body or another material, it is a different skill (cooking, medicine, etc.) which is exercised there. The mastery over wood, metal, vegetables, etc., is never merely destructive, but preservative, involving a positive care exercised upon the materials and tools. Therapeutic skills such as medicine are the clearest case of this component of care, but in fact it is present in all skills. Where the worker has a greater skill, he preserves his tools and materials better.

While a skill is tied up with a certain type of material and tool, it is not totally restricted to them. A particularly skilled worker is one who can specify new sorts of tools, materials and procedures for the purpose at hand. A given skill is defined not only by its materials and tools, it is a special type of *situation* which calls for, say, the builder's skill : man's need for housing. The skill's scope is defined by a type of situation, which is a lack or need of some sort. Thus the skill is not merely the mastery over a set of tools and materials, but over a definite sector of human life. The builder is a master of housing the physician of the body, the sailor of sea transport, and so on. The skill is a mastery or control over a sector of natural or social being. Within the particular sector, the skilled worker possesses authority. This is a power over it, which is convincingly manifested by being exercised in full public view, which is acknowledged by others as a matter of course, and requires no certification. The acknowledgment of his authority on the part of others contains an element of awe, but to the authority there is nothing mysterious in what he does, and the actual tendency of his work is to demystify his authority, to teach the skill by exercising it, to invite participation and collegiality on the part of others.

The project of an anarchist devolution is precisely not aimed at abolition of this kind of authority. The idea of liberation, in fact, consists in part of finding work that is worth doing, and that means work that brings human skills into play as well as satisfying other human needs and desires. This is what I call specific authority ; that means authority over a *sector* of nature or society. This, in fact, is roughly the original meaning of *authority,* but the course of history has been to change its meaning, so it is nowadays almost impossible to use the word in this sense. The term is now used mainly for the sort of authority that bosses have. Let us look into that.

In ancient times, productive tasks were pursued in shops, mines, factories and so on. In these settings we see an authority pattern of masters and workers. In many cases, the workers were slaves; the master owned them. Masters ordered the slaves to begin to work, to stop working, to make this rather than that. These relationships were an early form of the micro-state.

In other periods, workers were not slaves, but apprentices, journeymen, and so on. The masters did not own them, but they owned the shops, the tools, and the products were theirs to sell. Here again the master craftsman was situated in an authority rank within the shop, giving orders to the workers. And later, with capitalist relations of production, the pattern of authority alters in detail but not in substance.

The authority of the master (boss) **over the worker** is what we are concerned with. Let us imagine a stonemason's shop, in any period, with ten workers and one owner-boss.

The workers collectively possess a set of skills useful in this sector of production. Very likely the boss possesses some of them too, and may exercise them from time to time, working alongside his employees. It is quite indifferent to his authority qua boss whether he does or does not. The skills are employed upon a material and directed towards satisfying some need. They are engaged in their sector ; but his authority is directed to the *interior* of the shop. It is control, not over the sector (housing and stone) but over workers.

But the boss's authority does not exist only because there is this well-defined social unit, the shop. His authority does not spring directly from its unity. True, the relationship of authority only exists within a well-defined social unit, but it has a further condition. There are other shops, engaged in other sectors of production, which have a similar pattern of authority. There is a whole class of bosses, never merely one boss in one shop. In the authority relation of boss to worker, there is not merely a hierarchy in one locale, there is a relationship of his whole class to the whole of the working class. This is the external support of the interior relation of authority.

It is in the boss class that the links are made between shop and shop, they draw up contracts for deliveries of goods from shop to shop. To each

other they represent their respective shops. But the authority relation *within* each shop is the point where its interior is brought into line with its exterior. The exterior of each shop is a group of other shops, places where related work goes on. It is the boss class who organize these relationships. That means that the authority of the entire class of bosses is concentrated in the authority which the boss exercises within his own shop. But authority of the class is precisely not a mastery of a given domain or sector. It is an unrestricted mastery which the class has over the whole of the people's life. No one boss is master of the entire town, of course. What he does have is an authority over his workers, an authority which is unspecific in its origins.

The boss's authority within the shop is not equivalent to any of the skills which he might or might not practice there, for example, it is not the same thing as a skill in coordinating the various tasks that go on there. The authority of the boss is clearest when he *denies* a request, *refuses* authorization or orders his workers to stop whatever they are doing. Authority comes across most vividly in negations because its own nature is to be unspecific. Skilled activities ,as I sought to argue before, coordinate themselves to a large degree. Where they do not, for example, where the operation is too complex, and one worker cannot understand what another is doing, there is need for a coordinator. But coordination is not the same thing as authority, it is a specific task alongside others. In his essay *On Authority*, Engels identified authority with co-ordination, but thereby be slipped into a whole host of fallacies. I shall mention a few of them below.

The authority of masters over workers has been connected, in all periods of history, to the property system. If the workers were slaves, the masters owned them. If they were freemen or apprentices the masters still owned the shops, the tools and the products were theirs to exchange for their profit. In capitalist relations of production, the owners become separated to some degree from the immediate bosses, but they are there in the background. How the authority relation in the shop is connected to the master's *property* in slaves, the means of production, in products and in land is not a simple question at all. It is not enough to remark that authority relations are merely *reflections* or *expressions* of a property system. For there remains to be mentioned the crucial factor in all this, the authority of the *State*.

STATES AND MICRO-STATES

The authority exercised by the master in his shop would never have been possible were it not situated in a *State*. The rank of the master depended upon a recognition offered him in the city at large, as the master stone mason. But it was not mere recognition, in a loose sense, offered by *society* which sustained him in his rank. It was a sanction supported by the State, the threat of armed response from soldiers to mutiny or riot on the part of workers, particularly when the workers were slaves. And citizenship in the State was among the most important privileges of the master. What I want to argue is that the authority relationship within the shop stemmed from an antecedent authority relationship in the State. That is why I want to call such a shop a micro-state, to stress that the State is not a product of such shops as these, but that it is the other way around. That is also to say that the micro-state does not rise directly from the social relations of production. It is not a relationship which is native to production at all. It is a foreign graft upon the primary

craft relations of production. A type of authority stemming from the State has been infused into sector institutions, making them small scale copies of the State.

But it is more important to talk about our own situation than the past. The term 'State' is often difficult to understand, because one cannot see the State. This difficulty is increased in parliamentary systems, where the functions of the State are divided among many legislative, judicial and executive organs and it is compounded again in federal systems such as the Canadian one, where State functions are distributed among levels of government.

However, there is no difficulty in identifying a whole set of particular government organizations, cabinets, departments, agencies, etc. Anyone can name fifty of them, even if it is not so easy to see how they are all related. Let us simply use the term *State* for the *sum total of government institutions*. My claim is that however intricate the relationships among these particular organizations at bottom they are one and not many. They constitute together one single institution, the State. The intricacies are partly constitutional ones, but there are also informal ones. For example, there may be an alliance between the Nova Scotia Department of Labour and the R.C.M.P. These are connections among sub-institutions of the State.

Many branches of government have the same inner form as corporations. Many of them are really micro-states, that is, sector institutions supplying particular services the same way private corporations do, e.g. the CBC. But other government institutions are different. Courts, police, cabinets, have a unique sort of power which individuals experience in a very direct way—when they pay taxes or go to jail—and which other institutions also experience. It is in these very powerful agencies that the unity of the State is clearest. The State is not a sector institution but a total one.

Sector institutions like mining companies and law firms link up with each other and make all shorts of adjustments to each other in their formal organizations. But the government institutions do not merely crisscross, they form a unity. In regulating the affairs of the sector institutions, the State perpetually injects unspecific authority into their interiors. It certifies them, incorporates them, limits their growth from time to time, regulates their mutual adjustments and in all these ways it makes them, to a limited degree, its agents. It does not go so far as to seize their capital; it goes just far enough to reintroduce continually unspecific authority into them. The authority of the foreman on the job is a reflection of the authority of the cop on the beat. The places we work lie within the field of this magnet, the State and its peculiar forces touches everything in that field.

The peculiar force of the State, the unspecific authority of a total institution, is not a mysterious visitation upon mankind but something generated in the final analysis out of the skills practiced in various sectors. The authority of the sovereign power, which is inserted into the sectors turning them into micro-states was generated out of the sectors in the first place. But this historical process is not something we can deal with here.

Workers control and anarchy

While the micro-states have been infused from the actual State, they also help to sustain the latter. Authority relationships are complex. When they are not operational, they weaken, and therefore when sub-authorities are defied, the super-authority they have depended on tends to totter. Thus, while the micro-states cannot be abolished without abolition of the State, it is also true that successful struggle against the micro-states can lead to the abolition of the State.

Direct struggle of the people against the State itself seems hardly capable of success nowadays, its army cannot be defeated. But the interior of each and every micro-state is an arena where struggle can succeed. That is the struggle for workers' control. Micro-states of all descriptions, capitalist corporations which are economically productive and sector institutions which live off the surplus can be engaged in tactical battles of the sort which prevents the army from intervening.

In single-company towns, to mention only one example, the struggle for workers' control is at the same time a struggle for community control. When this demand is made, it is possible to prevent the army from intervening. Struggles for specific issues conducted within the corporations' walls do not need to bring out the army and combats of a limited nature, in which the local community gives its support, even when a limited violence is directed against company goons and local police, need not involve the army. The problem lies in selecting just that degree of pressure which can succeed against the company and the local police which does not bring the army out. Such a strategy adopted in town after town, and plant after plant can make a revolution. This rather than the demand for nationalization is what can return the economy of Canada to Canadians.

Anarchists have long proclaimed the program of abolishing the State but this is inevitably an abstraction unless the cutting edge of the people's movement is directed against the micro-states. Abolition of the State is a meaningless slogan unless it includes the revolution in the social relations of production where the micro-states have been broken. The Soviet Union will never attain anarchy until its micro-states have been broken down.

An anarchy is not merely a stateless society. It is a society in which unspecific authority in every locale has been abolished and every social and economic process is managed by the workers, i.e., by specific authority. The anarchist has to prove that no unspecific authority is required to manage individual sector activities and to correlate their relationships. This can be proved, I believe, but it goes beyond the scope of this essay. One of the distinctions that he needs to defend is the one between coordination which circulates information and authority which interrupts relations between worker and worker. Another point he needs to make is against Engel's pessimistic views on authority. Engles refers in his essay to the *authority of steam* i.e. to the element of necessity in the material world and the use of it in technology. This material system of forces is such that individual caprice cannot be tolerated in productive plants. Therefore there needs to be managerial authority. He is saying that because there is a material system that cannot vary beyond certain limits there needs to be a social system of the same sort. But this is not the case. It is the given material unity of a plant which can hold workers together. It is because the processes of production have an element of order in them which all can see that a secondary social order of the same type is unnecessary.

THE STATE AS SOCIALIZER: OFY and LIP PROGRAMMES

by Lorne F. Huston

LEAVING behind the tired, colourless image of the State, the government of the seventies has launched itself into the realms of the planning of imagination, enthusiasm and idealism. Qualifying its programmes Opportunities for Youth and Local Initiatives Projects as a kind of "Planned anarchism" [1], the State has sought to meet youth "where it's at." Most criticism of these programmes has revolved around four major points:

(1) that they are an expensive plaything for middle-class youth;

(2) that they are an election gimmick designed to woo the youth vote for the Liberals;

(3) that in Québec, the programmes are an attempt to re-establish contacts with a generation that regards Ottawa as superfluous;

(4) that they are designed to mask unemployment rather than to deal with the causes.

While these criticisms are generally valid, we think that there is a deeper and more coherent motivation than this. These programmes are part of a strategy of social control.

Our principal hypothesis here is that these programmes are much more a response to social instability than to an economic crisis as such. We suggest that they are not particularly effective from an economic point of view but that they are very effective

---

1. "Report of the Evaluation Task Force to the Secretary of State" February 1972, p. 7.

concerning their principal function : the integration of "marginals" into the main-stream of society. The simple existence of the unemployed does not threaten capitalist society. At certain times it can even be useful, by creating a large reserve of cheap labour and by "fighting inflation". What causes the problem are the social consequences of unemployment. Massive unemployment breaks some of the bonds which psychologically and physically bind the workers to the society. The control exercised through various social pressures in the work place is no longer present. This is even more true for youth who are generally more on the margin of society in any case.

In an extremely interesting book, Piven and Cloward suggest that when massive unemployment has undesirable social consequences, assistance programmes are established and expanded in order to control unemployment sufficiently to restore order. [2] An examination of the OFY and LIP programmes in the light of this hypothesis is fruitful. We begin with an analysis of the economic and social impact of these programmes. Secondly, we examine how social control is exercised through these programmes, and finally, we look briefly at their significance in the larger perspective of social planning.

PATCHING OR WEAVING SOMETHING NEW?

The "raison d'être" of these programmes cannot be grasped in an analysis of their economic impact. If the principal concern of the government were to reduce the rate of unemployment, it could have used much more effective instruments from an economic standpoint. This type of programme plays a bandage role by creating jobs, but in a capitalist society the role of governments in the economic system is largely that : to bandage the wounds left by private enterprise. If a mine's operations no longer fulfill the administration's criteria of economic behaviour, it simply closes down and leaves the government to pick up the pieces — whether it be through grants to companies or unemployment assistance. This role can hardly be said to be new to governments. However, there are some programmes which are better designed to reduce unemployment than others. It is interesting to note for example that the Trudeau government strongly opposed the "winter works" programme. This programme which encourages contruction and other related sectors which have a high multiplier effect on the economy contributes directly to an economic upswing. In the construction sector for example, materials are bought, processed and sold at a higher price. There is thus value added. An increase in construction generates benefits to all of the multiple related industries.

But in the case of the OFY and LIP programmes, this is not the case. There is very little material bought in relation to the total input into the economy (about 17%) and there is no production as such, thus no value added. The total buying power is not significantly increased since employees receive almost the same as the unemployment insurance benefits. Thus if it is patching, it is not even good patching. Instead, while still taking the major co-ordinates of its action from private enterprise, the government tries to weave together the loose strands. A policy dealing with the social consequences of unemployment must be integrated with an economic policy. Marginals, such as alienated youth, must be woven back into the fabric of society. The economic considerations are secondary in such programmes; their significance is

---

2. *Regulating the Poor : The Functions of Public Welfare*, Random House, (New York : 1971)

100

in their capacity to promote social stability. The government commissioned a task force to evaluate the Opportunities for Youth programme. They write:

"Although OFY did provide some income for some students, it did nothing to alter the conditions which create student unemployment. (...) Structured as it was, Opportunities for Youth can probably not be truly identified as an employment programme." (p. 83)

It is evident from the report that the main object of these programmes is to effect a change in the attitudes of the participants, referred to as the "target group". The success of failure of the projects is a completely secondary consideration. (pp. 68 & 84). As the report suggests:

"Crucial to an examination of OFY is an understanding of the government decision that the most appropriate method of alleviating student unemployment and possible unrest was the provision of 'meaningful activity'." (p. 84)

Indeed, the government felt "the distinct possibility that a combination of unemployment and 'inactivity' would lead to social unrest." (p. 16) The governement began to understand that a "hot" autumn in Québec didn't mean an Indian Summer. In the summer of 1968, various students groups were organizing. In October student occupations closed down the majority of the CEGEPS (community colleges) and the universities followed. The summer of 1969 was characterized by higher unemployment coupled with clashes between youth and the local elite in the Gaspé and a hunger strike by a youth committee in east Montréal to protest unemployment. The army was sent into Québec after police went on strike and students and workers attacked the offices of Murray Hill. In October, schools were paralysed again as 50,000 students took to the streets to protest the bill entrenching the anglicization process in the educational system. 1970 saw the P.Q. obtain 24% of the popular vote in the Québec election. Another hot October followed; the FLQ kidnapped Cross and Laporte. Student federations all over Québec came out in favour of the objectives of the F.L.Q. Youth were involved in citizens committees, forming Political Action Committees and working for FRAP.

In Canada, the "youth phenomenon" took different forms. Many were not interested in taking jobs for the summer. The Trans-Canada Highway was littered with scraggly transients. The committee on youth estimated that approximately 200,000 young people had been travelling in the summer of 1970, and expected the figure to jump to 300,000 in 1971. Clashes between youth and the local establishment became more frequent, particularly in Vancouver. Drug consumption spiraled and the Youth Report noted a serious degree of alienation among youth.

The government was not particularly concerned about the unemployed person that was actively looking for work (p. 16) but it had noticed a growing number of unemployed who were not even interested in joining the work force. Thus it was necessary to design a programme that would be directed particularly to this group. This is clearly expressed in the Task Force report on OFY and is equally evident in the LIP programme. The latter has the same perception of the problem. Not only is the form the same, but the very nature of the programme is designed for the educated unemployed, that is, those that can prepare, organize and administer a project. In both cases the target group is primarily those who constitute a threat to social stability.

To more fully understand the character of these programmes, it is useful to the conception of reality that inspires them. Today's technocrats are proclaiming the end of ideology. Problems that do come up have technical or "optimal" solutions that transcend idological considerations. Society is seen as a system composed of various sub-systems that correspond to the different groups or institutions in the society. The system is governed by a supra-rationality which is the efficient use of resources (human as well as physical). Thus, the interdependent, harmonious and integrative relationships between subsystems are emphasized. Problems are therefore situations which upset the equilibrium of forces. The Task Force underlines this perception of the problem:

"The committee dealt with the dissatisfaction, rather than the issues themselves as the problems." (p. 21)

According to the technocratic view prevalent in today's western capitalist societies[3], there are no fundamental contradictions within the system. There are *groups* in society which must *co-operate* in order for society to develop, but there are no *social* classes which are characterized by relationships of *oppression*. While wealth should be distributed in an "optimal" fashion in order to ensure the most efficient use of resources, the existing patterns of authority relationships cannot be questioned. Problems of a society are not due to contradictions inherent in a particular stage in the development of society or to conflicting views of reality, but rather to problems of communication. It is a lack of communication that prevents the integration of marginals into the society-system.

The problem of communication has two aspects. On the one hand, the State must find out as much as it can about each group in society, either by encouraging them to use the communication channels or by doing research. On the other hand, the State must make well known what it does. Of course, this perspective defines the State as a neutral arbitrator with no preference for certain types of information over others. The people in government become classless and are equally able to understand and act upon the problems of the rich as the poor.

The choice then, to encourage the participation of marginal youth now becomes clearly understandable. As the Task Force points out:

"For it was not unemployment per se which was seen as creating social unrest: but rather inactivity and non-participation in general." (p. 16)

Participation increases the flow of information in both directions and thus establishes a stronger presence of the dominant society.

"On the assupmtion that the more vocal young people are generally more conscious of social issues, it was argued that any programme which encompassed youth-initiated projets... would be seen as a model of government responsiveness... and hence create participation between government and youth in identifying and solving the problems of their society." (p. 18)

---

3. While this vision of society is found in almost all of the western capitalist societies, it is interesting to note that it marks the writings of Trudeau as well. See "Politique Fonctionnelle" in *Cité Libre*, juin 1950, "Politique Fonctionnelle II" *Ibid.*, Feb. 1951, & "Pour une Politique Fonctionnelle" with others in *Ibid.*, May 1964. Also see, Fred CALOREN, "The War Measures Act and the Politics of Functionalism" in *Our Generation*, Vol. 7, No. 3, Nov. 1970.

Thus the State elaborates programmes that seek to integrate the marginals. What is important in the eyes of the State is that the participants feel that they are doing something "meaningful". It is interesting to note, in passing, that one of the criteria for the projects is that they must constitute a "meaningful activity." This "concept", as vague as it is, is part of a whole vocabulary invented and first used by the counter-culture that has been rendered meaningless by its use in the dominant society. Its use as a criterion of evaluation of these projects illustrates the "imperialist" tendency of the government faced with the signs of a different definition of reality.

That the psychological satisfaction of the participants in the programmes is more important to the government than what is actually done in the projects is clear. These programmes are principally designed neither to reduce unemployment nor to help solve social problems; they are designed to impart a sense of involvement to marginal youth in society. Thus for example, when the authors of the Task Force interpret the estimations of the participants on the value of their project, they note a general satisfaction and they remark:

"It does not really matter whether or not this estimate is a realistic one; what is important is that they were enthusiastic and optimistic about the value of their summer employment." (p. 81)

What the participants do is not important [4], it is only what they *think* about what are doing that is important. Discontent is perceived as the problem; the causes of this discontent are neglected. In this sense, these programmes are more than just an expensive plaything for middle-class youth. It is primarily given to middle-class youth because they are the ones who are contesting society most loudly. While lower class youth suffer the effects of captitalist society even more, they have been less vocal in their rejection and thus are not perceived as a problem.

SOME EFFECTIVE TECHNIQUES

In the first part of this article, we tried to outline the general strategy of social control of which the OFY and LIP programmes are a part. In the following section, we shall examine the mechanicms through which social control is exercised.

We mentioned the double impact of these programmes above. One of the particular characteristics of the programmes is that the object of the programmes is also the subject of the projects. The client is also the administrator. As we have seen, this characteristic is necessary in order to give the impression to the administrator-client that he or she is involved in a "meaningful" activity. It is important therefore, to examine the framework within which his activities are confined in order to explore the nature of the possibilities open to him.

First of all, one might note that the participant plays a role in relation to the population that is similar to that played by the government in relation to the participants. While the government establishes its presence among the educated unemployed, the latter establish, in turn, a presence amongst other marginal groups. The projects that are concerned with pensioners or immigrants for example, are there to give a voice to those who have none.

One might think that the integration of marginals into the dominant society would be desirable but one must take another look at the nature of these program-

---

4. Unless, of course, they try to change the existing power relationships. We'll examine this point below.

mes. It is important to note that it is not a change in the power relationships of society that is envisaged by these programmes. The projects of OFY and LIP are there to provide a service or to do research but projects which seek to attack the structural causes (which are essentially political) are categorically refused. Consider now the definition of the activity of the participants since it constitutes one of the most important aspects of the programmes.

Perhaps one can distinguish two different ways to deal with social problems. One is primarily concerned with providing a service; the other is more concerned with creating a collectivity in order to facilitate a take-over by the population concerned of its own administration. The first alternative, in furnishing an individual service does not seek to attack the causes of existing problems but simply to help people meet their problems. In this sense it corresponds with the vision of society without conflict that we mentioned earlier. Specific cases of discontent can be overcome by simply furnishing the relevant information.

Thus for example, a Tenants Association following the first alternative, would furnish legal information to tenants concerning their rights, or their leases but it could not attack one of the main causes of the problems of tenants — that of the socio-economic inequality of landlords and tenants. Tenants are forced to submit to the demands of landlords as long as they are not organized collectively. One can know one's rights as a tenant backwards and forwards but this means little if the laws, leases and power relationships are clearly biased in favour of the landlords.

Take another example: that of medical clinics. Perhaps the clinics will be capable of distributing medical services more equally but they are incapable of attacking the socio-economic causes of sickness — poor housing conditions, malnutrition due to low salaries, dangerous working conditions, among others. In both case the socio-economic causes (the class character) of the problems are neglected because they are not services to be rendered but a call for political action, which is prohibited by the programmes.

Indeed, to ensure that these projects stay within the realm of furnishing services, there are several built-in safeguards which effectively prevent collective action.

1° *SELECTION OF PROJECTS:* The criteria of acceptance are sufficiently ambiguous to allow the civil servants to reject any project that could possibly encourage collective action, without their having to justify their refusal nor for the participants to defend their project. The obscurity of the criteria is important in another sense as well. It plays the role of the carrot before the donkey. A group that may have been refused a first time can always hope it will be accepted a second time and thus often it will submit to the conditions of the programme even when it is not financed by the government, in order to improve its possibilities of acceptance the next time. Also, the government can effectively decide what projects are most important in a given area as well as determining how long they shall exist, since in most cases, no grant means no project. This also gives the government a certain power to direct the use of energies. A project in an area tends to attract the most energetic people and prevent the development of other more autonomously defined projects.

2° *THE FLOOD TECHNIQUE:* When I was eight or nine years old, I was responsable for watering the garden but I hated cucumbers. At first, I did not water the cucumbers, hoping that they would not grow. However, after this was discovered, I was ordered to water the cucumbers. So I decided to flood them. I put the nozzle of the hose two inches from the ground and kept it there for fifteen minutes full blast, day after day. The cucumbers never came up.

In a sense, this has been the technique of the government as well. For a time, projects with a socio-political character were continually denied the financial nourishment that they needed. 90% of the time and energy of the people was spent seeking a solid financial base. Citizens committees and political action groups started, flourished briefly and died but the soil was getting richer and the State was faced with two alternatives : either stamp them out or flood them. The inefficient and highly visible repressive character of the first alternative, as exemplified by the repression of FRAP was less desirable. Throwing opposition candidates in jail the week before the elections, the jailing of the most active supporters and the harassing of others together with the seizure of printing equipment and materials is far less attractive to the proponents of the society without conflict.

Instead, where two or three full-time workers might be needed to run a committee, ten or fifteen were given. What is the effect of this ? To begin with, one of the essential characteristics of any socio-political action is that it involves the people who are oppressed in their own struggle. In other words, one of the basic tenets of political action is that the distinction between "helpers" and "helped" must be suppressed — that no professionals can define and execute the processes of the changing situation. A full time staff of a dozen workers effectively prevents this type of participation.

J. Grand'Maison, in his book, *"VERS UN NOUVEAU POUVOIR"* writes : *"A populist leadership is not born in superstructures — even the most democratic. A consciousness of its own forces and dynamism is necessary. Premature institutionalization strangles it because the organization is uprooted from its living environment and the full time employees... predominate."* [5]

A summary look at the socio-political projects of OFY and LIP confirms this theoretical observation. Time and time again, projects where the language may be "radical" are floundering in the bog of organizational problems and doing very little radical action. Personality conflicts, division and definition of tasks, and generally poor co-ordination characterize the vast majority of this type of project, especially, the most democratic and least hierarchical organizations. Consequently, little time is left to seek out prospective supporters and those that do come are usually unable to integrate since the organization is largely preoccupied with its own problems. Thus, the flood technique undercuts one of the major props of a socio-political organization.

Even social work programmes with trained professionals and a certain knowledge as to how to proceed go through a major upheaval when the staff is doubled all at once from four to eight. It is little wonder then, that the LIP and OFY projects are plagued by organizational problems when ten or fifteen inexperience people grope for a form of collective action.

3° THE LENGTH OF PROJECTS : Organizational or starting problems are exacerbated by the time element. When the Québec government decided to embark upon a co-ordinated, coherent plan of social animation under the B.A.E.Q. (Bureau d'Aménagement de l'Est du Québec) they divised a programme over three and one half years, not over three and one half months as these programmes would have. Of this 3½ years, 1½ years was spent just setting up the programme. Of course, the

---

5.   J. Grand'Maison, *Vers un Nouveau Pouvoir*, Hurtubise, Montréal, 1968, pp. 113-14.

programme was on a bigger scale than local projects but the fact remains that most of the eighteen months spent getting organized was spent learning about the localities and trying to get started.

The three to four month life span of most projects falsifies the time element of this type of work. The organizational obstacles, the training of the personnel, the knowledge of the problems involved and the network of contacts needed present an insurmountable obstacle to effective collective action.

But the short duration of the projects prevents a collective approach in another manner. Since the projects are of a temporary character, there exists an obstacle to a strong identification with the practical dimensions of the problems faced. This is as true for the personnel of the projects as it is for the community itself. On the one hand, it is difficult to put ones whole self into a project that one knows is temporary. On the other hand, there will always be a certain skepticism on the part of the community towards the project because it was parachuted from the sky yesterday and will disappear again tomorrow without any relation to the development of the situation it is meant to deal with. For the personnel, a project can only be an interesting way to spend the summer or to make some money during the winter. This is perceived by the population who know that they are only a secondary consideration in these programmes.

4° *OTHER FACTORS :* One might mention other aspects of these programmes used by the government — placards posted in the offices of projects proclaming "Canada works !", devaluation of the provincial government and revaluation of the federal government but the impact of these aspects is less clear and lacking a more systematic study of these factors, we shall simply mention them here. The "Agence de presse libre du Québec" (APLQ) has just published an excellent critique of these programmes entitled "Perspectives jeunesse : Le programme cool d'un gouvernement too much". While their approach differs slightly from the one we use here, they go into much more detail in certain areas. The Ottawa-Québec aspect is delved into more and there is an analysis of student unemployment over the past few years, together with a good list of other government summer programmes.

USEFULNESS AS A RADICAL STRATEGY

Let us introduce a long parenthetical comment at this point. Our priniple concern in this paper has been to show the State's strategy behind the OFY and LIP programmes and to show it works. However, some radicals have contended that it is possible to use these projects as part of a radical strategy. We briefly treat this point.

First of all, there is little or no evidence of which we are aware which leads us to agree with this contention. On the whole, the projects have been well-behaved, with radicalism being confined to the verbal level. In many cases the radical push comes from those outside the projects — and is largely swallowed up by internal problems. If anything, political action by youth seems to be on the decline or at least well away from the LIP or OFY projects. The strikes at the Universié de Montréal and the Université du Québec à Montréal were isolated and quiet. The more innovative actions of the students in the social work deparment at Sherbrooke and the CEGEP students in Rosemount who locked out the administration and set up parallel departments had little help from these governmental programmes.

Secondly, these contentions take little account of the radically different character of the two alternatives. The government programmes provide for projects oriented towards furnishing services, employing ten to fifteen people and lasting four months. Little citizen participation in the defining and running of the group is possible or needed. A collective political project, on the other hand, is oriented towards the transformation of the power structure through the collective action of a large group of people of whom two or three may be needed to supply the full time technical help needed. This type of project is of more or less long duration. Citizen participation is both needed and necessary. How is the second disguised as the first? The distance between the two is vast.

The government learned an important lesson from its experience with the Company of Young Canadians. In the case of the CYC, longer lasting projects, smaller teams and a fair degree of local control enabled some projects to become politically visible. It is not surprising then to see that none of these characteristics are found in the OFY or LIP programmes. The "reform" of the CYC was the answer to this type of freedom. Control was tightened, volunteers were fired or forced to resign, and the company was reorganized.

Finally, we can not say that no projects can ever mount a politically effective collective action. All we can say is that the odds are stacked high against it and that the occasional exception does nothing to undermine the arguments we have used here. The exception not only serves to confirm the rule but also re-enforces it since it creates a false sense of hope for so many others. Close parentheses.

CONCLUSIONS

We can conclude from the study of the framework of these projects that they are more or less limited to providing services. In this situation, the project often acts as a shock absorber between the problems engendered by the society and their effects on individuals. While we do not deny the sometimes urgent need for an emergency service for a number of problems, it should be noted that such a service can mask the causes of problems. In fact, it is even possible that people complain about the inefficiency of the shock absorbers rather than the shocks themselves; that is, it is possible that the population would complain about the less than perfect service rendered by non-professionals rather than the causes of these problems.

The service aspect of the projects tends to force the participants to integrate the population. The participants ease the effects of the problems without directly dealing with the causes and thus renders the problems more supportable. In this sense, the personnel plays a role of domination. The service aspect masks and obscures the problems and in no way furnishes the means for the population to resolve their problems. On the contrary, it keeps the population in a state of continual dependence. The projects are forced to reproduce the same distance that separates those that "help" from those that are "helped". What is tragi-comic in these programmes is that under the banner of the autonomy of youth is a call to participate in the domination mechanisms of society.

In sum, one notes that the State has constructed a safety valve that is very effective. These programmes, destined for those who constitute a threat to social stability, affectively channel discontent. What is even more remarkable is that this discontent is not simply rendered powerless — it is harnessed to work for the dominant society. One begins to appreciate the degree to which these programmes are refined instruments of a liberal society.

These programmes are not alone. Similar characteristics can be found in other summer programmes of the federal government. It would be interesting too, in the light of this approach, to examine the policies and actions of the Health and Welfare Department as well as those of Indian affaires. Furthermore, one can see the same strategy in many programmes of the Québec government such as Bill 65 (reorganization of medical services), Multimedia, Bill 10 (concerning legal clinics). All carry the same characteristics of an integrative participation.

Thus, it seems to us that with these programmes the capitalist State has entered a new phase in social planning. The "anarchy" of competition and private enterprize has been supplemented with the "planned anarchy" of social control policies. Ad hoc State intervention in the economy to re-enforce and support particular firms and markets became an accepted policy at the turn of the century. Then, with the economic crisis of the thirties and the anticyclical economic policy of Keynes, State support of capitalism took on an even greater dimension. It was no longer sufficient to intervene only in an ad hoc manner (although of course, this was and is still necesary). State support had to be regular and systematic. It seems that now we are faced with yet another dimension of State support for the economic system. On the economic level, the State progressively assumes the role of co-ordinator for private enterprise. Armed with such instruments as wage and price controls, already present in Europe and making their appearance in North America, the patching role that government has played is being abandoned for that of orchestra conductor. On the social level, programmes such as OFY and LIP signify an unprecedented concern for the control of social consequences of economic behaviour. The isolation of the marginals produced by capitalist society can no longer be left ignored. They must be integrated in order to eliminate any traces of a possible resistance.

ON REVOLUTION IN THE METROPOLIS

by Mickey Ellinger and John Rowntree

THE WORKING CLASS IN THE METROPOLIS

The United States is the metropolis of an imperialist economic and political system that is breaking down under the pressures of attack both from the periphery and from within. This essay, written from the metropolis, examines how the political economic pressures of a failing empire are felt at the center. It outlines the formation of the metropolitan liberation forces and what groups of workers will form the revolutionary socialist leadership.

This essay locates the United States as the center, the metropolis of world capitalism. From this angle of vision it is clear that the social problems of the United States are problems of monopoly capitalism under challenge by socialism. These problems lead to revolution because of how they affect the mass of working people, the agents of revolutionary change. Therefore, it is necessary to study how the people are reacting to the social problems of a faltering imperialism.

To study the United States as the metropolis of world capitalism brings its problems into focus so that the direction that events will take is more understandable. The near-sighted view that what goes on in the United States depends entirely on internal events makes it impossible to understand those events. But when we look at the world as a whole, locked in a battle between a social system that is dying out and a new one that is coming into being, we see that the problems of the United States today are the problems of a moribund capitalism whose final desperate gasps are throwing it into convulsions. This essay examines those convulsions, how the people of the United States suffer the failing capitalist empire, and how they can throw off the yoke of that empire, freeing themselves and at the same time striking a lethal blow against the international system of oppression governed by the rulers of the United States.

The problems of the United States today are those of the center of power of a dying social and economic system; the solutions can only be understood by seeing how the problems affect the working people of the United States who do the work that keeps the metropolis running and who hold the power to overthrow it. If we study how the system affects working people, we can avoid being misled by a narrow view of the elites who benefit from maintaining the system. Rather than studying the present structure of power, we want to examine the potential for changing that structure. That potential rests with the mass of people who work for wages and pay the increasing price of empire. To know how close the United States is to changing its social system from capitalism, based on profit, to socialism, based on labour, we must study the present situation of working people and how various groups of workers are reacting to that situation.

This essay is therefore a study of the development of a working class movement in the metropolis of imperialism. We discuss the political economy of the empire, its economic crisis, and the impact of that economic crisis on social and political formations of the working people. The rulers of the U.S. economy and society are on the defensive; to fend off the socialist challenge, the apparatus of the State has grown and become more all-pervasive. The State has grown in response to the external challenge of socialism and the internal crises of capitalism.

In some ways the history of the present period begins in 1917, when the first socialist revolution transformed the struggle between socialism and capitalism from a set of interconnected domestic struggles to an international struggle. This essay begins a little later, with the world crisis of capital-

ism in the 1930's and the solution to that crisis worked out in World War II. The depression of the 1930's demonstrated that capitalism was both an international system and a very fragile system; the World War of the early 1940's reorganized the shrinking international capitalist economy into a single system of power controlled by the United States. In the twenty-five years since the end of World War II, the domination of U.S. capital over other capital has been increasing, while the number of people and nations which have freed themselves from the domination of capital altogether has also been increasing. The result is not the polarization between two systems that is described by the rulers in the United States as the Cold War, but the attack on an increasingly unified and rigid U.S.—controlled capitalist system by a growing number of increasingly diverse and flexible socialist systems of economy and society.

The development of the United States as the metropolis of world capitalism also shows how the economic, social and political system of the United States has become more and more stereotypically bureaucratic, unresponsive, and intolerant. Since the United States became the undisputed metropolis of world capitalism at the end of World War II, the power of the State apparatus has necessarily grown dramatically. The State has assumed responsibility not only to defend the international capitalist economy in its external relations by military, economic and political means, but also to promote the internal health of the metropolis by programs of State investment that try to prevent the increasingly monopolized economy from succumbing to its own internally-generated tendencies to stagnation. The State has pursued Keynesian policies of active intervention to promote economic health. These policies and the programs that have been implemented have been financed by expropriating the productivity of working people. The number of workers has increased dramatically, as the self-employed have become wage workers and women have joined the work force. One result has been that the working class is practically synonymous with the people ; more than three-quarters of U.S. people are working class. This growing working class faces increasing expropriation through taxes to protect and extend the monopoly capitalist structure of investment inside and outside the country. These policies have been very costly to working people ; not only have their taxes paid for State subsidies to monopoly capital inside the country and imperial capital abroad, but also they have suffered under the militarization of the society and its increasing repressiveness. That price has been high ; we examine the costs to workers in the United States of living in the metropolis of world capitalism.

And yet, U.S. workers have not actively opposed capitalism. One of the fashionable contemporary myths is that the working people of this country support capitalism and oppose socialism. This essay examines the U.S. working class since the end of World War II. We have seen a period in which the majority of workers did not actively oppose, and had no forms through which to oppose, capitalism ; but that period is ending. The postwar experiments in Keynesian social democracy have demonstrated only that capitalism can be reformed to be more brutal and warlike than ever. The social upheavals of the last decade are the beginnings of a revival of active worker opposition to their exploitation by capital. The working class nature of these upheavals is far from clear on the surface. Yet, there is an under-lying unity to such apparently disparate events as the civil rights movement's development into a revolutionary movement for liberation of the black people, the student peace movement's growth from its pacifist origins to an increasingly anti-imperialist ideology, the sudden emergence of a broad and intense movement for women's liberation, the growing restlessness within the labour union movement, the rapid growth of new unions among public employees, and the widespread "taxpayer revolt." Each of these social groups—blacks and other colonized minorities, students, soldiers and other young workers, women, organized workers, public employees—has had a particular set of life and work experiences that grow out of the postwar State economic policy. (Many of their experiences are not shaped by Keynesianism ; but we concentrate on those that are.)

Capital has become more centralized and more closely tied to the State institutions. The increased investment promoted by the joint efforts of capital and the state has been made possible by a great increase in labour productivity in consumer goods industries, itself in part the result of the reorganization of capital under State auspices before, during and after World War II. This increase in the productivity of workers producing food, clothing and other consumer goods has been so great that it was possible not only to finance more investment and a growing State to absorb surplus labour and to protect the structure of capital, but also to grant an increase in real wages to workers in all sectors of the economy. In other words, the postwar "prosperity" of 1945 to 1965 was the result of an increase in the productivity of workers in the consumer goods industries that was so great that real wages of workers rose in spite of the increased expropriation of surplus value by capital to expand investment and by the State to absorb surplus labour and to protect that expanded investment. This "prosperity" created a set of institutions—strong trade unions, expanded education, a large standing army, decaying cities and sprawling suburbs, new and bigger government bureaucracies—that today are the arenas of growing social conflict.

The increasing cost to workers of supporting a more and more costly extension of investments under State protection was disguised by a reorganization and division of the labour force that hid the growing problems of finding investment outlets and creating new jobs. These problems were hidden by the ideological blinders of a culture that accepted the inferior status of blacks, women and youth, and could define as "prosperity" a period in which the situation of more than half of all workers was at least problematical and more likely deteriorating. The same blinders have made it difficult to see that the revolt of blacks, youth and women is a revolt against being particularly victimized by the growing economic problems of the United States as its metropolitan role becomes more costly. The social unrest in the United States today is not a crisis over race, sex, or generations, but a job crisis and a crisis of the standard and quality of life for all workers.

The response to the economic crisis is complicated by the divisions among workers. Workers are divided along sex, race and age lines, so that women workers are concentrated in the low-paid clerical and service occupations, black and other minority nationality workers in the low-paid service and unskilled labour jobs, while young workers are kept out of the labour force by longer schooling and forced labour in the military before entering the growing fields of the services and public employment. Workers are also divided between the private sector and the tax-financed public sector and between the highly productive manufacturing workers and the less productive service sector. These many divisions result in a complex mosaic that makes it hard to see a basis for working class unity on economic issues. The economic crisis hits workers in different ways—rising unemployment, falling real wages, deteriorating standard of living. And often each group blames other workers. Black workers blame their problems on the racism of white workers, and white workers blame the deterioration of their real wages on the competition of black workers. Women blame men for keeping them in boring, badly paid jobs ; men blame women for the growing job shortage. Young people are convinced that they are subjected to high unemployment rates, conscription and persecution for their tastes and preferences because the older generation is jealous of its privileges. Older workers fear the competition of the young for their jobs, while resenting the tax costs of keeping them in school or the army and out of the labour force. Workers in the private sector blame the wage demands of workers in the public sector for their skyrocketing taxes ; public employees resort to strikes that, by depriving other workers of public services, both demonstrate the power of public employees and increase the resentment of other workers against them. Lower-paid workers accuse the higher paid of joining the forces that are trying to deprive them of a decent wage. All these conflicts are real ; that is, are really happening ; yet the only beneficiary of divisions among workers is capital, which is able to exploit all workers more because they cannot offer a united resistance. The existence of these conflicts is a sign that the divisions are breaking down.

All workers pay not only politically but also economically for their division : that is, both black and white workers are penalized by racism, both men and women by sex discrimination, both young and old by the exclusion of young people from productive jobs. The costs of discrimination—of hiring workers at jobs that are less productive than those they could do with adequate training—are borne by the better-paid workers through their taxes. Taxes on better-paid workers finance the welfare programs that keep alive an underclass created by capitalism's inability to offer productive jobs to all. Taxes pay for the military machine that supports U.S. capital's domination of the non-socialist world, for the schools that absorb the unemployable labour of millions of young people, for the police apparatus that persecutes the poor who are created by a stagnant economy. Taxes support a growing public sector that relies heavily on underpaid women—the taxes of the husbands pay the low wages of their wives. Workers experience the State as an agent of increasing exploitation and, as they resist State demands for ever more taxes, come to see that the State, acting in the interests of capital, is exploiting all workers and that workers are not exploiting each other. This recognition makes alliances of workers possible ; instead of conflicts among workers, the State's own policy is increasingly raising the possibility of a metropolitan liberation front of workers in alliance with each other facing capital in alliance with the State.

The price that workers pay for discrimination is hidden by ideological blinders ; so is the price that workers pay for imperialism. The vast military, economic and political machine that allows U.S. capital to dominate the world, impoverishing workers of other countries, is financed by taxes on U.S. workers. This cost was hidden for 20 years under the ideological blinders of patriotism. Under the guise of "defending the Free World," U.S. workers were induced to support the pattern of investment that created the warfare State. The labour unions were a major institution that forced workers to support the programs of imperialism. These ideological blinders were fairly effective until about the mid-1960's, when it became necessary to take the lives as well as the taxes of people to fight socialism. The war in South East Asia has cost about 50,000 lives of U.S. soldiers, has created a million and a half veterans of that war, has disrupted the lives of millions more young men through conscription or enforced schooling in the attempt to avoid conscription, and has disrupted the lives of their parents, wives and employers. Further, the United States is losing the war, demonstrating to its own people that no amount of military might can defeat a people committed to liberation from imperialist domination.

Workers are shedding their ideological blinders because of their experiences of the State. As the illusory postwar "prosperity" evaporates in inflation, unemployment and war taxes, workers become more conscious of the growing costs—economic, political, personal—of a stagnant monopoly capitalism and an embattled imperialism. Workers shed their ideological blinders as they learn that the State is the enemy of its citizens, supporting the exploitation of labour by capital at home and abroad. The breakdown of capitalism and imperialism is accompanied by a breakdown in the legitimacy of the government and an increase in the resistance to the State. This widespread resistance is rapidly being transformed into active opposition led by revolutionary socialists from the ghettoes, the schools and the armies.

Workers are only beginning to shed their blinders. We are at the beginning of a period of tremendous unrest and internal conflict. As some workers begin to abandon racist, national chauvinist, anti-woman, anti-youth attitudes, others feel acutely threatened and become more attached to the security of those attitudes, even to the extent of being willing to fight to preserve the power of capital. Growing militance and radicalism does not automatically lead in a straight line to working class unity. Battles for racial and sexual equality, battles for student power in the schools, draft resistance and organizations of soldiers, public employee strikes, wildcat strikes of organized workers, and taxpayer revolts may heighten divisions among workers in the short run. But these struggles are brought together by their common target—the State—and by workers' growing perception that the State's active role in imperialism, racism, sexism and the suppression of youth stems from its complicity with capital.

Dissatisfied groups of workers are beginning to see that their problem is capitalism and that the solution to that problem is socialism. Growing worker pressures lead to a struggle for socialism as the only way to free workers from the costs of international and domestic exploitation and to make possible the human use of the U.S. economy's vast resources. The United States is in a state of permanent war because it is at war with socialism and self-determination throughout the world. Workers, as they begin to refuse to continue to support war, support socialism by refusing to allow their government to oppose it. Passive resistance to imperialism becomes active opposition and active struggle for a socialist organization of the economy and society as the consciousness grows that the profit system leaves more and more socially necessary tasks undone while leaving more and more workers unemployed or underemployed. U.S. capital could be put to social uses throughout the world ; but these tasks, not being profitable, are not being done. More and more workers do wasteful jobs or are being forced into the growing ranks of welfare clients and other unemployables. Workers are imprisoned by past investments and cannot do what needs to be done as long as the profit rate determines the tasks that workers will take up. Workers cannot even reallocate the taxes they pay to stop financing racism and other forms of inequality. Under capitalism there are no mechanisms by which workers can determine how the social surplus will be spent. Before the State became such a large active partner in the process of extracting and allocating the surplus, the helplessness of workers was justified by the ideology of the rights of private property. However, since the end of World War II the privacy of that property has been exposed as a myth. It is harder to use the old rhetoric to deny that the social product is socially produced but privately appropriated. When the State, nominally responsive to the wishes of the people, becomes actively involved in denying the people any participation in the process of allocating the tax-generated surplus, people confront the conflict between democracy and capitalism. If they want to achieve democratic forms, it becomes increasingly clear that democratic control over the economy is imperative and that socialism is necessary to make that control possible.

The growing pressures toward socialism will be expressed in a great many ways, all of them disruptive of things

114

as they are. The particular ways in which capital has captured the machinery of government shapes the growing pressures for socialism around growing resistance to the state-capital alliance and a breakdown of the distinction between political and economic action. Workers, increasingly frustrated with the growing costs of their subjection to capital and the State, resist with strikes, tax refusals, refusal to cooperate with the war, etc. Since the laws protect capital, workers break the law. When they do they are repressed ; even if they do not break the law's letter, the State recognizes correctly that even technically legal strikes and demonstrations violate the pro-capital spirit of the law. Socialism will not be granted peacefully ; the forces of capitalism command an army and, even at the height of the civil war, will retain the loyalty of at least part of that army. The forces of capitalism have a police and intelligence net bent upon crushing socialist organizations in their infancy. Socialism declares private property to be a privilege to be overthrown rather than a right to be upheld ; the owners of private property cannot be expected to surrender just because they are in a minority. They have been in a minority all the time they have been in power. If their power is overthrown, it will only be because the working people fight and win.

The struggle for socialism within the United States has begun ; but it is far from over. This essay examines the basis for a metropolitan liberation front in the United States today. The origins and character of the U.S. metropolis and divisions in the U.S. workers and the way these divisions are being overcome are developed. First the social divisions within the working class are laid out and the basis of those divisions in the work-life experience of different groups of workers is exposed. The origins of those divisions are examined as one result of the State economic policy formulated out of the experience of the depression and World War II. Then the contemporary economy is described, with a discussion of the inextricable interdependence of domestic monopoly, imperialism, and the State. While each of these three pillars has always been a part of capitalist development, the giant State is the most rapidly growing and dynamic part of the contemporary U.S. economy and is therefore given separate treatment. The ways that the State promotes the exploitation of labour by capital through its tax and monetary policies and the growing porblems of that form of State exploitation are discussed in detail. Then we turn to the social crisis of the metropolis. We outline the revolutionary socialist movement that is developing under the leadership of blacks, youth and women. Then we examine how this leadership spreads beyond the ghettoes, the armies, the schools and the family to lead an attack on the bureaucracies of the labour unions, the political parties, and the State agencies themselves. Finally we examine the context in which a metropolitan liberation movement must overcome the divisions in the working class and forge a revolutionary alliance that can open an internal front in the war against the imperialist system.

DIVISIONS IN THE WORKING CLASS

The working class is a larger percentage of the population of the United States today than ever before, so that wage labour is an experience shared by the great majority of adults. At the same time, however, the working class is divided along social lines of race, sex, and age, and also according to whether they are organized or unorganized, or working in the public or private sector of the economy. The result is that within the working class there is race conflict ; conflict over the role of women ; conflict about the status of young people ; conflict about the relation of organized workers to their trade unions and of unorganized to organized workers ; conflict between workers as taxpayers and other workers as tax-supported public employees ; and conflict of all workers with the tax-financed State institutions.

These divisions are real and often intense ; but they must be set against the backdrop of a working class that is growing in size. Farming and other non-farm population has disappeared peared ; so has the small business enterprise that allows its owner to be self-employed. Regional variations in living patterns have become less important as more people move to large metropolitan areas. Even the number and variety of employers is declining.

The division between the farm and nonfarm population has disappeared as a major economic, social an political division. For most of U.S. history, the major issues of economic policy-prices, wages, tariffs, taxes—have been debated between the farm and urban blocs. Yet by 1968, farm population had fallen to less than 10.5 million, only about 5.5 percent of the total population. [1] So no matter how much the interests of farmers may still differ from those of the rest of the population, farmers are so few and their numbers are decreasing so rapidly (at about 5 percent a year) that they are no longer an important source of social conflict.

The small businessman is going the way of the farmer. The number of self-employed has fallen ; not only as a percentage of the labour force but also in absolute numbers, decreasing more than 1.2 million between 1960 and 1968, from 10.4 percent to 7.1 percent of all non-agricultural workers. The age of Horatio Alger has long been over ; it is no longer realistic to aspire to become self-employed. The economic and political interests of small businessmen—in promoting competition, reducing government interference in the economy, etc.—no longer have support from a social base ; and although the goals of small business may be a part of the rhetoric of most politicians, they are not part of the matrix of power within which politicians work.

The decline of farming and small business means that more than 90 percent of the U.S. working people are wage and salary workers who own no capital. It is difficult to get an exact measure of the working class. However, in 1968, out of a labour force of more than 82 million, there were more than 75 million civilian and military, employed and unemployed, workers who earn their livings by selling their labour power. Of these 75 million, about 10 to 12 million are managers, high or petty civilian and military officials, high-prestige professionals and the like, who, although technically wage workers, exercise power over other workers or have high social status and are more likely to think of themselves as part of the ruling than the working class. This leaves about 63 million workers, fully three-quarters of all who work, who are *only* wage workers ; these workers are individually powerless before their employers and supervisors and before the ruling corporate, union, and State bureaucracies. Our concern here is with the patterns of life-work experience of these 63 million workers in the metropolis of imperialism and how their lives are intertwined with those of students, welfare recipients, and others who are unpaid members of the producing and consuming relations

116

that define the present structure and future direction of this society. Workers are sharply divided ; and yet these divisions themselves are part of work and life patterns that are growing more rather than less similar. U.S. workers live more concentrated in metropolitan areas than ever before, and work for fewer employers than ever before ; the divisions, then, are thrown into relief against a growing uniformity.

Most U.S. residents, about two-thirds, live in metropolitan areas of more than 50 thousand people ; more than half the U.S. population, 113 million people, lives in the 110 largest metropolitan areas with more than a quarter of a million residents. As these metropolitan areas have grown, they **have become more alike** ; the most significant variations in life style are found within each metropolitan area, not among them. In the central city live a few very rich and the mass of the very poor, including half of all black people and the bulk of single young people living on their own. In the suburbs live the most prosperous quarter of the white working class in the culture of mortgages and car payments. Even the small independent businesses that used to give variety to neighborhoods have been replaced by chain stores ; the ubiquitous green sign of the freeway exit looks the same from San Diego to Maine. A person's life style is more significantly affected by whether he lives in the central city or a suburb than whether he lives in metropolitan Seattle or metropolitan Miami.

The homogeneity of work and life experiences in the United States is increased by the number of workers that work for the same handful of giant corporations and State agencies. The largest 500 industrial corporations hire more than two-thirds of all industrial workers, some 14 million. [2] About 18 million people work directly for the federal, state, or local governments. About 4.6 million work for the U.S. Department of Defense alone. So although the working class is very divided, these divisions stand out against a social and economic reality of increasing concentration, centralization, and standardization.

Yet the divisions are central to an understanding of the dynamics of the working class in the United States today. As the working class has grown as a percentage of the working population, the life and work experience of specific groups of workers has become more and more different. Some of these groups are overlapping socially defined ones : blacks, women, and youth. Others are defined by the sector of the economy, public or private, in which they work. Others are defined, regardless of sector, by whether they are organized or unorganized. The grouping and separation of kinds of workers by race, sex, age, sector, and organization has created a mosaic of overlapping and interdependent categories of workers in conflict. Mass politics in the United States today and tomorrow depends for its character and direction on these divisions, their origins, the role they play in the economy, society and political system, and how that role is changing.

The particular work and life experiences of blacks, women and youth are marked by their relatively recent and historically specific entry into the labour force and the traditional cultural attitudes to these workers. Together these forces have shaped the particular occupations that are open to them. Black men and women workers, for example, joined the urban labour force in large numbers during and after World War II. Women, both black and white, began to flow into

117

the labour market about the same time. And youth, black and white, men and women, are the traditional new entrants into any labour force. These new entrants face particular barriers. They are channelled into the growing occupations as determined by three factors : capital's need for workers ; the cultural definitions of the labour appropriate to each group ; and the preparation for the workplace the society offers each kind of new entrant. The channelling of blacks, women and youth into unskilled and badly paid jobs in services and public employment shows that the economy has not been able to provide enough productive jobs to employ new entrants to the labour force. In a period of relative labour surplus the groups who will get the worst jobs are the traditional victims of discrimination.

During World War II, black workers left rural labour and went to work at the bottom of the urban labour force in the worst-paid and most insecure jobs. Today more than three quarters of the black population lives in urban centers and works and lives in the urban industrial economy. Not surprising in light of the history of black exploitation, urban blacks are almost entirely working class or chronically unemployed lumpenproletarians. Blacks are roughly 11 percent of the population and the labour force, but nearly 15 percent of the working class ; less than two percent of the urban black labour force are self-employed, and less than 10 percent of the black workers are employed in those professional, technical, and managerial high-status occupations that employ more than 20 percent of white workers. Further, blacks are not only the poorest U.S. workers. Because blacks have been enslaved and because of their history in the U.S., they are in many ways a separate people, an exploited national minority as well as a discriminated-

against racial minority. (Other national minorities—Latin Americans, Asians, and native Americans—also have distinctive experiences within the U.S. working class. But neither space nor information makes it possible to give separate treatment to these smaller, but very important, groups.)

Even more than whites, then, blacks are overwhelmingly urban and working class. Their entry into the urban labour market in wartime during an acute shortage of industrial workers, plus the effect of racist patterns of employment, housing and education, has locked black workers into unskilled manufacturing and service jobs, high unemployment rates and continued poverty. Table I shows that nonwhites, 92 percent of whom are blacks, are concentrated in the most poorly paid sectors of the industrial and service fields and are largely excluded from the growing professional and "white collar" fields. Two-thirds of urban non-white workers are operatives, labourers and service workers (maids, janitors, hospital workers, etc.), compared to one-third of urban whites.

A look at Table I will help clarify why the median income of non-white families in 1967 was $4,919 compared to $8,274 for white families ; why the average of non-white wages has remained at less than 60 percent of the average for white workers since the early 1950's ; and why even the underestimated official unemployment rates for non-white workers have been twice as high as those of whites since the beginning of the 1960's. Three-quarters of non-white workers are semi-skilled or unskilled blue collar and service workers, compared to less than half of white workers. More than 11 percent of non-whites work as labourers, with a median 1967 income of $3,979 for men and $2,628 for women ; and

118

10 percent of non-white workers, mainly women, work as private domestics at wages of $765 a year; another 20 percent of non-white workers are other kinds of service workers with a median wage of $3,645, about the 1967 poverty line for a family of four. And within each occupational category, non-whites are concentrated at the bottom, holding the lowest paying jobs.

Black workers not only have the worst jobs in the urban industrial economy; their jobs are being elim-

inated by technical changes and by the decline in manufacturing employment because of its monopolization. Racist housing, education, and job opportunities converge to put many blacks out of steady work altogether, throwing them onto the urban scrap heap of ghetto hustling, welfare, and hopelessness. About 2 million U.S. blacks live so far outside the bureaucratic-money economy that the 1960 Census neglected to count them. One in six black men between the ages of 20 and 39 was missed by the enumerators [3]

Table 1 Non-agricultural White and Non-white Occupational Distribution, by percentage, in 1968; and Median Income of Persons with Income by Sex and Occupation, 1967. (Stat. Ab. 1969, tables 322 and 482)

Occupation	White Employment Share (%)	Black Employment Share (%)	Median Income Men 1967	Median Income Women 1967
Total	100.0%	100.0%	—	—
White Collar	51.9	25.5	—	—
Managers, etc.	11.6%	2.9%	$9267	$4474
Professionals	15.0	8.2	9370	5210
Sales	6.9	2.0	6814	2116
Clerical	18.4	12.4	6380	3844
Blue Collar	37.2	44.7	—	—
Craftsmen, etc.	14.5	8.4	7224	3826
Operatives	18.5	25.0	5858	3218
Labourers	4.2	11.3	3979	2628
Services	10.9	29.8	—	—
Private house	1.5	10.0	—	765
Other	9.4	19.8	4532	2076

As soon as black workers joined the urban labour force in appreciable numbers they began to function as that "last hired, first fired" labour pool that is necessary to a capitalist system. The gap between the unemployment rates of black and white workers opened during the depression; in 1935, for example, the percentages

of workers looking for work or engaged in "emergency" work (work relief) were 36 percent of black men, 28 percent of black women, 21 percent of white men, and 19 percent of white women. [4] The gap closed somewhat during the acute labour shortage of World War II, but then widened again at the close of the

Korean War. The official unemployment rates of black workers have been at least twice as high as those of whites since 1954. [5] These official rates minimize black unemployment, not only because of the under-counting of blacks, but also because the unemployment statistics themselves are gathered and interpreted in such a way that the under-employment of black workers and their despairing abandonment of any effort to find a job are not counted in the statistics. For instance, the labour participation rate of young black men (20-24 years) has fallen steadily since 1953, much faster than for young white men, even though the increase in school enrollment for young white men of that age is much greater than for blacks. Many young black men have so little hope of finding a job that they no longer look for work. Many more black workers, young and old, men and women, work part-time because they cannot find full-time jobs. Involuntary part-time employment rates for blacks are probably about 50 percent higher than for whites. These and other factors combine to boost the real black unemployment rates close to three times those of whites. [6]

Even when black workers have jobs, their wages are much lower than those of white workers. The average income of black men was 54 percent of the average for whites in 1947. It rose to 62 percent of the white average by 1951, but fell back to 55 percent by 1962. With the high demand for labour in the early Viet Nam war years, black income has increased to about its 1951 Korean War ratio. [7] The median income of black families follows the same pattern ; it stood at 62 percent of the median income of white families in 1968. Almost a third of black families, 32.5 percent in 1967, are poor by the government's official definition, four times the rate for white

families. And although this poverty is in most cases the result of high unemployment rates, one-sixth of poor black families had the income of a full-time wage earner all year and still could not rise above the poverty line ; this is five times the incidence of working poverty for white families (3.1 percent).

The abject poverty of blacks in the United States is only the most easily measurable cost of racist exploitation. There would still be poor if the U.S. were not a racist society, since a capitalist economic system based on profit thrives on an ample pool of badly paid workers who can be subjected to low wages and job insecurity with a minimum of social and political repercussions. Capitalist production requires a bottom to the heap. But racist blinders have made it easier for this poverty to persist and have promoted and perpetuated the capitalist exploitation of labour ; if white workers had experienced the poverty and unemployment that would have been their lot if the casualties of capitalism had been integrated, they would have been less willing to settle for New Deal reforms, business unionism and the Cold War instead of a democratic restructuring of the economy to serve the needs of workers.

While the work and life experience of blacks in the United States has set them apart from whites so much that the white majority can be practically oblivious to the exploitation of the black minority, the work and life experience of women workers is so closely tied to that of men that their exploitation is hidden not by separation but by intimacy. The exploitation of black workers in hidden by racism and segregation ; the exploitation of women workers is hidden by an ideology of the role of women in the home and economy that plays down the

120

importance of their labour and permits women to be victimized by the profit system and to support that system themselves by thinking of their paid labour as secondary to their roles as wife and mother.

Economic necessity has been a major factor in women going to work outside the home. In 1940, only one-quarter of women worked, and only 10 percent of women with children under 18 years of age. By 1968, about 40 percent of women worked, including 40 percent of mothers. More than half of women between 18 and 64 years old work in any given month, and women are about 38 percent of the civilian labour force. During the 1960's, the number of women in the labour force grew three times as fast as the number of men. This rapid increase in the number of working women represents an increase mainly in the percentage of married women who work ; the labour participation rate for single women has increased only slightly in the last 30 years (from 48.1 percent in 1940 to 51.4 percent in 1968, with considerable fluctuation), while that for married women living with their husbands has tripled in the same period and that for women with children has gone up four times. And, while the labour participation rate for black women has always been higher than that of white women, testifying to the greater poverty of black families, the gap is narrowing. In 1950, 40 percent of black women and only 30 percent of white women worked, a 25 percent difference ; by the late 1960's that difference had been reduced to 20 percent, as half of black women and 40 percent of white women were at work. While in 1940, married women were only about a third of all working women, by 1968, they were almost two-thirds ; single women, on the other hand, who were half of working women in 1940, were less than a quarter in 1968.

As women have entered the labour force they have found jobs in the expanding white collar and service work occupations. However, within these sectors, women work in the occupations with low median earnings, low status, and little power. Fewer than 3 million working women are managers, high-status professionals, or in self-employed small business. So while more than 20 percent of the male working population is either a capitalist, large or petty, or a relatively high-status worker with some power over other workers, only about 10 percent of working women hold either capital or status or power ; and only an insignificant number of black women are not working class. While about 60 percent of women are white collar workers, two-thirds of these, more than 40 percent of all working women, are poorly paid sales or clerical workers ; almost a quarter of women are household and other service workers ; for black women in particular, less than a quarter are white collar and almost 60 percent are household and other service workers.

Women workers, like black workers, have largely been by-passed by the labour unions. Only about a sixth of women work in the blue-collar occupations that account for 80 percent of union membership ; most white women work in the white collar occupations that account for only 14 percent of union membership, and most black women work in the service occupations that account for only 5 percent of union membership.

Concentrated in the low-paying jobs, neglected by unions, women's wages average about $3,300 a year, less than 60 percent of the average for men. Table I shows that women earn less than men in every occupational category. These low wages are a subsidy to profits ; yet neither men nor women workers have been willing or able to demand equal work and equal wages for women. Even though women's wages are low, their contribution to family income is substantial. In 1966, working wives contributed 22 percent of the family's total income, and they contributed 36.8 percent if they worked full time all year. This contribution made a difference of $2,100 in median family income in 1966 (between a $7,128 median for one-earner families and a $9,246 median for families with two earners). Officially-defined poverty in families fell in the 1960's by 8.7 million family members, no doubt in large part because 4.7 million more married women living with their husbands went to work during the period. By 1966, two-fifths of families whose income was above poverty levels had two earners, and almost 45 percent of families with incomes above $7,000. [8] Today about 23 percent of personal income goes to pay mortgage and installment debts ; thus the working husband is able to provide food, clothing, recreation, etc., while the wages of the working wife frequently pay for the house, car, and other consumer durables bought on credit.

Women's entry into the labour force is another aspect of the job crisis that the economy has been facing since the middle of the 1950's. On the one hand, there are not enough jobs ; on the other, "prosperity" (and profits) depends on the purchases by consumers of more houses, cars and other consumer goods. Government economic policy has tried to help keep up purchases in two ways : by providing jobs and sources of transfer income such as welfare, social security payments, and unemployment benefits ; and by promoting a pattern of investment that forces workers to buy houses and cars. Tax money has gone for highways, not public transportation ; housing loans

have made it more profitable for contractors to build single-family homes for sale than apartments for rent. So families have had to buy more expensive consumer durable goods, which has meant increased family indebtedness and an increased number of workers per family. As the number of children per family has declined and the years of education have increased, mothers have gone to work while their children spend more time in school. When women cannot find full-time jobs or cannot take them on in addition to their home role, they work part-time ; most part-time workers are women. Working women, then, help finance the purchases necessary to sustain the consumer economy and also, through their taxes and contribution to family income, finance the schools that absorb surplus labour and train workers.

Women's exploitation in the labour market is part of the growing job crisis of a stagnant economy. This increased exploitation compounds and, increasingly, defines the crisis of expectations faced by more and more women. Although more women work for a longer part of their lives, their primary labour is still assumed to be the unpaid work of housekeeping and child rearing. This work does not have a market value, which in a market society means that it has little prestige and receives a small share of the social resources. In 1968 there were about 35 million women who were not in the labour force because they were "keeping house." A society based on exchange value cannot recognize the production of use-values ; women cannot be paid for their labour in the home. And yet a crucial part of the postwar "prosperity" has been the purchase of expensive appliances to lighten household labour (as well as the purchase of the house itself). To afford these expensive goods, women

122

have had to moonlight, in effect, by getting another job outside the home to finance the tools for the job inside the home. So married women increasingly hold a job and a half or two jobs and are paid about 60 percent of one job. And costs of child care must come out of these low wages, since the care of children is a family (i.e., a mother's) responsibility. Government estimates are that there are 5 million children under the age of 6 with mothers who work, and only half a million of these children have adequate day care ; the other 4.5 million are cared for in other ways at a great cost out of a woman's small paycheck.

Women's entry into the labour force has meant the taking on of another job besides unpaid household and maternal labour. Although the mechanical part of household labour has perhaps been lightened with the appliances that have been bought with the working woman's paycheck, the social part of woman's unpaid labour cannot be mechanized. When married women with children go to work, their social function as a tension manager for their husbands and the teacher of social values to their children is seriously impaired. Much of the current emphasis on home and family in clear disregard for the reality of women working stems from the hoped-for function of women as easers of the men's tension from their jobs. But when women work too, neither partner is in a position to manage the tension of the other. Nor can women invest the time in socializing their children that is prescribed by social values, or that is in fact necessary to prepare them to be good and passive workers in the relatively sophisticated kinds of technological jobs that the economy needs and to accept their social roles without question. Children are learning their social values in

school, in the streets, and from each other, not from their absent parents. Young people are being tossed out of the atomized family units. Increasingly, the school has replaced the family as the place where social values are learned. The results are just beginning to disrupt the social fabric.

The root of women's oppression as women is the responsibility of the mother for child rearing within the nuclear family. Women's entry into the schools and labour force drive them into contradictions between their market and family roles. But the schools and workplace also collectivize women, who are isolated in the nuclear family, and make it possible for them to attack their oppression through these collective institutions. Demands for child care facilities, etc., show how central the child rearing problem really is, and also how inadequate the institutions of monopoly capital and the State are to care for children.

Women workers will continue to increase as a part of the work force ; so the conflicts between their market and non-market roles will increase, as will the pressures on the economic system posed by their labour. On the one hand, it is only profitable to employ so many women because their wages are so low ; on other, these low wages cannot generate enough purchasing power to keep up consumption, essential to maintaining profits. The family, instead of being a refuge from the pressures of the market, becomes more a part of these pressures.

The social divisions between black and white workers and men and women are very different kinds of social divisions, one so great as to approach a caste in the workplace and a nation in the society, the other a combination of different niches in the labour heirarchy and different roles in the same home. The youth division is of still another kind. Youth live intimately with their elders, so the division between them is not like that between black and white. On the other hand, while the exploitation of women is justified by a traditional set of values being eroded by the realities of the contemporary economy, the exploitation of youth is justified by a new definition of their role. This new definition of young men and women as "youth" rather than adults, cloaked in the ideology of patriotism and "educational opportunity," has helped obscure the job crisis and the postponement of entry into the labour market since the end of World War II. The reaction of youth to their experiences of work, school, army, and unemployment is often misinterpreted and misunderstood by older workers with a different set of life-work experiences.

The distinctive life-work experiences of youth revolve around three events for men—school, the draft, and unemployment—and three for women—school, the home, and unemployment. In these ways young people are forced to absorb stagnation by staying out of the paid civilian labour force (or, in the case of students, interpreting the low-paid work they do to get through school as secondary to their main occupation of being a student, a rationale not that different from the one used to explain away the low wages of women). All three of these experiences—longer schooling, virtually comprehensive conscription for men, and high unemployment rates—have developed since the end of World War II and become truly general in the 1950's and 1960's. Both the schools and the army are institutions for the oppression of the young ; they therefore are also the institutions from which the young can organize against their oppression.

In schools young people not only

disguise their own present unemployment but at the same time are trained for the jobs that will be most profitable to monopoly capital, at their own expense and that of the taxpayers, not at the expense of the employers who will profit from their training. This way of paying for the training allows employers to discriminate against well-trained blacks and women at the expense of the taxpayers and the victims of discrimination themselves. The draft is even more exploitive than other wage labour. It postpones young men's entry into the labour force and takes two years of the lives of almost two-thirds of young men (and all the lives of some of them) to protect the imperialist system for capital, so that it will be profitable to hire them after they have finished their stint in the military. The imperial tax on young men is paid directly by them and also by other workers' taxes, not by the monopoly corporations that profit from imperialism. The third experience that sets young workers apart from older workers is their high unemployment rates, which are about three times as high for young as for older workers, failed to come down very much during the "prosperous" 1960's, and were in fact one of the conditions of the "prosperity" for older workers.

The educational system is in many ways an ideal institution for obscuring the stagnation of jobs, since education is sacred in this capitalist system as the church was in the feudal system. Criticism of education can be stifled by dismissing it as heresy rather than confronting it at all. Critics of the church were burned at the stake ; critics of education are branded as anti-intellectuals. However, the idolatry of education has obscured an extension of the years of schooling to meet the demands of capital for labour that is not only specifically better trained but in general made adaptable to the technologically sophisticated kinds of labour needed by the economy. The definition and content of education has always been determined by the needs of the production system ; the better educations of U.S. workers are often credited with making them more productive than their European counterparts. And the expansion of education since the end of World War II reflects in part the need for workers with a fairly high level of conceptual skill (not the mere literacy that is more than adequate, from the capitalist viewpoint, for unskilled labour).

The education industry produces human beings to fill social roles. Students are both the labour power and the commodity produced. If in the industrial process man becomes the appendage of the machine, in the contemporary school the aim is to make man himself a machine, a self-correcting cybernetic mechanism who can bring to his alienated labour an alienated but nonetheless human intelligence and spirit. The tools for producing this human capital output are intellect in the service of the *status quo* and in opposition to imagination. For instance, economists can discuss the elimination of poverty, but never the liberation of man from economic necessity itself. Psychologists study the psychological pre-requisites to living and working in society as it is, but never the social requirements of a liberated psyche. Engineering and the sciences are designed to harness creativity to the needs of capital and the State, not the needs of human beings ; weapons research is well supported, oceanography and food sciences virtually ignored. The educational system is supposed to be able to build people capable of self-direction and then compel them to freely choose to uphold the system. The problem is summarized by the radical French writer André Gorz : "Out of fear of

creating men who ... would refuse to submit to the discipline of a too narrow task and to the industrial heirarchy, the effort has been made to stunt them from the beginning : they were designed to be competent but limited, active but docile, intelligent but ignorant of anything outside of their function, incapable of having a horizon beyond that of their task. In short, they were designed to be specialists." [9] However, to try to teach ignorance at the same time as knowledge, dependence at the same time as intellectual autonomy, even within narrow limits, exposes one to the risk of provoking an uprising against these limits. These contradictions are exploding at high schools and colleges as students begin to realize the alienation of producing one's self as a commodity for corporate use.

In addition to extending the training in skills and discipline, educational institutions in the last twenty years have also absorbed a tremendous amount of labour in teachers and students that would otherwise have been unemployed. One in six new jobs created between 1950 and 1968 was in public educational employment. In the same period the number of people between the ages of 18 and 30 who were in school increased about 3.2 million, from 13.5 percent of the age group in 1950 to about 22 percent of the age group in 1968. The increased *percentage* of young people (14 years old and older) in school absorbed more than 5 million people who would otherwise have been part of the full-time labour force. Education in a capitalist system is always designed to meet its needs, so one cannot disentangle the training in skills and discipline from the labour-absorbing function of the expanded education. But it is clear that most education past the mid-teens is surely unnecessary to train all but a very few workers. Millions of restless high school and college students know that their schooling is boring, irrelevant, and personally and socially undesirable, and that the expansion of education is not the great opportunity that the ideology proclaims. Much of what has been called "the expansion of educational opportunity" is the expansion of schooling to disguise the job crisis by decreasing the percentage of young people who are in the labour force—lowering the labour participation rate for men 20 to 24 from 91.2 percent in 1955 to 86.6 percent in 1964, for instance—and also by increasing the number who work part-time. [10] Students, especially college students, work when they are in school. In 1968, more than half of 20 to 24 year old men in school also worked; and 43.6 percent of the women in school worked too. [11] But few work full-time and even fewer think that their jobs define them as workers; instead they think of themselves as students, working their way through school.

The expansion of education and the greater reliance on the educational system to absorb surplus labour has the greatest effect on young white men, who are about three-quarters of the 20 year old school population. The failure of blacks and white women to get and keep jobs can be obscured by racism and sexism, but young white men are traditionally considered entitled to productive work. So as a stagnating economy makes it more difficult to provide that work, the educational mystification is important to hide from young men that they are impoverished and under-employed. Men stay in school so much longer now that the educational attainment of men and women has evened up, ending the traditionally higher educational attainment of women. More women than men still finish high school; but of the men and women who go to college, the men

stay longer, still believing their college degree will increase their lifetime income, while the women drop out. Ironically, the myth of education is self-destroying for blacks and white women. A standard apology of liberals is that the lower wages and higher unemployment rates of blacks and white women is not because of discrimination but because they are badly educated and trained. And yet the higher unemployment rates are true at every level of education. In fact, while the official overall unemployment rate for black men is twice that of whites, the unemployment rate of black college graduate men is three and a third times as high. Similarly, the overall unemployment rate for black women is twice that of white women, but for women with one to three years of college the figure is almost three times as high. Unemployment rates for white women, too, are higher than those for white men at every level of education. [12] Wages of blacks and white women are, too, lower than white men's wages at every level of educational attainment. This discrimination is costly in social terms, since education costs money that can only be re-couped from the increased income and taxes of the educated worker, which in turn can only be achieved by employment in a high-productivity occupation. But, because of the ideology of education as an opportunity and a social asset instead of a business investment, the costs of this discrimination are borne not by the employers but by the taxpayers who finance the educational institutions and by the victims themselves, who are never able to make up in wages the personal and social cost of their staying in school.

Schooling is the most sophisticated disguise of the crisis in youth employment. The expansion of the military machine is a much more obvious way to absorb surplus labour on the one hand and to force young men to do a kind of work they would not do voluntarily on the other. Since 1950, before the start of the Korean War, the size of the U.S. standing army has more than doubled, from 1.650 million to 3.535 million in 1968. This increase has eliminated the need for another 2 million jobs in the economy. More than two-thirds of young men are inducted into the army ; of those who are not inducted, almost all are rejected as unfit. Only a small group, less than an eighth of whites and a twelfth of blacks, escape through exemption or deferment. Student deferments do not lead to escape from the draft except for an insignificant half of one percent ; most who escape have hardship or fatherhood deferments. About ten percent of whites avoid regular service through reserve programs (only about two percent of blacks are able to use this escape route), and about four percent join officer programs and become wielders of power over other soldiers (only half of one percent of blacks have this option). The overwhelmingly majority (more than two-thirds) of young white men, and half of young black men, then, are held out of the civilian labour force for two years by means of conscription and enlistment in the armed forces.

Absorption of surplus labour, while an important part of the size of the military, is only part of the reason for the large standing army. The absorption is done by the military rather than other institutions because the military machine is a crucial element of the power of the United States over the other countries in the capitalist world and of its challenge and threat to the socialist countries. The army is the first and last resort of an expanding and embattled imperialism. The ideology of patriotism is used to justify the costs of the armed defense of imperialism by taxes on workers and by

two years of the lives of millions of young men for the benefit of the international monopoly corporations. For those young men themselves, military service is a microcosm of bureaucratic and racist society. Although more blacks than whites are rejected for military service, most on the grounds of a mental test designed to fit white culture, so few blacks participate in reserve or officer programs that black soldiers are 12 percent of all regular draftees or enlisted men.

The two-year imperial tax paid by young men is not justified on the grounds of "emergency" as conscription was in earlier wars. The Cold War ideology of permanent emergency against an invisible aggressor has simply made the army a part of the life of every young man, to be reckoned with as a given. Young men cannot be accepted into the labour force until they have discharged their two-year tax ; they carry into the rest of their work and life experience the memory of two years of regimentation and oppression at wages so low as to add insult to the danger and degradation of the experience. Particularly as the unending wars against socialist revolutions, not only in South East Asia but elsewhere as well, continue, more and more veterans will be veterans of combat against whole peoples. Some of these veterans will be used against rebellions inside this country ; others will join those rebellions.

The job crisis of the United States economy has become so acute that even the massive absorptions of young labour power in schools and the army, even the blinders of racism and the oppression of women, cannot disguise the growing problems of providing jobs for new entrants into the labour force. The final way in which the life and work experience of young people is set apart from that of older workers is the growing gap between the unemployment rates of workers under and over the age of 25. In a last effort to confine the effects of the economy's failures to the groups of workers with the least social status and political power, the unemployment rate for workers under 20 years of age has been allowed to remain at Great Depression levels since the early 1950's. Even during the 1960's, when the absolute number of unemployed fell from 4.7 million to 2.8 million, the number of teenage unemployed actually increased slightly, from 827 thousand to 835 thousand, while the percentage of all workers under 20 that were unemployed fell slightly from 16.8 percent to 12.6 percent. Young blacks experienced no real improvement at all : the absolute number of unemployed young blacks increased, while the unemployment rate fell only barely, from 27.6 percent in 1961 to 24.9 percent in 1968. The overall unemployment rate for all workers in 1968 was low for the United States, 3.6 percent. But in 1968, the last year of the great prosperity before the fight against inflation began to create more unemployment, the unemployment rate for young whites, 10.9 percent, was three times as high as the average, while that for young blacks was seven times the average. [13]

In addition to these spectacular unemployment rates, even by the minimized official figures, young workers are underemployed. They take part-time jobs because they cannot find full-time ones ; they abandon the search for jobs and drop out of the labour force and the statistics ; and, increasingly, they find jobs not in the private economy but in public employment that, for a variety of reasons, cannot pay wages as high as those in the private sector. While the age composition of the labour force in various occupations has not been studied, it

is obvious that new entrants will go to work in the growing sectors of the economy, and in the growing occupations within those sectors. Older workers will thus tend to be found in mining, construction, and manufacturing, transportation and public utilities, which occupy a decreasing portion of nonfarm employees, while young workers will tend to be an increasing percentage of workers in trade, finance, services and government employment. Of these growing industries, government is the largest and fastest growing ; the work and life experience of many young people is often a life totally within the public sector, first as a student, then, for the men, as a soldier, then as an employee of a local, state or federal government agency. Young white women, who tend to work either in clerical work or teaching, are likely to work exclusively in the public sector ; but young white men and young black men and women, too, are more likely to be in the public sector than older workers. Better educated young blacks are likely to work for governments because they are somewhat less discriminatory than private industry.

These three social divisions within the working class—black-white, women-men, young-old—differ in their origins and in the kind of hardships they cause, but they have closely connected political implications. The stagnant economy cannot provide enough jobs. The job crisis is imposed on blacks, women, and youth because this is a racist, age-dominated and male-dominated society and culture. But the job crisis itself is caused not by these ideologies but by the capitalist economic system. An economy that determines what is to be produced on the basis of profit also determined how many workers to hire and what they should be paid on the basis of profit. Capitalists pay their workers what is necessary to sustain and re-produce their labour ; they pay their workers what they must to get the kinds of labour that will maximize profits. Wages tend to be heirarchical, with a few workers at the top who are well-paid and more at every step down the scale who are paid less. This heirarchy is shaped by many factors, all of them governed by the requirements of capital, the structure of industry, etc. Some of these factors are intrinsic to monopoly capitalism, such as the tendency for the more monopolized firms to employ more capital per work-er and to pay higher wages than more competitive firms. Out of monopoly profits, higher wages can be paid not only to the workers who do the work but also to the executives, supervisors, and foremen who discipline the work-ers. However, while the heirarchy of wages is molded by the degree of monopoly power of the firms, the amounts of capital used by workers, how much profit the workers can produce for the firm, etc., the places in that heirarchy are filled according to a complex of social and cultural factors. Capitalism determines that there will be a pyramid, racism that blacks will be on the bottom. Discrim-ination and the traditional attitudes to women channel them into the low paid occupations. This wage heirarchy is inevitable as long as the rate of profit is the guide to what is produced and how. Racism, sexism, and age-domin-ation are essential parts of U.S. monopoly capitalism. Their function is to impose poverty and misery on groups declared to be inferior so as to hide the extent to which the capit-alist economic system depends on this pyramid of poverty.

These ideologies are embedded in institutions that organize the mistreat-ment of blacks, women and youth so that they will be the ones who stay at the bottom of the capitalist heap.

Thus the institutions of school and housing segregation facilitates a smaller investment in the living standards and education of blacks, so that the social tax cost of forcing them into the least productive worst paid jobs is lower than it would be if black schools and housing were allocated a fair share of the social investment. Curriculum differences in the education of men and women channel women into lower-paying jobs. The nuclear family forces women to work without wages in the home and at low wages outside it. Education and other social institutions make it likely that the high-prestige professional, technical and managerial servants of the ruling class will be older white men by patterns of social-ization, education and training that encourage white men and discourage blacks and white women from aspiring to such positions. Labour unions have kept youth, blacks and women out of the best-paid industrial jobs. These institutions, supposedly the represent-atives of the workers, have, partly consciously and partly by accident, protected and preserved the better-paid industrial jobs for the workers with the most social and political power and denied them, as much as possible, to their wives and children, as well as to most black workers. The social power of the unions rests on their concentration in the highly monopolized, highly productive, highly profitable industries ; but this power is challenged as the continuing growth of monopoly power restricts the number of workers in large plants covered by union contracts.

Labour union membership is a small and declining proportion of all wage workers. Union members were their largest percentage of all non-farm wage workers, 35.8 percent, in 1945. They have declined slowly but steadily since to 28.1 percent in 1966, about 18 million workers. These 18 million

129

workers are concentrated in the three sectors of the economy where productivity and wage rates have grown the fastest : manufacturing, construction and transportation. Labour union membership is concentrated in certain sectors of the economy, and in the largest firms in those sectors. In 1953 a survey found that while about 90 percent of the plants employing 1000 or more workers were covered by union contracts, only about half the plants with 51 to 100 workers were covered. [14] Unions have not expanded beyond the large plants, which accounts for their decay. Larger plants have more monopoly power, so they can pay higher wages than smaller competitive firms. In 1968, for example, the 200 largest manufacturing companies, almost all of which are covered by union contracts, hired 31 percent of all manufacturing workers, but paid 39 percent of total wages and salaries in manufacturing. It has been estimated that organized workers receive on the average 10 to 15 percent higher real wages than unorganized workers. [15] Union membership is also concentrated in the big cities of the Northeast, Midwest and the West Coast ; workers in the South and in smaller cities and towns have lower union membership.

The minority of industrial wage workers (about a third) that belong to unions are disproportionately white and men. While black workers (men and women) are about 11 percent of the total labour force, and women (black and white) are 42 percent of the total labour force, black workers are only about 8 percent of organized workers and women are only about 16 percent. The unorganized two-thirds of urban wage workers, on the other hand, are about 20 percent black (man and women) and 50 percent women (black and white). Obviously these proportions do not draw a caste-like race or sex line. Some black and women workers are organized ; a great many white men are not. But, in combination with the other major social institutions, segregation, the nuclear family and the educational system, the labour unions help to allocate the jobs that pay the highest wages to white men, the workers with the highest social and cultural status. Thus, the labour unions have attempted to reduce class consciousness and conflict by making it seem to white men in the wage labour working class that their position is relatively good. This kind of division draws attention away from the essentially exploitive nature of labour and draws the worker into the kind of one-dimensional thinking in which he feels good because his situation is not as awful as another's, instead of confronting his own exploitation.

The particular social power of the trade unions comes from the way they expanded at the end of the depression and during World War II, drawing into their ranks, not only the skilled craftsmen who had been union members since about World War I, but also the masses of relatively new industrial workers in the giant factories who were the leaders of class-based political and social action in the 1930's. The industrial unions, finally seizing on the organizing opportunities offered by the change in the production process from craft shops to assembly-line production, were able to tap the power of a mass of workers, who, although relatively unskilled, were working with the most advanced capital of the economy, in the most monopolized sectors, and could, therefore, demand the highest wages, not (as for skilled craftsmen) because they had a rare and therefore valuable skill but because they were productive and the employers could afford to meet their wage demands. A few other institutions came along with wages—grievance procedures, seniority rules for promotion and firing, increased job security—but mainly the unions provide a regular, dependable, disciplined work force for large corporate organizations that need many workers to work with large capital. The location of the labour unions in the most monopolized and productive industries determined that wages would be their major success and therefore their major focus.

However, the same characteristics that gave the labour unions their power when they were increasing their membership rapidly in the decade from 1935 to 1945 are costing them their power as the growth of jobs shifts away from the high-productivity manufacturing industries to the services, especially public services. For twenty years, more than two-fifths of the new jobs have been in direct government employment—military personnel, school teachers, clerical employees, service workers in government buildings, etc. These new jobs have absorbed black workers, women workers and young workers; many of the social divisions created in the rest of the economy overlap in government employment, which is the most racially integrated of any sector, hires a higher percentage of women than any other sector except finance and services, and, since it has been the fastest growing, has hired more of the young workers of both races and sexes than any other sector. The social composition of the public sector is therefore very different from the private sector and particularly different from the unionized private sector.

There are almost 15.9 million public employees working for the federal, state or local levels of government. Almost 30 percent of them work for the Department of Defense, 3.5 million as soldiers and another million as civilian employees. Another 30 percent

work in education, as teachers and other school employees. The remainder work as police and firemen, social workers, clerical workers in all levels of government bureaucracy, maintenance and other blue collar workers. About three-quarters of civilian federal government jobs are white-collar, the other quarter blue-collar; state and local ratios are probably about the same. Women are 42 percent of all government employees; blacks are 15 percent of all civilian federal employees (concentrated, of course, in the lower wage levels) and more than 11 percent of military employees. And although no general figures are available for the age composition of government employees, the falling median age of 43 years to 36 years) reflects the great flow of new entrants into that field and suggests what is happening throughout government employment. [16]

New workers—blacks, women, youth—are concentrated in the public sector. But while in the 1930's the new workers were concentrated in the industries that were most able to respond to wage demands, today the wage demands of new workers raise problems very different from those of thirty years ago. First, public employment is much more labour-intensive than private and cannot realize the kinds of productivity gains that are possible in the private goods-producing sector. Second, the wages of public employees are tax-financed, so that the demands of public employees for wage increases are demands on the real wages of other workers. Public employment is almost entirely service employment, much of it the provision of a personal service—such as teachers, social workers, hospital personnel—and the rest a kind of service that depends more on labour than capital. Only where an increase in capital investment can greatly increase product-

131

ivity can an increase in workers' wages be granted without decreasing the real wages of other workers (through the increased prices of the good or service produced) or reducing profits. Public employment is non-profit ; so, in effect, the only wage gains the public employees can make either decrease the number of jobs in the public sector or reduce the real wages of workers in the private sector. (For instance, if an office installs an automatic typewriter to answer form letters, it can afford to pay the operator more than a regular typist because the machine reduces the number of typists needed.) But since the public sector has the responsibility to capitalism of absorbing the surplus labour that cannot find work in the private economy, public employment tends not to be automated, since that would eliminate jobs. Therefore increased wages for public employees brings them into conflict with workers in the private economy who must pay higher taxes if public employees are to get higher wages.

This built-in conflict between public and private employees over the wages of public employees has not kept public employees from organizing in unions, demanding higher wages and other benefits, and even, in defiance of the ubiquitous laws against strikes by public employees, striking to back up their demands. But the conflict limits wage gains that public employees can hope to get from their elected employers who must offset voter anger at a strike in the public services against their anger at increased taxes. It also poses the problem of the contemporary State in one of its most politically explosive forms. The huge growth of the State has been for the benefit of capital and not for the working people. So public employees find themselves, as workers, called upon to perform services to capital under the guise of providing a public service. So, although wage demands bring public employees into conflict with workers in the private sector, demands to make the government serve the people and not capital brings public and private workers together. Public employees may therefore be able to play a very important role in taking workers' organizations (not the labour unions of today) beyond selfish and short-sighted wage demands and into a struggle for control of the economy by the people who do its work.

The experience of workers today has two sides. On the one hand, the number of people who work for wages is growing and the experience of being a worker is reaching a broader segment of the population than ever before. Women are entering the labour force, and fewer workers escape the experience of wage labour by farming or managing their own small business. Although perhaps as many as a quarter of white male workers have jobs that give them some nominal power, only a handful have independent self-employment. Regional differences, which once were great enough to spark regional war, have been greatly reduced. On the other hand, this very decrease in diversity makes it undeniably clear that broad social divisions of race, sex, and age run through the society and are acute symptoms of social crisis. These divisions have been used by an increasingly monopolized capitalist system that depends on having a heirarchy of workers, ordered according to their productivity and contributions to profits as dictated by the needs of capital, and paid in roughly that order. This heirarchy is made more socially acceptable by putting those with the least social power whose disadvantages can be most easily overlooked at the bottom. Racism has made it possible to ignore the poverty of black workers, to minimize its hardships, or to blame it on inadequacies of blacks. The traditional attitude that women are not full-fledged members of the work force excuses their low wages and confinement to jobs that are not only badly paid but boring, routine and dead-end. The worship of education and the conviction that "a man should serve his country" combine to excuse the exclusion of young workers from the labour force. By concentrating the consequences of stagnation on these groups at the bottom of the social heap, the job crisis facing the economy has been hidden. The labour unions have been complicitous in racism and the discrimination against women and the young and have hidden the job crisis from the white working men in the United States. Growing dependence on public employment is partly exposing the job crisis by breaking down the divisions among workers.

The job crisis, how it has been hidden and how it cannot be hidden any longer, is all closely related to the growing role of the State in the management of the economy. This role came out of the lessons learned in a decade and a half of depression and war.

REVOLUTION IN THE METROPOLIS

SOCIAL CRISIS, SOCIAL DIVISIONS, AND SOCIAL POLICY

The economic and political impact of social divisions depends on their relation to the economic and political system. Some divisions, such as those among immigrant groups, are no longer used to divide workers between the better and less well paid, and therefore have lost their political economic importance. Other divisions, such as those between men and women or between younger and older people,

have developed new political economic significance in addition no their traditional social and cultural importance. Still others, such as the division between black and white, have remained integral to the political and economic experience even though the nature of the relation has changed. Today the social divisions provide social support for the Keynesian economic solution to the crises of the 1930's and 40's. Government and business were unable to resolve the crisis of the 1930's until preparation for World War II showed how massive State investment could simulate recovery from the stagnation crisis. The new State economic policies had three parts : exporting stagnation ; subsidizing stagnation by taxes on the most productive workers ; and disguising stagnation by visiting its effects on blacks, women and youth. Labour unions were one of the most important institutions for implementing these policies ; purporting to represent the workers who were called upon to pay for the "solution", they could have led a resistance, but instead led compliance. Nor did socialists resist the implementation : the social democrats embraced Keynesianism ; the revolutionary socialists were divided by internal quarrels : the adherents of the Third International's "socialism in one country" policy abandoned efforts to build mass support for socialism in the United States. No effective opposition was mounted against allocating the economic burdens of a stagnating economy according to social power. For fifteen years these social and economic policies shaped the contemporary economy.

Today's social and economic crises are the breakdown of Keynesian economic policy and pluralist social policy. These policies themselves were a response to the great crisis of monopoly capitalism and imperialism in the 1930's and 1940's, the Great Depression and World War II. In the 1930's all the capitalist governments exhausted the remedies, short of war, to their internal economic crisis ; World War II was fought to decide which capitalist country would be the metropolis of a unified imperial system struggling to save capitalism and to wage war on socialism.

The Great Depression of the 1930's was the most serious economic crisis ever to befall capitalism, threatening every country of the capitalist world with literal economic collapse. In the United States, as in most other economies, the crises capped more than a decade of rapid monopolization and the saturation of investment. The automobile and electric power industries generated a large part of the new investment opportunities of the 1920's. Yearly auto output increased more than ten times between 1914 and 1929, generating (directly or indirectly) more than 45 percent of the new jobs for the period. [17] These new jobs were not only in the automobile industry itself, but came from the forward and backward linkages that changed the whole economic environment, opened up markets that could not be reached by water or rail, and set off a huge wave of secondary private investment in oil, rubber and glass, as well as public investment in highways. Electrical power industries were also important ; the production of electric power doubled in the 1920's and the value of products of the electric equipment industry almost tripled. This period of rapid investment was also a period of rapid monopolization. The number of automobile firms was reduced from 88 in 1921 to about a dozen by the end of the decade. [18] More than 3700 public utility companies disappeared during the 1920's : the market share of the 16 largest more than doubled, from 22.8 percent of the country's generating capacity in 1915 to 53 percent by 1925. In 1936,

the Federal Power Commission found that 90 percent of the generating capacity of the United States was held by 57 companies, of which 12 controlled 49.7 percent and one, 11.5 percent. [19] Monopolization went on throughout the economy in the 1920's, increasing profits for the remaining firms, who increased their market power and raised prices above the competitive level. But it also raised such high barriers to entry that new investment was curtailed, so that capital turned from investments in industry into banking, the stock market, and foreign loans, inflating the paper values whose collapse signalled the onset of depression.

The depression brought the economy to a virtual standstill. Between 1929 and 1932, national income fell from $83 billion to $40 billion, farm income from $12 billion to $5 billion, exports from $5 billion to $2.5 billion, and investment from $16 billion to less than $1 billion. The index of industrial production fell from 110 to 57, and durable goods from 132 to 41. [20] A third of the labour force was unemployed and 20 percent of the rural population was on relief. Recovery was slow and halting. Ten years after the crash, after a decade of unprecedented government activism, personal consumption expenditures were finally 6 percent above their 1929 level in constant prices, but non-residential fixed investment expenditures were still 42 percent below the 1929 level, and residential construction was 20 percent below. [21] Not until the United States began to rearm did economic recovery actually begin.

The private economy lay in ruins, unable to initiate a revival of investment ; first government officials refused to believe that there was anything they could do ; then they failed to concentrate on the massive stimulation of investment that was necessary for

134

recovery. At first, neither the Hoover administration nor the state governments thought that government intervention could help. Committed to the traditional laissez-faire view that all government intervention hurt business and the strict view of the Constitution that seemed to prohibit the intervention of the national government in State concerns such as welfare, national government officials watched impotently as the relief funds of towns and states were exhausted and the unemployment rate climbed. Even when public works programs were begun, they were limited in scope by the laissez-faire economists' horror of deficit financing.

The new Roosevelt administration was little more imaginative, relying for the most part on orthodox strategies to promote recovery : restoring confidence in the monetary system ; expanding international trade ; providing relief ; subsidizing business and agriculture ; and providing employment through public works. Only after the recession of 1937-38 showed that the economy was still on the verge of collapse did it become clear that massive government spending to underwrite investment and generate employment was a stark necessity.

Confusion about what caused the depression can be seen in many of the measures aimed at curing it. In the first place, most were not spending measures at all, but rules and regulations to make transactions more orderly, such as the Securities Act of 1933, the Banking Acts of 1933 and 1935, and the Securities Exchange Act of 1934. These measures were based on the presumption that the crash was the result of unsound business practices rather than the exhaustion of the whole engine—investment—of the system ; these laws had no effect on recovery. Another set of non-spending measures sought to reorganize world trade, again on the assumption that the collapse of trade was a cause rather than a symptom of the crash. These measures, too, had to wait on recovery to be effective. The kinds of regulation and rationalization of business envisaged by the National Industrial Recovery Administration (and by many of the production control measures in agriculture as well) were similarly aimed at reorganization and only accidentally at investment stimulation. These measures tried to cure the crisis of monopoly with more monopoly : restriction of output in agriculture, artificial maintenance of prices, cartel-type agreements to eliminate cut-throat competition. These measures were not so wrongheaded as they were inadequate, because they promoted centralization of existing capital without offering an outlet for new investment ; they made the stagnation more orderly without helping the economy overcome stagnation.

The spending measures were mostly as inadequate and misdirected as the reorganization measures. Government spending during the 1930's aimed at maintaining purchasing power, assuming that if people had enough money in their hands, they would demand the goods that would stimulate business recovery. But, while increased consumer demand could keep business from total collapse, it could not by itself stimulate growth and new investment, since the excess capacity in the economic system was more than enough to provide for consumers' day-to-day needs without more investment. The $18 billion given in relief between 1933 and 1939 was a stimulus to business, but did not create a demand for new investment. Even the "pump-priming" government investment in public building, power facilities, highways, etc., did not demand enough investment goods to use even existing excess capacity, much less stimulate a revival of investment. About $21 billion was spent on public works between 1933 and 1939; but excess capacity was still so great in 1939 that industrial output could double between 1939 and 1941 after a decade of almost no new capital investment.

The New Deal's economic programs had little effect on the economy; but the crisis of the Great Depression did reveal many of the social divisions that, incorporated into the postwar "solution" to the stagnation problems, would become an integral part of the problems of the economy and society of today. The gap between black and white unemployment rates began to be significant during the Great Depression, concentrating hardships, when possible, on black workers who were least able to resist. The complete failure of the economy to provide new jobs for four years meant, of course, that young new entrants were subjected to overwhelmingly high unemployment rates. The National Youth Administration and the Civilian Conservation Corps were set up to deal particularly with the problems of youth unemployment. The emerging problems of women in the labour force began to show up in the 1930's. In spite of the job crisis, the labour participation rate for women rose over the decade as women were driven into the labour force by changing social patterns and increasing family need. The craft unions, weakened as they were by the early years of the depression, nonetheless protected some of the older white men from some of the harships by visiting those hardships on younger workers, women, and blacks. The industrial unions offered a new form through which workers with the highest rate of productivity growth could be led into donating those productivity increases to paying for the costs of stagnation.

By the end of the 1930's it was painfully clear that the private economy could not recover without massive State spending to underwrite investment and generate employment. This State spending would have to be for an expanded military apparatus to establish the dominance of the United States against its challengers inside the capitalist world and to begin the war of aggression against socialism that was lauched at the same time.

During World War II the internal and external struggles of capitalism coincided. The crisis of capitalism in the 1930's hit every economy in the world except the state-run economy of the Soviet Union. International trade and finance were immediately curtailed; every capitalist country attempted an internal national remedy to its economic problems. Each capitalist country faced a growing internal socialist threat; economic crisis was a powerful stimulus to socialist mass movements. Rulers in every country discovered that the private economy could only be revived by massive State intervention to underwrite investment and generate employment. As each State began a campaign to stimulate investment, it was necessary not only to help rationalize capital inside the country through more monopolization, but also to promote expansion to overseas markets and resources. Some States colonized and annexed directly—Italy in Africa, Japan in Manchuria, Germany in the Sudeten, etc. Other States were more indirect and subtle, concluding trading arrangements, loans, treaties about the international monetary system, etc. Inevitably, these "solutions" led to conflict, Each group of national business and political leaders sought to solve their nation's internal crisis by expanding its boundaries, its markets, or both. International capitalism was not organized under the hegemony of one nation.

136

Great Britain had a relative hegemony in the pre-World War I years, maintained by "balance of power" mechanisms; but the depression and the beginnings of nationalist movements in the British Empire weakened her power. The United States and the Axis were the two candidates to inherit that leading role and to make it more explicit and well-organized. World War II determined that the United States would stand at the peak of international capitalism and that the Axis powers and the other European capitalist countries would be satellites and sub-metropolises for an imperial system headed by the United States. For most of the poor, imperialized capitalist countries, this period resulted only in a change of masters; for some, the disunity among the advanced countries provided the opportunity for revolutionaries to begin a war to liberate their nations from imperialist control. In China, the war of national liberation neared its victorious conclusion during the war among the capitalist powers in Europe and Asia.

The longer and more important war that began at the end of the 1930's was the imperialist war against socialism. Each capitalist government was fighting the socialist movements inside the country and mobilizing political support for the government's intervention on the side of capital. Each government tried to mobilize support for the necessary international alliance of capitalist countries by holding up the threat of socialism not only as an internal but an international movement. The existence of the Soviet Union internationalized the struggle between capitalism and socialism by making it a struggle among, rather than just within, nations. One way to look at World War II is as an interlude in the struggle between imperialism and socialism made necessary by the desire of each advanced capitalist country to

be the dominant imperial power. This struggle had to be settled since it led to absurdities such as the supposed alliance among the Soviet Union, England, and the United States. This alliance was more nominal than real; as soon as possible, even during the war against Germany, England and the United States were trying to find ways to contain, control and undermine the Soviet Union. As soon as the war was over and Germany and Japan defeated, the United States began to exercise its hegemony to make the interests of U.S. capital supreme in the newly organized international order of the capitalist world.

The crisis of the 1930's and 1940's was resolved by a reorganization of capitalism on a world scale. The United States became the undisputed metropolis of world capitalism and promoted the recovery of its private economy by a three-pronged attack on the problem of stagnation. The solution was to export the stagnation, to subsidize it, and to hide it. By becoming the metropolis, United States capital in league with the State was able to organize and finance a temporary resolution of the crisis by using existing social divisions and creating new ones to support its international domination.

The most visible solution to the stagnation crisis was the export of stagnation through the new institutions of empire. The advanced capitalist countries were on the brink of collapse; the underdeveloped capitalist countries of Asia, Africa and Latin America were either in the throes of revolutions for national liberation or were following pseudo-nationalist policies that left them even more deeply imperialized. With an economy whose output more than doubled during the war when the output of the other advanced countries was smaller than before the war (in Germany's case, only a quarter of pre-war levels), the dollar as the official international currency, and 77 percent of the gold reserves of the capitalist world, U.S. capitalists were able to export the stagnation of the U.S. economy by monopolizing the rest of the capitalist world along the same lines as the United States itself.

This monopolization proceeded by direct foreign investment, subsidized where necessary by grants of U.S. workers' tax money : to restore the shattered pre-war economies of Europe to sufficient health to support new investment ; and in the underdeveloped countries, to put in place the rudimentary social overhead capital needed to make direct foreign investment profitable. These tax-financed grants for economic aid and technical assistance—that is, aid to pay the salaries of U.S. experts to recommend which U.S. company to invite to invest in the imperialized country, and aid (mostly loans) to buy goods from U.S. firms—have cost U.S. workers about $50 billion in taxes since World War II and brought U.S. firms about $50 billion in sales. About a third of this aid, $17 billion, was concentrated in Western Europe in the first four years after the war and fostered enough recovery to absorb monopoly capital that the U.S. needed to export. After 1947, foreign investment, which had scarcely changed since 1930, began to grow at more than 10 percent a year. By 1950, U.S. direct investment in Western Europe was 20 percent above its 1940 level ; after 1950 it grew even more rapidly. (22) Direct investment in the poor imperialized countries also began to grow ; giant U.S. corporations, backed by treaties between the United States and the imperialized governments guaranteeing the corporations against expropriation, exported their monopoly power.

The institutions for the export of U.S. monopoly power worked smoothly not only because the United States came out of the war in a position of political and economic dominance, but also because this dominance was enforced by the Bretton Woods Agreement of 1944 that set up an international money system, putting the U.S. dollar on a par with gold as an international currency. United States investors could use the new international pre-eminence of the dollar to buy up the world in their own currency, a unique advantage, and to keep their gold monopoly much longer than they would have been able to do if they had to trade gold itself for titles to ownership of foreign investments. The dollar monopoly, and the virtual U.S. monopoly of gold reserves, financed the great wave of foreign investment and the growth of U.S. military power.

The economic, political, and military institutions of empire can hardly be distinguished, since they have operated as an integrated configuration. The export of U.S. monopoly would not have been possible without the establishment of the U.S. international military apparatus through agreements to maintain standing armies and to equip those armies with material received from U.S. arms manufacturers. The armies—NATO in Europe, SEATO in Asia, etc.—were set up to menace the Soviet Union, China and other countries and to suppress revolutionary movements wherever they appeared. These military institutions have spent more than $30 billion in military aid since the end of World War II ; this has been as loans or grants to other governments so that they can buy arms in the U.S., or direct shipment of the arms from government stores. Further, the U.S. military apparatus has spent from $1 to $4 billion outside the United States every year since 1950, pumping more dollars into international transactions to increase U.S. dominance.

138

The export of U.S. monopoly power was imposed on other capitalist countries which were too weak to resist. Workers in the United States were told that the tax cost of foreign aid was a necessary cost of fighting socialism, and that they benefited in some way from the international dominance of U.S. capital. The old argument that workers have a stake in the profits and prosperity of business was revived and refurbished by the labour union bureaucracies as part of the new postwar ideology of class harmony. This ideology was directed at workers with the highest productivity, who worked in the manufacturing industies and who produced the most profits for capital. They were paid the highest wages and convinced to finance through their taxes a massive subsidy to their employers, both inside the United States itself and in the rest of the capitalist world.

The massive state subsidy to capital, financed by taxes on workers, has had four main aspects : the redirection of a full tenth of all production to military uses ; the launching of a program of investment in education to absorb stagnation and train workers ; the investment by the State in expensive highways that have underwritten the expansion of the structure of private investment in automobiles ; and the pursuit of a complex of economic and social policies that have fostered the expansion of an economy that rests on consumer durables. Justified by the ideology of a new, active State that used Keynesian economic tools to avert another depression and to promote "welfare," the governments were able to extract more and more taxes from workers to subsidize an increasingly monopolized private sector.

Military spending is the largest single subsidy to capital in the Keynesian State. Military spending finally promoted recovery after a decade of depression. Under the stimulation of defense contracts, already amounting to $10 billion in 1940, industrial production doubled between August 1939 and December 1941, when the United States entered the war. [23] The government bought $186 billion in arms during the war ; direct purchases of war goods and services alone accounted for about half the gross national product in 1944 and 1945. The government spent $16 billion on new plant during the war. Giant corporations ran the plants during the war and bought them at its end for a fraction of their market value. The war spending was a successful promoting of monopoly power, continued after the war on a permanent basis. During the war, the largest one hundred industrial corporations received two-thirds of all the prime contracts ; the top 33 corporations received more than half ; and the top ten got fully 30 percent. The largest 250 corporations ran 79 percent of the government-built plants and acquired 70 percent of those disposed of in 1946, even though they only owned 65 percent of the nation's other manufacturing facilities. [24] The average sale prices of the government built plant and equipment after the war were about 30 percent of original cost. [25] The large-scale subsidy to the monopoly private sector through military spending was continued after the war, when government purchases of war goods and services remained high, reflecting the military side of the new institutions of empire. The taxing-spending machinery of government has forced the workers to tithe to militarism and imperialism. Workers have paid for private profits in the wars against socialism, with their taxes and with the lives of their young men. Military spending has also been a way to export, subsidize, and hide the job crisis by expanding the standing army.

Workers have also paid with their taxes and distorted lives for a costly expansion of the education system to absorb surplus labour and to train people at the workers' expense for the jobs that monopoly capitalism makes available. Educational spending tripled between 1950 and 1960, and more than doubled again between 1960 and 1970. The school expansion went with a longer school experience ; median school years completed increased from 9 years in 1947 to 12.1 years in 1968. This increase in schooling is one of the most important ways that the job crisis was hidden ; the absorption of surplus labour as teachers and students, as well as employment in school construction and school equipment manufacturing, etc., were a significant part of the worker-financed state subsidy to the private economy after the war.

Workers have also paid to finance housing and transportation policies that have distorted society's resources to extract a continuing subsidy to capital from workers through the purchase of consumer durables. At the war's end, there was a tremendous backlog of pent-up consumer demand and an acute housing shortage. To satisfy the demand for housing, state policies encouraged the construction and purchase of single family homes. Mortgage guarantee programs underwrote the mortgage market, greatly increased the volume of mortgage debt and the number of workers who had mortgaged twenty or thirty years of future labour for a place to live. The number of families who "owned" their own homes, which was lower in 1940 than it had been in 1890, 43.6 percent, jumped dramatically to 55 percent in 1950, 62 percent in 1960, and 64 percent in 1967. At the same time the percentage of homes that were mortgaged increased from 45 percent in 1940 to 57 percent in 1960, and the median ratio of debt to value climbed

from 43 to 53 percent. This housing policy was enmeshed in a whole network of causes and consequences. Single family homes were built on vacant land in the suburbs. Suburbanization compelled a massive tax subsidy to capital for highway and street programs ; workers bought cars to get to work from the house they had to buy to have a place to live. Racist banks and real estate institutions and the low income of black workers (because of racist hiring practices) meant that mostly whites moved into the new suburban homes, leaving blacks in the central cities. The growing debt burden of working families increased the likelihood that both husband and wife would work, which in turn increased the demand for cars and labour-saving household appliances. So capital has received a continuing subsidy from all the expensive purchases that have been made necessary by the original social policy of encouraging individual mortgage ownership of suburban homes.

The subsidy to capital under the institutions of the new metropolis of the capitalist empire was larger than workers realized. But since the productivity of workers in manufacturing was increasing very rapidly, both profits and wages rose, and the most productivity most highly paid workers were able to pay more taxes and still receive real wage increases. These highly paid workers did not feel a job crisis in the private economy until much later (the late 1960's) when the burdens of stagnation had become so great that even the most highly paid felt them. Highly paid workers were willing to subsidize the stagnation, in part because until recently the costs were experienced by workers outside the highly paid sector. Besides exporting stagnation into the new empire and subsidizing stagnation inside the metropolis, the job crisis was hidden

140

by the creation, reinforcement and perpetuation of the social divisions whose breakdown today has led to social crisis in the United States. The costs of stagnation were borne by blacks, women and youth through unemployment, under-employment, and unpaid labour; their situation was hidden by the ideological blinders that made it possible for others to ignore their problems or to explain them away on grounds made reasonable by racism, sexism, and seniorial chauvinism.

At the end of the war, returning veterans reclaimed their jobs, throwing the blacks and women who had replaced them out of work. Since race bars were just beginning to bend a little in the early 1940's, many of the displaced workers were black who had first gained industrial employment when the war created a serious labour shortage. Some effort was made to soften the blow of unemployment for women with an increased emphasis on the joys and delights of motherhood and family and for youth with expanded educational opportunities, such as the GI bill for veterans and increased low-cost or free education for everyone. Blacks were largely neglected or ignored. The median wage of the black worker fell as soon as there was no war to create a labour shortage; all through the 1950's when the U.S. economy was enjoying unprecedented prosperity, the relative wages of black workers deteriorated and the gap between black and white unemployment widened. Women returned home after the war, but came back into the labour force in increasing numbers after 1950 to help with the growing level of family indebtedness. Women's entry into the labour force, seemingly to stay, made it necessary to develop increasingly rigid patterns of job discrimination if the crisis of stagnation was to be hidden by confining its impact to workers with secondary status.

The key to hiding the job crisis, however, was the redefinition of youth and the expansion of the educational system and the standing army. The exploitation of blacks was limited, not by benevolence or even by fear of black resistance, but by the small size of the black population. Unemployment, under-employment and low wages for a tenth of workers was not enough to absorb stagnation in a private sector that could not provide enough new jobs. Excluding women from the labour force would curtail family purchasing power and threaten the consumer economy, so women had to be employed even if at low wages. The most successful part of hiding the job crisis was the invention of "educational opportunity" and the lengthening of school attendance. By extending the median years of schooling since the war's end, three years have been subtracted from the time that a person is or thinks of himself as a full-time worker. Labour participation for students is lower than for workers of the same age who are not students; and, when students do work, they often do not realize that their low wages are absorbing the job crisis of stagnation. The expansion of teaching jobs with the expansion of education has not only hidden the unemployment of students but that of their teachers as well. Education expansion was encouraged in the early postwar years by payments to veterans under the tax-financed GI Bill provisions; later the Sputnik-inspired National Defense Education Act financed still more expansion. After 1965, the poverty program's "work-study" provisions created a class of badly paid jobs to keep working class youth out of the regular labour force. People were also forced to stay in school by the growing youth unemployment that first became a serious problem in the late 1950's. Youth unemployment, the failure of the system to provide enough new jobs, was explained by the familiar ideology that education and training are necessary in a technologically advanced society. (This argument was also used to justify the unemployment and low wages of blacks and women, in spite of how easy it was to provide necessary training on the job during a labour shortage, such as during World War II.)

The strategies to combat stagnation were enthusiastically supported by labour union leaders. The new industrial unions organized during the crisis of the 1930's and 40's were incorporated into the social and political structures of the Keynesian solution. Before the crisis, labour union struggles had been largely those of craftsmen—carpenters, machinists, etc. —and had been more concerned with the pay and status of the crafts than with the conditions of all working people in the United States. The socialist minority in the American Federation of Labour was consistently outvoted ; the principles of business unionism and labour-management cooperation were firmly entrenched. The economic crisis of the 1930's damaged the AFL ; union membership, which had declined slowly during the prosperous 1920's, fell still further during the depression and was lower in 1933 than in 1917. Yet the vested interest of the AFL leadership in protecting the crafts was more important to them than organizing workers, and the leadership of the AFL hampered the efforts of organizers to take advantage of the possibilities offered by the giant manufacturing plants that brought thousands of workers together. Only when the industrial union organizers in the Committee on Industrial Organization, led by John L. Lewis of the Mine Workers, finally organized workers along industrial lines in defiance of the AFL leadership and were expelled

from the organization in 1935, did union membership begin to grow again. [26] The independent CIO, armed with the newly passed Wagner Act guaranteeing workers the right to organize, conducted an organizing drive that more than doubled union membership between 1935 and 1938. Union membership, which was less than 14 percent of the non-farm labour force in 1935, grew to embrace almost 36 percent of non-farm workers by 1945. But then it levelled off, and has declined slowly but steadily since 1954. Giant union bureaucracies to control labour are a significant feature of the economy and political system. The leaders of the labour unions have joined State officials in a campaign to convince union members, who tend to be the best paid workers whose taxes finance the imperial economy, that their tax burdens benefit them in some way.

The labour unions became a tool of monopoly capital at home and abroad. Bitterly anti-socialist, labour union leaders supported the use of their members' taxes to fight aggressive wars against socialism abroad ; they also spent their members' union dues money on programs to subvert the labour movements of other countries and to subject foreign workers to manipulation by U.S.-financed labour unions. The labour union leadership attacked the socialists in U.S. unions, expelling unions from the AFL and CIO (in some cases setting up competing unions) rather than accept their socialist leadership. Internationally, too, the AFL and CIO preferred to split the labour movement rather than work in an international federation that would be governed by its socialist majority. Since then, working through the U.S.-dominated International Confederation of Free Trade Unions, and in Latin America through the American Institute for Free Labor Development of the AFL-CIO, the leaders of U.S. labour unions have actively helped export the stagnation of the U.S. economy.

Inside the metropolis, the labour unions have promoted programs to subsidize a stagnating capitalist economy through taxes on workers. The labour union leaders have been vocal supporters of increased military spending, public highway construction, school spending, and "welfare" programs that help absorb surplus labour and disguise the private sector's inability to provide new jobs. The labour unions have also helped to hide the stagnation by pretending to speak for all U.S. workers when in fact they have never been able to silence many more than a third and today control few more than a quarter. To the extent that the labour unions pretend that their members are the typical workers of the country, they help to obscure the situation of blacks, women and youth by making them invisible or by redefining their life activity as not work. The craft unions are and always have been racist and sexist. They have only recently been willing to formally renounce these policies; in practice the crafts remain white male occupations. The industrial unions, although not as exclusive as the crafts, nonetheless value the preservation of the seniority system much more than reducing the unemployment of blacks, women and young workers. Further, since labour unions have not organized the fastest-growing sectors of the labour force, their membership has become disproportionately older, male and white, reinforcing the impression that other members of the working class are somehow not really workers.

It is not surprising that the labour unions, which (except for the IWW) have always been explicitly on the side of capital in the United States, collabor-ated with the State's program to export, subsidize and hide the stagnation of the capitalist economy. But the new programs and policies were also embraced or at least not steadfastly opposed by U.S. socialists. The policies carried out under the New Deal and World War II attracted many socialists directly into government employment, especially during the war when the United States gave the illusion of an alliance with the world's only non-capitalist country. Others went to work in the union movement, especially in the new industrial unions. They got caught in the dilemmas of supporting those organizations, to which they were fundamentally opposed, so that they could continue to work within them and use them a vehicles to reach workers. Reformist socialists were dumbfounded by the explosive growth of State power and allowed themselves to believe that their dreams were coming true. Their fundamental misconception that capital would relinquish control without a battle allowed them to mislead themselves (and others) into believing that some shift of power had taken place. But the rise of the U.S. metropolis was so rapid and took place in such a novel setting that even many revolutionaries were misled. This problem was made much worse by the policy of the Soviet Union at that time, which proclaimed that the duty of socialists was to defend the Soviet Union and preserve "socialism in one country". Those who were loyal to the Soviet Union defended that loyalty before doing mass socialist organizing. These socialists even opposed strikes during the war, leaving militant workers to the kind of economist leadership that would only press demands without any class content. Further, the whole policy of "socialism in one country" caused socialists who were critical of the Soviet Union to spend tremendous amounts of energy attacking its supporters rather than pressing forward with a revolutionary program for the United States. Deluded and divided, no successful socialist opposition was mounted against the Keynesian offensive.

In summary, the fifteen years of the Great Depression and World War II threatened mortal crisis for monopoly capitalism. Stagnation and crisis seemed about to triumph. The crisis was averted only by the forcible centralization of capital throughout the world under the domination of the United States. The governments of the United States assumed a new importance as the governments of the new metropolis. The national level of government, which had not previously been considered the most important, eclipsed the state and local governments when it assumed its new metropolitan responsibilities. Officials, bankers and generals from Washington assumed commanding roles in the diplomatic, financial, and military battles against socialism and in support of monopoly capitalism and imperialism. United States capital exported its stagnation crisis to the rest of the world by extending its monopoly power both in the industrial capitalist countries and in the underdeveloped ones, where patterns of U.S. exploitation deepened the underdevelopment (and accelerated the processes that would in time lead to socialist resistance).

Inside the new metropolis, political power was centralized so that the new State economic policies could subsidize stagnation through massive outlays of workers' taxes to underwrite investment and generate employment. The size of the national government's employment went up six times between 1930 and 1945, while state employment only increased about 50 percent. Similarly, while state and local government spending increased only slowly

in the crisis period, national government expenditures skyrocketed.

Centralization was justified not only positively but negatively through fear. Waves of anti-socialist ideology washed across the country. At the same time that socialism was declared treasonous, another ideological effort was made to immunize workers against the socialist virus by insisting that the United States was in fact a "middle class" and not a working class nation at all. A national cult was established to glorify the single family home, the family, and church attendance ; personal non-conformity was as suspicious as outright political deviance. The centralization of the political institutions was reinforced ideologically as well as economically. A vast expansion of corporate, union, and State bureaucratic rule, along with the militarization of U.S. society, was established under the name of liberalism.

The crisis in the United States today signals the exhaustion of the remedies to the crisis of 1930-45. To understand today's crisis it is necessary to characterize the contemporary economy and its major contradictions, which are set forth in the next section.

THE PILLARS OF THE METROPOLITAN ECONOMY

The economic organization of the United States shapes the society we live in. We live in the metropolis of imperialism, in a setting of large monopoly corporations, imperialist expansion and a vast State apparatus supporting domestic monopoly and foreign imperialism. These three pillars of the economy hold up the social structure in which working people live under the dictates of the corporate and State bureaucracies. The particular stresses and strains in those pillars point to how the structures can collapse and make it clear why the first groups of working people to attack the structures are blacks, youth and women.

The United States is a capitalist economy. Investment and production decisions are made by privately owned firms according to their owners' and managers' estimates of profitability. The livelihood of all the people depends on the decisions made by these businesses. Workers are hired only when profits are expected to be reaped by hiring them. Government activities depend on tax and debt financing, and so rest on the prosperity of the private economy, the ability of workers to pay taxes and the willingness of banks, business, and wealthy individuals to hold government debt. However, the power of capital goes far beyond just determining the extent of prosperity. The power of capital is the power to shape the future by means of investment decisions based on profit expectations. These investment decisions determine the outlines of how we live and how we will live, what jobs will be available, what kinds of goods and services will be offered to consumers, what our daily lives will be like. There is a housing shortage and high war spending because businessmen cannot make as much profit in housing as in making war goods. There is a shortage of parks and mass transportation but not of parking lots and automobiles for the same reason. Capitalism is not just a way of doing business ; it is a way of life. As the metropolitan economy has developed in the last thirty years, the tremendous growth of three features stands out : monopoly power ; imperialism ; and the State. Monopoly, imperialism, and the State are the pillars of the metropolitan economy, the sources of its strengths and weaknesses. Monopolization has gone on so rapidly that by 1969 fewer than 2600 corporations held 86 percent of all manufacturing assets and received 88 percent of the net profits of all manufacturing corporations in the United States. Foreign holdings are so massive that foreign subsidiaries of U.S. corporations have sales of more than $200 billion a year, more than a fifth of the gross national product of the United States. The State is so large that governments hire directly 20 percent of the employed labour force and generate the jobs held by another 8 percent, purchasing the goods and services they produce. The sheer immensity of these magnitudes shows the importance of these features of the metropolitan economy. This section explores not only the importance but the character, dimensions, interdependence, and indispensability of these three pillars of U.S. monopoly capitalism.

The first pillar of the metropolitan economy is monopoly, the control of investment and production decisions in a few hands. Big business is very big, very powerful and very profitable. By every measure of business activity, a few large corporations are in control. The manufacturing corporations, the banks and other financial institutions and even the distribution channels are highly monopolized, closely interlocked, and becoming more rather than less centralized. At the beginning of 1969, the largest 87 manufacturing corporations, those with more than one billion dollars in assets, owned 46 percent of all manufacturing assets and reaped 50 percent of all manufacturing profits in the United States. The smallest 192,000 manufacturing corporations, with assets of less than 10 million dollars, held only 14 percent of assets and made only 12 percent of all manufacturing profits. At the very bottom of this heirarchy of capital were about 175,000 manufacturing businesses classed as proprietorships and partnerships, which held about 1 percent of all manufacturing assets, or less than one-third of those of Standard Oil of New Jersey. [27] Out of more than 369,000 manufacturing firms in the United States, 87 corporations made half of all the profits and 2593 corporations made 88 percent of all the profits.

Monopoly power is the ability not only to make profits but to dispose of them freely. Very few centers of economic power make the basic social decisions about what is produced and how. In 1968, the *Fortune Directory* reported that the largest 500 industrial corporations made 74.4 percent of industrial profits on 64 percent of all industrial sales ; the top 50 made 39.8 percent of all industry earnings on 30.9 percent of the total sales of all U.S. industrial corporations. [28] The 500 largest industrial corporations hired almost 14 million workers in 1968, almost 69 percent of all industrial employment and more than 18 percent of all civilian employment. In 1963, the largest 200 manufacturing corporations produced 41 percent of the value added by manufacture, but with their monopoly profits were able to make 46 percent of the new capital expenditures in manufacturing. This is one way the big get bigger. The value added by manufacture by the largest 200 companies increased from 30 percent in 1947 to 42 percent in 1966.

Monopoly power is not limited to manufacturing. In every sector of the economy a few firms are so large that they dwarf the others. In 1968, there were 13,698 commercial banks. Of these, the 10 largest held nearly 24 percent of all bank assets, and the 50 largest held 41.5 percent. Of the 1775 life insurance companies, the 10 largest controlled more than 58 percent of all insurance assets, and the 50 largest controlled about 84 percent.

Even in the relatively more decentralized area of retail trade, with about 1.7 million establishments, the largest 50 companies accounted for more than 18 percent of the 1968 retail sales. American Telephone and Telegraph, the world's largest corporation, with more than 40 billion dollars in assets in 1968, had more assets than the next largest 21 utilities and made more profits than the next largest 31 utilities in 1968.

These data on the concentration of monopoly power are impressive, but ties among corporations increase this concentration still more. The largest 100 manufacturing corporations reported 239 billion dollars in assets in 1968, but they held about 25 billion more dollars in investments in unconsolidated subsidiaries, affiliates, or companies. [29] Further, the large corporations are linked to each other through their boards of directors and company officers. A staff report to the Antitrust Subcommittee of the U.S. House Committee on the Judiciary examined 29 of the largest industrial and commercial corporations in 1962. [30] They found that of the 463 members of the Boards of Directors of these corporations, 220 sat on 314 boards of banks and financial institutions, 91 were directors of 132 insurance companies, and 239 sat on the governing boards of 717 other industrial and commercial corporations. Another study at the same time found that the 50 largest industrial corporations had 520 interlocks (through directors or company officers) with the 1,000 largest manufacturing firms ; 134 of these 520 interlocks were with companies in the same general product line. The largest 200 industrial corporations had 476 interlocks with each other and a total of 1,450 interlocks among the largest 1,000. [31] Still another study found that in 1965 the 200 largest non-financial corporations had 1720 interlocks, and the 50 largest financial corporations had 760 interlocks. The financial and non-financial corporations are also closely linked. The total liabilities of non-financial business are about 500 billion dollars. About one-third of the assets of the 200 largest non-financial corporations are financed on credit ; these 200 corporations interlock 616 times—roughly one-third of their total interlocks—with the 50 largest banks and life insurance companies. [32] A staff report of the Federal Trade Commission on corporate mergers supplies a good example : "General Motors Corporation, the country's largest industrial corporation when measured by sales, was interlocked with 7 of the 100 largest industrial corporations, with the nation's largest railroad, and with the largest telephone company. All told, the 63 corporations with which General Motors was interlocked in 1962 had combined assets exceeding $65 billion." [33] Corporate power is further centralized by the partial integration of separate corporate enterprises through joint ventures. Between 1960 and 1968, the 200 largest manufacturing corporations of 1968 formed at least 705 joint ventures, involving 1,153 intercorporate ties ; about one-fifth of these joint ventures linked the 200 largest corporations with each other. [34]

Monopoly power is concentrated in very few hands ; and the centralization of economic power is continuing. The tendency to monopoly is inherent in capitalist development. Monopolists re-invest their super profits for rapid growth and have the financial base to acquire other firms. The power of the giant corporations continues to grow. The Federal Trade Commission study on corporate mergers in 1969 concluded : "At present the top 200 corporations own over three-fifths of all manufacturing assets, or more than

the share owned by the 1,000 largest companies in 1941. Moreover, the top 100 corporations now hold a greater share of the nation's manufacturing facilities than the largest 200 owned in 1950." [35] The share of corporate manufacturing assets held by the 1,000 largest corporations grew from 61.6 percent in 1941 to 80.8 percent in 1968. Monopoly power continues to grow because it is self-reinforcing. In 1968, the top 500 U.S. industrial corporations accounted for 64 percent of industrial sales, but made 74.4 percent of all industry profits ; these figures mean that the largest 500 corporations made more than 63 percent greater return on sales than the rest of industry. These high monopoly profits make further monopolization possible. Finding profitable investment outlets for these surpluses becomes increasingly difficult, since the monopoly corporations must protect the value of their existing investments. For example, General Motors cannot invest in an electric car or mass transportation because that would threaten the value of their investment in the individually-owned gasoline engine automobile. And yet profits must be reinvested to realize still more profits. Increasingly, monopoly corporations acquire other firms rather than make new investments. Since the boom cycle begun in World War II, mergers have become more and more important as outlets for capital. Between 1948 and 1952, acquired assets averaged less than 3 percent as much as total new capital investment for the economy ; this percentage increased by an average of about 18 percent annually until 1967 ; and by 1968, acquired assets reached at least 55 percent as much as total new capital investment. [36] Thus the stagnation of monopoly power breeds more monopolization.

The second pillar of the metropolitan economy, imperialism, is the external face of the domestic growth of monopoly. The increasing centralization of capital that has gone on inside the United States has also gone on throughout the capitalist world. The same large corporations that control the U.S. economy have also eclipsed the capitalists of other nations. The search for profits and investment outlets does not stop at the national boundaries. Almost half of the gross product of the capitalist world was generated in the United States in 1967, more than $800 billion out of a total of about $1,700 billion. But further, more than 20 percent of the gross product of the rest of the capitalist world was produced by foreign affiliates of U.S. corporations. Foreign subsidiaries of U.S. corporations produce more than $200 billion in sales ; this is larger than the gross product of all economies in the world except the United States and the Soviet Union. With less than 10 percent of the population, U.S. capital controls and profits from about 60 percent of the output produced every year by the entire capitalist world. Harry Magdoff, in *The Age of Imperialism*, attempted to estimate the size of the foreign market, including U.S. exports. He concluded that in 1964, the foreign market was equal to about two-fifths of the entire domestic output of farms, factories, and mines. [37]

The centralization of U.S. capital outside the United States is even greater than inside the country. In 1957, 163 firms accounted for about 80 percent of total U.S. foreign investments. These are, of course, the largest firms. Of the 200 largest corporations in the United States, about 85 percent have one or more foreign subsidiaries. "In all Western Europe, 20 United States firms account for two thirds of United States investment." [38] Only 70 U.S. firms account for nearly half of U.S. investments in the underdeveloped countries. [39] It has been estimated that about 75 U.S. corporations make more than 25 percent of their sales in foreign markets. [40]

U.S. capital affects all levels of the world economy, from the extraction of raw materials to manufacturing and the banking system, in both underdeveloped and developed countries. About one-third of U.S. production abroad is in Canada, one-third is in Europe, and one-third is in the rest of the capitalist world. About 40 percent of U.S. direct investment abroad is in manufacturing, 30 percent is in oil, and 30 percent is in other activities.

U.S. corporate control over the capitalist world's oil production offers revealing examples of the scope of U.S. economic imperialism. The foreign investments of the U.S. oil industry are about 30 percent of all U.S. foreign investments and provide about half of all foreign profits to U.S. capital. In 1967, Standard Oil Company of New Jersey had operations in 45 countries, Mobil Oil Company in 38 countries, and Gulf Oil Company in 48 countries. Although in 1968 only 25 percent of the capitalist world's oil production came from the United States, 71 percent was produced by U.S.-owned firms as recently as 1964. The companies candidly explain that they are keeping the U.S. oil supply "in reserve ;" that is, they plan to exhaust the irreplaceable oil resources of other countries before those of the United States. Standard Oil Company of New Jersey sold about 40 percent of the capitalist world's oil in 1968. Only about 18 percent of this was produced inside the United States ; another 5 percent came from holdings in Canada and Europe. The remaining production came from foreign holdings in the underdeveloped countries—32.4 percent from Latin America, more than 31 percent from the Middle East, and

148

almost 13 percent from Libya. More than half of Standard Oil's net income in 1968 came from abroad. [41]

U.S. capital is deeply involved in most of the capitalist economies of the world. In Canada, where the United States holds more than 80 percent of all foreign investments, foreign subsidiaries held 26 percent of all the assets and made 40 percent of the profits of all corporations in 1967. Foreigners controlled 60 percent of the Canadian mining industry, 57 percent of manufacturing, 83 percent of chemicals, and 99 percent of petroleum and coal products. [42] In England, U.S.-owned firms generate about 10 percent of the annual gross product. In Italy, in 1967, U.S. corporations owned at least 6 percent of all corporate investments. [43] In all of Latin America, where exports amount to about 20 percent of total output, U.S. corporations accounted for about one-third of Latin American exports to the world in 1967. [44] In Brazil, where about half of the foreign capital comes from the United States, foreign capital in 1968 controlled 40 percent of the capital market, 62 percent of the foreign trade, 82 percent of the maritime transport, 100 percent of motor vehicle and tire production, more than 80 percent of the pharmaceutical industry, nearly 50 percent of the chemical industry, 59 percent of machine production, 48 percent of aluminum, and 90 percent of cement. [45] Outside of North America and Europe, U.S.-owned corporations control and profit from more than a quarter of the annual production of the capitalist world.

Even these figures understate the extent of U.S. corporate control over the capitalist world's economy. Uncounted are the sales of unconsolidated affiliates in which U.S. firms hold only a minority interest, joint ventures, and foreign firms operating under copyright and patent agreements. Between 1960 and 1968, 164 of the 200 largest U.S. manufacturing corporations engaged in joint ventures creating 572 ties with foreign companies. [46] The full extent of U.S. corporate involvement in foreign economies is not known ; however, an example will show the variety of ties that reinforce direct U.S. majority ownership. North American-Rockwell Corporation is the 8th largest defense contractor and the 29th largest U.S. industrial corporation. Itself a merger of two large U.S. corporations, North American-Rockwell acquired 5 U.S. firms in 1968. Its international dealings are carried on in 20 countries, and it has ties to 40 foreign firms : 10 subsidiaries in which it holds at least a 50 percent interest ; 15 affiliates in which its interest is less than 50 percent ; and 15 licensees from which it receives royalty income. With its British affiliate it holds a controlling interest in a West German firm as a joint venture. [47]

U.S. banking operations abroad have expanded to keep pace with, and to help, U.S. extractive and manufacturing corporations exert control over foreign economies. In 1967, the largest U.S. banks had 298 branches in 55 countries. The number of branches outside the United States increased about 2.7 times between 1955 and 1967 ; the volume of foreign operations probably increased much faster. For example, between 1957 and 1967, deposits in the foreign branches of New York banks rose from $1.35 billion to $9.5 billion ; and in mid-1960's these deposits were growing at a rate seven times greater than deposits at home. During that period the foreign business of Manufacturers Hanover, the fourth largest commercial bank in the United States, increased from 10 percent to 25 percent of its total business. [48] Further, by 1967, U.S. banks had set up 52 subsidiary corporations in international banking. These subsidiary corporations engage in a wide range of foreign financial and investment activities, including direct investments in industries abroad. [49] Control over banking and finance abroad gives U.S. capital tremendous control over the direction of investment spending in the imperialized economies. With the aid of U.S. banking interests abroad, U.S. corporations can take over foreign firms or expand existing operations with little capital from the United States. Recently, U.S. corporation affiliates abroad have been financing between 80 and 90 percent of their new capital expenditures from local sources.

U.S. corporations have expanded abroad much faster than inside the United States. Total U.S. direct investments abroad have increased more than eight times in book value since 1945 ; since 1950, they have been growing at more than 10 percent a year. In 1961, 460 of the 1,000 largest U.S. corporations had a subsidiary or branch in Europe ; this had risen to 700 out of the largest 1,000 by 1965. [50] In 1967, U.S. industry acquired 508 foreign firms, and 708 in 1968. Magdoff has calculated that while domestic manufacturing sales rose by 26 percent from 1950 to 1964, exports plus foreign sales rose by more than 50 percent more. Exports plus sales of foreign based U.S. firms rose from 15 percent to 22 percent of total manufacture sales between 1950 and 1964. [51] From 1958 through 1968, U.S. manufacturers expanded their overseas capacity 471 percent, as compared with a 72 percent increase in domestic capacity.

This imperialist expansion has, of course, been driven by the search for profits. Profit rates on U.S. investments abroad are probably about twice as high as in the United States, and

higher in the underdeveloped than in the developed countries. Foreign investments yield extremely high profits partly because the investments are concentrated in the most monopolized sectors of the foreign economies. For example, in 1967, in Canada the mainly-U.S. foreign subsidiaries accounted for 40 percent of the profits while controlling only 26 percent of the assets of all corporations ; thus, the profit rates on assets are about 90 percent greater for the foreign-owned operations in Canada than for the Canadian-owned. In the underdeveloped countries the super-profits on U.S. investments are so great relative to further profitable investment opportunities that between 1950 and 1965, almost three times as much money was taken out in earnings as was put into these countries by new direct investment ; even with this tremendous outflow of profits, the value of U.S. direct investments in the underdeveloped countries increased almost 2.6 times in the same 15 year period. [52] Between 1950 and 1964, earnings on foreign investments of U.S. corporations operating abroad rose from 10 percent to 22 percent of *all* domestic non-financial corporate profits, showing that U.S. monopoly capital's dependence on foreign operations is increasing. [53]

This spread of U.S. monopoly control over the entire capitalist world, now producing output abroad exceeding $200 billion in sales value each year, has been very profitable for U.S. capital. It has provided the major avenue for expansion of monopoly power during the past 20 years, while the U.S. private economy has increasingly stagnated under the weight of its own monopolized economy. The people of the United States spend more than 10 percent of their total labour each year to maintain the military establishment that protects the U.S.-

owned foreign assets that produce that $200 billion for capital. Most of the imperialist profits are used for further investment and imperialist expansion abroad, although enough of these profits are repatriated to more than repay the outflow of direct investment. Between 1950 and 1969, income on foreign direct investments returned to the United States exceeded the outflow of direct investments from the United States by about $21 billion. [54] This $21 billion was to the profit of monopoly corporations, but it was earned at the cost of almost $1,000 billion to the society taken by the U.S. government from workers' taxes to defend the U.S. capitalist empire during the same period.

The third pillar of the metropolitan economy is the State, which actively supports monopoly and imperialism. Governments in the United States are very large ; hardly a day goes by in which some government does not impinge on ordinary life activities. Governments affect economic life in particular ways that are closely related to the growth of domestic monopoly and foreign imperialism.

The most obvious impact of government on the economy is its tremendous demand for goods and services. Government purchases of goods and services, financed primarily by direct or indirect taxes on workers, generates some jobs for workers and more profits for business. In 1968, all levels of government purchased 23 percent of all the goods and services produced by the economy, $220.3 billion out of a gross national product of $865.7 billion. About $95.2 billion of this government spending was for compensation of general government employees ; the remaining $105.1 billion, primarily purchases from business, amounted to about one-seventh of all final business sales in 1968. This government spending generated about 28 percent of all jobs in the entire economy in 1968. In that year there were about 79.5 million employed workers in the United States. More than 12.3 million of these were civilian employees of the federal, state, and local governments ; and more than 3.5 million men were in the military. Governments hired directly 20 percent, or one in five, of all workers with jobs in 1968. Further, more than 1 million out of the 3.3 million construction workers in 1968 owe their jobs to governments, since about one-third of all new construction was publicly financed. The Department of Labour has estimated that in 1968 another 3 million private industry jobs were directly generated by the demand of the Defense Department for the war-related goods and services these workers produced. Finally, all other federal, state, and local purchases from private industry generated about 3.3 million additional jobs. So in 1968, about 6.4 million, or 8 percent of all jobs, were jobs in private industry producing goods and services purchased by governments. Thus, State directly hires or purchases the output of about 28 percent of all employed workers in the United States. Workers at the remaining 72 percent of jobs in the economy must be able to produce enough goods and services to meet their own consumption needs as well as those of the 28 percent working for State. The productivity of workers in the private sector also underwrites the monopoly profits of the corporations that support the consumption of the capitalists as well as the production of the investment goods that add to corporate wealth.

Direct job creation is only part of State activity that creates jobs and incomes. Subsidy programs to the private sector, including foreign aid which almost all returns to the United

States to purchase U.S goods, generate still more tax-financed jobs. And more than 45 million men, women, and children stand in a client relationship to some government institution, receiving tax-financed incomes as beneficiaries of social insurance, public assistance, veterans benefits, unemployment insurance, etc. Further, nearly 8 million people over 17 years of age are enrolled in schools, the socialized apprenticeship centers that receive about half of their financing from taxes. Thus, completely aside from the use one makes of government agencies every day, *probably about half of the people of the United States depend directly or indirectly on the State for their occupations or for a large part of their incomes.*

The State's role in the economy is not only large but rapidly growing. Over the entire period from 1950 to 1968, State purchases of goods and services amounted to about 20.5 percent of gross national product. However, State purchases as a percent of gross output increased from 13.3 percent in 1950, to 19.8 percent in 1960, to 23.1 percent in 1968. Even more important has been the role of State in new job creation. In 1950, the governments in the United States directly hired or purchased the output of about 16.9 percent of the employed workers ; this increased to 28 percent by 1968. There were almost 60.8 million jobs in the economy in 1950 and almost 79.5 million jobs in 1968, an increase of 18.7 million jobs in the United States. Civilian employment by governments increased from 6.4 million in 1950 to more than 12.3 million in 1968 ; the military increased from 1.65 million in 1950 to more than 3.5 million in 1968. There was a total increase in government payrolls of more than 7.8 million jobs, or about 42 percent of all new jobs created in the economy over the 18 year period.

During the same period the number of jobs producing output to be sold directly to the State rose from more than 2.2 million to about 6.4 million, accounting for almost 22.4 percent of the new jobs created in the economy. The increase in State purchases of goods and services between 1950 and 1968 directly created 12 million out of the 18.7 million new jobs ; this is 64.3 percent, or almost two-thirds, of all new jobs over 18 years. [55]

The State's purchases have generated almost two out of every three new jobs since 1950, without including any multiplier effects of these purchases on the rest of the economy or any new jobs created to supply the consumption needs of these new workers. Nor does this include the indirect creation of the jobs of those who had to produce the capital goods or the factories and equipment for the 4.2 million government-generated private sector new workers to work with. Nor does this include the additional government-generated jobs that were partly supported by tax-financed government subsidies to the private sector of the economy. Nor does this take account of the effect of government transfer programs, which encouraged earlier retirement throughout the period and reduced the number of jobs needed ; and school enrollment of people over 17 years old increased by about 5 million, further reducing the demands for new jobs since 1950.

The monopolized private sector of the economy, on the other hand, has been largely unable to create new jobs. The State's payrolls increased by over 7.8 million between 1950 and 1968. Of the almost 10.9 million new private sector jobs created, almost 4.2 million, or 38.6 percent, were increases in jobs to supply State demanded goods and services. More than a third of the new private sector jobs created between

1950 and 1968 were only part-time jobs, mainly in wholesale and retail trade. There have been no truly epoch-making, investment and employment generating innovations since the automobile. Recall that between 1914 and 1929, the heyday of the automobile industry, more than 45 percent of all new jobs created in the economy were due directly or indirectly to the automobile. With the high and increasing degree of monopolization of the economy, monopoly capitalism, concerned with protecting the values of its existing highly centralized investments, has faced a chronic stagnation problem. Between 1950 and 1968, total manufacturing, mining, and construction employment increased by 28 percent, creating only 5.17 million new jobs. (Probably two-thirds or more of these new jobs can be attributed to increased government purchases, since most of the 4.2 million new government-generated private sector jobs during the period were in manufacturing and construction.) While employment in these industries increased only 28 percent, the total increase in goods output plus new structures built increased by 88.3 percent, from $237.8 billion to $447.7 billion in 1958 dollars. Automation and labour saving investments have had the effect of eliminating 11.1 million jobs in manufacturing, mining and construction since 1950 by finding ways to increase output without hiring more workers. If the State had not rescued the stagnant monopoly capitalist economy, the failures of a system based on the private appropriation of profits would have been abundantly clear to millions of unemployed workers.

The State penetrates every aspect of economic life. Accounting for 23 percent of gross output and 28 percent of all jobs, and two-thirds of all new jobs created for 20 years, the particular relations between the State and the rest of the economy show up in every kind of economic activity. The three pillars of the metropolitan economy—monopoly, imperialism, and the State—are inextricably bound to one another. The vast expansion of monopoly and imperialism in the past 20 years was only possible because the State appropriated huge amounts of the economic surplus through workers' taxes to be used in support of that monopoly power and imperialism.

Today, 28 percent of workers are able to purchase the consumption goods produced by workers labouring for the monopoly corporations only because they receive tax-financed incomes. The State supports monopoly capital even more directly by not engaging in any direct production of goods and services that would compete with private corporations. Purchasing output from monopoly corporations uses workers' taxes to support monopoly profits and further monopoly growth. When the State wants to expand the production of war goods to protect corporate profits abroad, it uses workers' taxes to make it profitable to those same corporations to produce more war goods and fewer consumption goods for workers.

An examination of the activities actually performed by the State shows that it primarily subsidies monopoly and imperialism. The construction companies profit directly from the one-third of construction activity that is tax-financed ; but the automobile, oil and transportation industries also profit from the public construction of the highways, and all industry benefits from the cost reductions of improved transportation facilities. Industry also benefits from the tax-financed training of workers in the schools; and from the federal government's financing of about 70 percent of all research and development each year, including more than 50 percent of all industrial research and development. About one-eighth of industry is "regulated" by State agencies : the electric power, gas, water, transportation, telephone and communications industries have State sanctions and support of their monopoly position and monopoly profits. The State gave $3.5 billion in farm payments in 1969 ; the top 4 percent of the receivers got one-third of the total. Between 1955 and 1968, the federal government's foreign aid programs financed 29 percent of all agricultural exports. The highly monopolized oil industry operates like a cartel under government supervision. Although U.S. corporations control more than 70 percent of world oil production, import quotas keep the domestic price high, and oil depletion allowances reduce the taxes on oil producers. *Business Week* has summarized the impact on the oil industry ; "Both the import program and the tax incentives that center around the 27½ percent depletion allowance [reduced to 23 percent in 1969] are designed to foster the domestic oil producing industry. The first involves a transfer of $4 billion from consumers, in the form of higher prices ; the second, according to Treasury estimates, involves a transfer of $1.6 billion from other taxpayers. Together, they total close to the net profits for the entire industry." [56] Many corporations profit by using State-owned plant and equipment. Robert J. Gordon calculated that the U.S. government has purchased $45 billion of plant and equipment (in 1958 prices) for the use of private firms between 1940 and 1965 ; between 1945 and 1965, the State, at an original cost of some $12 billion, built plant and equipment for the use and profit of private operators in the defense, atomic energy, and space-related industries. [57] Examples of the State support of monopoly capital can be multiplied at length.

The State also supports monopoly power by its fiscal and monetary policy. State purchases of goods and services from business (excluding compensation of State employees) amounted to about one-seventh of all final business sales in 1968. However, Harry Magdoff has calculated that in 1963, the federal government directly or indirectly purchased 36 percent of the output of the highly monopolized producers durable goods industries ; besides underwriting the profits of these industries, this concentration of federal spending in this most volatile investment goods sector of the economy has helped to reduce the volatility of economic activity during the past 20 years. [58] Banking, credit, and financing activities are regulated by the Federal Reserve system, but monopoly power in banking is not curtailed ; in 1968, the 10 largest commercial banks held nearly 24 percent of all bank assets. In addition, when monopoly corporations raise their prices too rapidly to suit the stabilization goals of the State, the Federal Reserve system tightens credit by raising interest rates which hurts the small investor rather than the monopoly corporations who have little need for external financing because of their high monopoly profits. These same restrictive monetary policies discourage imports of consumption goods from abroad, while encouraging exports of the monopoly corporations and facilitating foreign investment.

Some of the most intimate links among the three pillars of the economy are forged by federal defense spending. Defense spending alone generates more than 10 percent of the total jobs in manufacturing. This spending is extremely profitable. Murray Weidenbaum, Assistant Secretary of the Treasury in 1970, found that from 1962 to 1965, defense firms had a profit rate on net worth of 17.5 percent, while non-defense firms had only a 10.6 percent return. [59] These high returns reflect the high degree of monopoly power in the defense industries. Defense procurement by the federal government now amounts to almost $40 billion a year ; however, only 18 percent of the defense contracts go to firms with fewer than 500 employees. In fiscal 1969, the top five contractors received a greater share than all the "little" firms put together, 18.9 percent of the total. The top ten contractors received 29 percent of all defense contracts, and the top 50 got 56.7 percent. Many of the defense contractors profit directly from their defense production inside the United States and profit again by the U.S. government military protection of their investments abroad. For example, General Electric, the second largest defense contractor in fiscal 1969 and the fourth largest industrial corporation in the United States in 1968, profits from the 20 percent of its business that is for war, as well as from the military protection of the 25 percent of its total business that is done abroad. United Aircraft, the fifth largest defense contractor and the thirty-third largest industrial corporation, does 56 percent of its business with the Defense Department and another 25 percent abroad. Raytheon, the eleventh largest defense contractor and the seventy-ninth largest industrial corporation, does 58 percent of its business for war, while 10 percent of its total activities are outside the U.S. These particulars should not obscure the general subsidy that the State gives to the whole $200 billion imperialist market ; each year workers pay taxes to finance $80 billion in defense spending and $8 billion in veterans benefits to insure the maintenance and expansion of U.S. corporate imperialism. Imperialism is costly to the workers in the metropolis, and the State is the major ally of expending monopoly capital at home and abroad.

In addition to this expensive protection of imperialist expansion, the State provides many services for U.S. monopoly capital abroad. These services include the State's foreign aid programs, the control of tariffs and international trading agreements, and, primarily, the dominance of the dollar as the world currency and the U.S. control over the world monetary system. Harry Magdoff, in *The Age of Imperialism*, gives a thorough analysis of the many State aids to imperialism.

We have explored in some detail the three economic pillars of the metropolis of imperialism. Neither monopoly nor imperialism are new ; however, they have obviously continued to expand their control and power in the United States and abroad. Today the largest 100 U.S. corporations control more than a quarter of the wealth of the entire capitalist world. While the State in capitalism has always promoted capitalist expansion, in recent decades the continued expansion of monopoly and imperialism has increasingly depended on State power. The growth of each of the pillars of the economy is indispensable to the growth of the others. We turn in the next chapter to examine some of the problems faced by the vast and continually expanding State in the capitalist and imperialist context in which it is enmeshed.

THE NEW STATE AND SOME OF ITS CONTRADICTIONS

State power has grown in the twentieth century to meet the needs of continued monopoly centralization and imperialist expansion. A decade of monopoly-bred depression was followed by the war from which the United States emerged as the economic and

155

military center of the capitalist world. To meet its increased economic and military responsibilities, the State became a major participant in the web of social and economic relations of the country. Although these political and economic responsibilities were expressed by forms that pretended to be autonomous and independent of both labour and capital, the structure of the State institutions in fact bound the State to promote the interests of capital. Today, these ties to capital have become the cause of the State's economic problems. As State power has continued to grow, the State institutions have become enmeshed in the very contradictions they were set up to resolve. Established to prevent economic and social crisis, the State's economic policy has become part of the crisis.

This section and the next are two parts of a single discussion. This section focusses on the problems of domestic fiscal (taxing and spending) activities of the State, while the economic problems of the increased imperialist commitments of the State are generally reserved for the following chapter. Both sections analyze how the State institutions increasingly become part of the economic, political, and social crisis of capitalism.

The fundamental economic problem of monopoly capitalism is that corporations with increasing monopoly power find it difficult to sustain new investment programs which maintain aggregate demand and high levels of employment while at the same time maintaining profit rates on existing investments. [60] The Great Depression made this abundantly clear. The new Keynesian State economic policy implemented during and after World War II must continually confront the problems of keeping a monopoly capitalist system running in defiance of its

own inherent tendencies to stagnation. To understand these problems we must explore the character, structure, and diminishing efficacy of these new State economic policies. As the Keynesian solution begins to wear itself out, the probability of a world-wide capitalist economic breakdown increases, although it would be futile to attempt to specify its timing or dimensions. The nature and contradictions of the new State policies and institutions are themselves generating some of the economic problems and social conflicts that define the revolutionary context of U.S. politics today.

Capitalism poses the perennial problem of poverty in the midst of plenty. The fundamental problem of private ownership of capital is to reap the productivity of the social capital while maintaining private profits. Capital is employed in production only when its owner receives a sufficient profit. When the structure of ownership and debt is highly monopolized and the capital already in use is highly productive, there is a growing problem of finding further profitable ways to expand investment and production. Monopoly capital was failing in its task of extracting sufficient profits from workers to keep up investment while maintaining aggregate demand ; the Keynesians discovered that the State could help capital by using its taxing and spending abilities for three tasks : to extract economic surplus from workers ; to hire directly workers who could not find jobs in the private sector ; and to underwrite the profitability of further investment and production of monopoly capital. This State appropriation and allocation of part of the economic surplus can go on as long as the productivity of labour increases fast enough to pay the rising taxes and as long as State programs support rather than inhibit the profitability of monopoly capital. As capital

156

continues to concentrate and centralize, the State must expand its activities to maintain aggregate demand and employment; but its expansion is increasingly inflationary, which narrows its ability and opportunities to support monopoly profits. As the State expands its activities under capitalism, it does not eliminate the contradictions of monopoly capital; instead, the State itself becomes more enmeshed in those contradictions.

Keynesian economic policy has three inter-related objectives. First, the State tries to protect the domestic structure of investment and debt and promote new domestic investment. Second, the State tries to protect the present structure of foreign investment and ownership and promote its expansion. Third, the State tries to protect and promote its own activities. To accomplish these goals the State uses taxing and spending measures to shift resources from workers to capital and money measures to protect the value of contracts and debts. These objectives are riddled with contradictions. It is a very delicate task to promote any new investment without upsetting the existing structure of contracts, titles of ownership, debt, and profit rates. Likewise, accomplishing one of these objectives often makes it harder to accomplish another.

While in a formal sense the State may have great freedom in its financing and spending policies, it is in fact severely limited by its commitment to the preservation of the existing structure of property rights and the incomes, or profits, derived from that ownership. The aid of the State's financing and monetary activities is to promote confidence in the existing debt markets. The State cannot produce goods itself; it can only spend directly for activities such as education that, while unprofitable, service private production. State spending must foster the consumer economy of single-family housing, automobiles, and consumer durables. If these measures do not provide enough employment, the State absorbs surplus labour in ways that do not conflict with existing capital and debt structures; the State creates new industries such as defense that do not compete with old industries; and it absorbs labour directly by conscription and increased schooling. The State uses its taxing and spending to share the increased productivity of workers producing consumption goods with workers in State-financed activities and with the owners of the capital employed in supplying State purchased goods.

The formal economic role of the State is to act as an autonomous mediator between labour and capital and as a stabilizing influence on the economy. The language of the Employment Act of 1946, the statutory basis for much of the State's role, charges it with the responsibility of "creating and maintaining, in a manner calculated to foster and promote free competitive enterprise [sic] and the general welfare, conditions under which there will be afforded useful employment opportunities, including self-employment, for those able, willing, and seeking to work, and to promote maximum employment, production, and purchasing power..." This role assumes that capitalism is compatible with the general welfare and that class harmony can be achieved within a capitalist framework. But, since the reality of capitalism is one of unrelenting conflict of interests between capital and labour, State policies cannot be neutral. State action is pro-capital because of the very structure of State institutions and the impact of State programs.

The State in a capitalist economy

157

is itself a capitalist enterprise that operates according to sound business principles. It pays wages to its workers and interest to the owners of its debt. Except for conscripted labour, the wages paid by State bureaucracies are roughly equivalent to those paid by profit-making private sector employers. When its current expenditures exceed current revenues, the State sells its debt in private debt markets. State investment decisions are guided by cost-benefit decision-making criteria analogous to private calculations of profitability. The primary difference between State institutions and private businesses is that the State does not have to sell its services to obtain operating revenues, but can use its coercive legal powers to tax workers to finance its activities. Workers would not voluntarily pay for most State activities, since they are for the benefit of capital and not workers. This dependence on taxes gives the State a financial interest in promoting "maximum employment, production and purchasing power." So even though the State cannot sell its services to workers, it has as great an interest as business in promoting capitalist prosperity, encouraging profitable expansion opportunities for business, and so forth.

Since taxing profits would discourage capitalist expansion, State spending is primarily financed by taxes on wages. Personal income taxes are directly on wages. Sales and excise taxes are paid by workers, since they are incorporated into the prices they pay for goods and services. Social security and other payroll taxes are direct reductions in workers' wages. Property taxes are primarily taxes on the homes of working people, and renters pay the landlords' property taxes in their rents. Corporation income taxes and other business taxes are built into the prices of the products

that workers consume ; despite increased corporation income taxes, after-tax corporate profits were a greater percentage of national income in the 1960's than in any earlier decade.

Although taxes on workers are the primary means of State financing, debt sales are also used. State sells debt to finance long-term projects such as school building programs, water plans, and highways ; they also resort to debt-financing in periods of war or recession, when worker resistance to increased taxes is high. Although the interest costs of debt are borne by workers' taxes—almost 7 percent of the federal budget goes to pay the interest on the national debt each year—debt-financing puts the State squarely in the middle of the social relations of capital itself. The Federal Reserve System holds much of the State debt ; it maintains its control over the monetary system by its purchases and sales of this debt. When the State sells debt and increases the amount of debt (reducing the money supply outstanding), it must avoid upsetting the values of private debt, which represents the titles to ownership of capital. The fetish of the balanced budget and the horror of State deficits comes from the fear that if the State does not extract enough taxes from workers to offset the injections of new spending into the economy, State debt will compete with private debt and after the values of existing ownership patterns in the economy.

Just as high profits in the private sector depend on prosperity, the tax-financed State institutions depend for their solvency on capitalist prosperity. State institutions have an interest in paying the same low wages to its workers that are paid by private employers. Both governments and corporations prefer workers to have high incomes, but low wages.

While one-fifth of employed workers receive their paychecks from governments in the United States, with minor exceptions these governments do not engage in direct production of goods. Instead, all manufacturing, mining, construction, and the distribution of goods, as well as finance, real estate, and insurance activities are governed by the laws of profits, the rules of capital. State employees work in bureaucracies that provide services to capital necessary to promote continued profits and accumulation of capital. These services include the education and training of much of the labour force, the maintenance of a postal system, the provision of police to protect private property, the establishment of a court system to enforce contracts, the maintenance of harbors, airports, and highways to promote commerce and trade, the maintenance of a social welfare and public assistance system to underwrite the lowest wage and most underemployed segment of the labour force, and so forth. Faced with stagnating opportunities for domestic profits, monopoly capital needs a large military and diplomatic corps to police an expanding imperialist market. All these are traditional government services to capital ; but they have expanded tremendously since the 1930's. Along with the dramatic increase in tax-financed, otherwise unemployable, workers providing these services for business was an even more dramatic increase in the capital expenditures required to expand these services, particularly in defense, education, and transportation. The State uses increased taxes on workers to underwrite the profits in the private production of war material, missiles, highways, school buildings, paper clips, etc. Today, when 10 percent of all workers in the private sector of the economy are supplying goods and services to governments, the State must be cautious as it reallocates among the services it provides to business or it can disrupt the structure of private ownership of capital, defeating the original purpose of these services.

The State machinery and the power of capital are completely interdependent. Monopoly capital demands a vastly expanded State apparatus to service and promote prosperity, profits, and capital accumulation at home and abroad. The increasing size of the bureaucracies that provide these services, because of the tremendous effect on employment, incomes, and prices, uses up the alternatives and limits the flexibility of the State bureaucrats in supporting capital. As the increasing stagnation of monopoly capital generates an increasing fiscal crisis of the State machinery, much of the finesse of the new monetary and fiscal policies of Keynesianism will have to be abandoned ; wage, price, and more forceful credit controls, along with more State sponsored centralization of capital, will become necessary simply for the bureaucracies to be able to maintain their support of monopoly capital. The current fiscal and social crisis of the State has been caused by the State reaching the limits of the Keynesian solution.

State efforts to shore up a stagnating monopoly capitalism have led to chronic inflation. For 20 years the governments of the United States used taxes on workers to pay for about two-thirds of all new jobs created in the economy. Almost two-fifths of the new jobs created in the private sector of the economy owe their existence directly to the increased State purchases of goods and services from the private sector. Each shift from private to State financed employment is inflationary. Wages must increase

159

enough so that taxes on those wages can support more workers for government or on government contract. Fewer workers in private production must experience enough increased productivity to support more workers in the State production of services to capital. Increased taxes have also had to finance welfare programs to support the vastly increased number of underemployed and underpaid workers who are victims of the stagnation in new jobs. Profits in the consumer economy have depended on this taxing-spending redistribution of worker productivity among workers to maintain consumer demand for goods and services.

Perhaps even more important than these shifts has been the increased dependence of private profits on direct State purchases. While only 10 percent of all private jobs are generated by State purchases, about one-fifth of all manufacturing and construction jobs are generated by State purchases. Since State purchases are concentrated in the most highly monopolized sectors of the economy where profits are the highest, somewhat more than one-fifth of all manufacturing and construction profits can be attributed to tax-financed State purchases. And, over the past 20 years, the *increases* in State purchases alone have accounted for a much larger proportion of the increases in profits in private manufacturing and construction. If the State tries to curb inflation by cutting back on spending, as it is doing currently, it must not only hold down the wages of State workers, but also constrain the size and growth of private profits. Even if the State could find new projects so that it could continue to create two-thirds of all new jobs, the mounting inflationary crisis would mean that its new projects would end up undermining the values of private debt and capital instead of enhancing them. Attempts to curb the inflation by

holding down State employees' wages or raising taxes meet public employee and taxpayer resistance ; if they succeed at all, it causes consumption to fall, which undermines the profits in the consumer goods sector of the economy. Consumers go deeper into debt to keep up their consumption level, which temporarily postpones the problem, but intensifies it in the long run as worker resistance to higher prices and increased indebtedness grows with each successive year. On the other hand, if the governments try to fight inflation by cutting purchases rather than or in addition to cutting payrolls, monopoly profits will fall in manufacturing and construction which will create a further lack-of-jobs crisis in the private sector. If the State slows its expansion relative to the private sector, even, say, to create only half instead of two-thirds of new jobs, the unemployment crisis of monopoly stagnation will reappear, and even more inflation will be created as unemployed people apply to the social welfare-transfer institutions. These considerations define the fiscal context in which the State finds itself in a stagnating monopoly capitalism.

The State's inflation-producing problems are made worse by the power over prices held by the monopoly corporations and the labour unions. State purchases in the most monopolized sectors increases the demand for basic goods, so the big corporations raise their prices. All industries that use basic materials face higher costs and raise their prices, etc. Price increases spread like ripples in a pond. But when the State cuts its demand, this does not lower prices because the monopolies are not under pressure from competitors. So they cut output and lay off workers but do not lower prices (and may raise them to maintain profits on smaller outputs). The result is the 1970 pattern of unemployment and recession combined with continued inflation.

The fundamental contradiction of capitalism between the social nature of production and the private ownership of the means of production is revealed in the era of monopoly capitalism as a monetary and fiscal crisis of the State, bringing the social conflict into the political arena where the workers confront the State as the enemy. There would be no fiscal crisis if workers controlled production through a democratic administration of the economy ; but production is guided by the profit considerations of monopoly corporations, and the State is merely a political and economic weapon in the arsenal of capital. The unfilled needs of millions of people in the United States and the world cannot be met by capital, for it is not profitable ; they cannot be met by State planning, for the State only plans for the profits of capital.

Although we have scarcely distinguished between the federal, state, and local governments, it becomes necessary to do so in order to examine more closely the particular ways that the fiscal and social crisis affects the government machinery. The most important spending program of the federal government, discussed more fully in the next section, is the warfare program. War spending accounts for about 40 percent of all State purchases of goods and services, provides about 30 percent of all direct State employment, and generates more than 10 percent of all manufacturing jobs in the private economy. War spending is the core of the federal government's domestic fiscal crisis ; it is also the crucial link between the government's domestic and international problems, the crisis of imperialism. In order to fulfill its commitment to imperialism, the federal government uses its authority over the monetary system to ease its own fiscal problems by adding to those of state and local governments. So state and local governments must operate in a setting of chronic inflation, tight-money policies, and high interest rates.

Although the state and local governments are closest to the people and provide most of the public services that people experience in their daily lives, these governments are weak in their relations to business and the federal government. Their revenues come primarily from local sources— sales taxes, property taxes, and fees for services—with about one-sixth of their revenues coming as transfers from the federal government. Yet they provide at the local level services which primarily serve the highly monopolized corporate structure that operates in the national market. Local governments are no match for the corporations. General Motors alone had net sales in 1968 that were almost two and one-half times as large as the total revenue of the State of California ; and its net profits after taxes were exceeded by the total revenues of only 9 state governments. The state and local governments are the tools of national monopoly capital. They are powerless to deal with the increasing national monopoly capital. They are life ; they have only become more deeply imprisoned in the contradictions of the system. Their fiscal dependence forces them to acquiesce in, if not promote, the allocation of resources that is most profitable to monopoly capital. They finance the construction and maintenance of the highways and streets and other essential services to accommodate the move to the suburbs, while bearing the increased costs of police and welfare to cope with the poverty of the central cities. State and local governments have also paid for the expansion of education, which,

161

second to war spending, has been the most important subsidy to monopoly capital and "solution" to the job crisis of stagnation.

State and local governments are fiscally weak, subordinate to federal monetary and fiscal policy, and particularly vulnerable to the vagaries of business conditions and to taxpayer resistance to increased tax bills. Between 1950 and 1968, state and local government debt increased by six times, more rapidly than any other category of debt. But they are having trouble getting voter permission to increase their indebtedness ; voting against bond issues is one of the few ways workers can express their resistance to increasingly costly government services to capital. Further, this debt competes in debt markets with other government and private debt, so that taxpayers are subject both to the demands of the wealthy debt holders and to federal monetary policy regarding the prevailing level of interest rates. In addition, state and local governments depend on the particularly regressive sales and property taxes, which means that their financing weighs particularly hard on those workers least able to afford it ; and, unlike the income tax, inflation does not increase the revenue yields of these taxes as fast as the costs of government programs go up with rising prices. State and local governments hire about 60 percent of all direct State employees, about half of whom work in education. Their activities are very labour intensive, which subjects state and local governments to severe cost problems when their workers strive to keep their wages up to the levels in the private sector ; unlike workers in the private sector, it is difficult to increase the productivity of teachers, social workers, policemen, firemen, typists, accountants, public

health workers, and maintenance workers.

The state and local governments also carry out the details and bear the burdens of federal government policies, acting as administrative units for the national government. The federal government's highway and housing policies after World War II forced the state and local governments to take on a tremendous job of supplying the necessary services to the suburban developments, while leaving their central cities and ghettoes to decay and further increasing costs for police and welfare. The federal government established the welfare state, with standards and subsidies, but the state and local governments were left with their poverty pockets, a declining tax base, and an increasingly costly welfare program. Inflation and high interest rates saddle the state and local governments with swelling costs, inflexible revenue sources, and tight debt markets. The federal government's monetary policies promote high interest rates, which not only pressures state and local governments, but also is largely responsible for the spread of the housing shortage from the ghetto to the suburb. In periods of tight money the small debt sellers suffer ; home buyers and state and local governments are victims of the central monetary authority.

The welfare state programs managed by state and local governments with substantial aid from the federal government are a major example of how the State's fiscal crisis leads to social crisis. The same conditions—underemployment, low wages, and poverty—that increase the need for welfare transfers also cause the low incomes and deteriorating tax bases that make it difficult for the state and local governments to finance such transfers. In inflationary times, public employees and welfare clients press for increased welfare allocations, while taxpayers resist these increases, each for the same reason—declining purchasing power of their dollars. In recession and periods of unemployment the number of workers needing welfare grows, while the number of relatively prosperous taxpaying workers declines. In a time like the present, when inflation and recession are combined, the public agencies in fact face both these contradictions at the same time. The programs of the welfare state cost more and more, while the state and local governments are having growing difficulties with their employees, clients, and taxpayers. It is far from clear that the planners of the Keynesian welfare state policies can deliver on their promises of a poverty level income to all the underemployed and underpaid workers in a stagnating economy.

Education spending is the most important contribution of the state and local governments to easing monopoly capital's job crisis. About 40 percent of all state and local government spending now goes to support the educational system. Since 1950, one-sixth of all new jobs created in the entire economy were increases in educational employment by state and local governments. About 6 percent of all new construction since 1950 has been state and local school construction. Increased schooling has eliminated the need to find jobs for millions who otherwise would have been in the job market. In 1968, there were more than 5.5 million students 14 years old and over who would have been in the labour force seeking jobs if the 1950 proportions of adults in school had prevailed. In other words, since 1950, the growth in the *proportions* of adults working for or enrolled in schools absorbed more than 8.5 million adults, approximately the same number as the total new jobs created in the private sector of the economy that were not directly generated by State purchases.

Even though monopoly capital has profited from the increasingly well-educated new entrants to the labour force, it has been able to create fewer and fewer jobs as a proportion of the adult population. Even if the proportion of adults working for or enrolled in schools were to remain at the current levels, the job crisis would reappear on a monumental scale. Yet, by the late 1960's, even with the massive war spending, private industry was having difficulty in providing jobs for new entrants to the labour force. And the productivity and wages of the productive private sector workers are not increasing rapidly enough for these workers to afford the increased taxes necessary to finance the increasing proportions of unproductive workers and students in education. Workers in general are resisting tax increases, while education workers are pressing to keep their wages up to the levels of private sector workers. In the expansion of education, then, state and local governments have spent their way into an inflationary fiscal crisis that they cannot spend their way out of.

When monopoly capital could not keep up high profits and enough investment to maintain high levels of employment, the State responded with a temporary fiscal solution by "socializing" the costs of monopoly capitalism. Since workers already produced so much with existing capital that monopoly corporations could not profitably invest further, the State increased taxes on workers to finance State underwriting of further monopoly expansion and profits. The State machinery provided cost-reducing and demand-creating programs for capital; however, the relative shrinkage of the private goods producing sector of the economy has made the continued State fiscal expansion increasingly inflationary, so that the fiscal solvency of the State institutions comes into contradiction with the profits of monopoly capital. State monetary policies have always accommodated to the trends in private credit, supporting inflation or deflation as private capital dictated. So it should come as no surprise to find that the State's fiscal institutions cannot solve the contradictions of monopoly capitalism ; they can merely share in them. Monopoly capitalism's stagnation and the ensuing job crisis is revealed in a fiscal crisis of the State institutions.

This crisis shows up at all levels of the State as workers resist tax increases while inflation pushes up the costs of State programs. State efforts to fight inflation fail since the State cannot reverse the historical process of monopolization in the private sector and centralization in the public that has made inflation a chronic condition. The State can only cause inflation and recession to coincide. When we turn from the strictly domestic to the international dynamics of the State-monopoly crisis, we see that the unfolding insoluble economic crisis of the State is accelerating the growth of revolutionary forces within the U.S. working class. The metropolis of the empire is breaking down, not only from within, but also from without.

CRISIS IN THE METROPOLIS

The crisis of State power in the United States is a crisis in the metropolis of the world system of imperialism. While in the last section the focus was on the contradictions generated by State action to protect and promote monopoly capitalism inside the country, here we focus on the contradictions of the position of the United States as the seat of empire. This is a view of

imperialism from within the metropolis, an examination of the economic and social costs of imperialism to workers in the United States. The failures of imperialism are experienced in the United States in two inter-related ways : as economic failures of monopoly capitalism and as growing militarism and war. The imperial commitments to fight socialism, to protect and promote U.S. foreign investments, and to uphold the dollar as the instrument of U.S. control of the international transactions and debt markets are the international aspects of the domestic commitments to maintain monopoly capitalism. The state bureaucracies are deeply involved in both commitments ; and just as the State has become a crucial part of the domestic crisis, it is also the arena in which the crisis of an embattled imperialism is fought out. Continued imperialist expansion, essential to the profits of U.S. monopoly capital, impoverishes workers ; economic and social forces in the United States and abroad are undermining the continued success of imperialism. National liberation struggles in the underdeveloped countries, restiveness among the workers in the other advanced countries as they resist the increasing costs of living in sub-metropolises, and growing domestic economic, social, and political pressures all demonstrate the failures of imperialism. As the imperial policies fail, the rulers of the metropolis turn more and more to military solutions to political problems, to more force to uphold contracts, to internal repression and global war to defend their increasingly precarious position. The State struggles to meet the imperial commitment by war ; but imperialism limits its own capacity to prosecute the growing war that it must continue to fight.

The imperial commitment has three inter-related parts. First is the commitment to defend the capitalist world's economic system and class structure against socialism by a network of military and political institutions. Second is the commitment to protect and promote the foreign investment of the same U.S. monopoly corporations that are protected by the State's domestic economic policy. Third is the commitment to protect the international monetary system through which U.S. capital exercises its hegemony in the international capitalist economy. These external responsibilities of the State reinforce and are a part of the responsibilities to monopoly capital as it operates within the United States. But while all levels of government are involved in implementing the domestic economic policy that leads the State into crisis, the imperialist responsibilities are almost entirely those of the federal government. *This imperial commitment is the major cause of the centralization of political power in the United States and the end to any real system of federalism. These responsibilities also promote, and are the consequence of, the centralization of economic power in the United States.*

The main economic effect of the imperial commitment inside the United States has been to deform the internal economic structure to serve the demands of the war industry and the militarized State. Of course, militarism and war have always been an integral part of capitalist expansion, and no history of the accumulation of capital would be complete that did not incorporate war as a major determinant. [61] However, it is only since World War II that the capitalist world economy went on a permanent warfare footing. In the United States before the buildup for World War II, less than one percent of annual gross output went for war. But since 1940, about 10.6 percent of annual gross national product has been devoted to war. Since 1950, one dollar has been spent on war for every seven spent on personal consumption. Since the war in which the United States achieved capitalist world hegemony, the United States has become a permanent war economy to avoid economic stagnation at home and to promote imperialism and fight socialism abroad.

The growth of the war industry was a remedy to the problems of monopoly. The monopolization of the highly productive social capital limited further profitable investments ; economic stagnation was the price of monopoly. Tax financed State war spending unlocked the productivity controlled by monopoly capital in three ways : by using taxes to share workers' rising output and wages with other workers in war industries ; by opening up profitable investment outlets for industry ; and by giving military support for imperialist opportunities abroad since domestic "peace" markets did not offer enough profitable opportunities. Militarism and imperialism offered ways to export the stagnation of monopoly. Workers financed this profitable expansion by taxes, while keeping some of their increased productivity for themselves in rising real wages. The job crisis that threatened to become politically untenable was temporarily postponed. War spending was the most important government program designed to underwrite monopoly capital. As with other Keynesian State spending programs, its continued growth is crucial to alleviate the problems of stagnation associated with the increasing centralization of capital. But war spending becomes increasingly inflationary, a self-defeating policy. The contradictions of war spending are multiplied because of its impact on the empire.

The impact of the war industry on the economy and on peoples' lives can hardly be overstated. It has been the major avenue for the federal government's use of Keynesian policies to absorb the surplus labour that has been excluded from the private sector by the growth of monopoly power. The federal government has purchased almost a trillion dollars in war goods and services from the private economy since 1950. The Department of Defense is the largest single institution in the United States. It employs 4.6 million workers (5.8 percent of all employed workers in 1968), nearly as many as the 30 largest U.S. industrial companies combined ; it has assets of $200 billion, more than the 75 largest industrial corporations combined. Its operations extend to every government in the nation and to more than 100 other nations. [62] War has been a major growth industry, growing more than twice as fast as total gross national product. While GNP grew about 4 times in dollar terms between 1947 and 1969, and personal consumption grew only 3.6 times, war spending grew 8.7 times. The U.S. economy today allocates about as much to war as to the personal consumption of food. The private war industry is the largest single complex of industries in the private economy ; more than 10 percent of all manufacturing output and employment is war generated. By comparison, even the output of the giant automobile industry accounts for only about 4 percent of GNP.

The war industry is not only important in itself ; it is also closely tied to the other major government spending programs. The "national defense" ideology has been used to justify State spending on education, highways, research and development, and many other programs. This expansion has distorted these expenditures, adding to their cost and to their social contradictions.

War is the crucial element in the imperialist commitment ; it is closely tied to the second commitment of promoting foreign investment by U.S. corporations. Workers' taxes finance U.S. military operations to protect U.S. capital against nationalization in more than 100 countries. The United States maintains over 429 major and 2972 minor military bases throughout the world. Since World War II, about 80 countries have received a total of $50 billion in U.S. military aid ; the militarization of U.S. society has been shared with the entire capitalist world. [63] The war spending subsidy to U.S. capital also provides the profit base from which U.S. corporations have extended their foreign investment. Many large corporations are not only important defense contractors but also large foreign investors. More broadly, the promotion of foreign investment is based on the U.S. government commitment to combat socialism in every possible way. This commitment is kept not only by the threat of military force but also by the network of political and economic arrangements, such as foreign aid and trade agreements, negotiated with the compliant governments of other nations. Ever since the Marshall Plan, the government has used workers' taxes for grants and loans to countries for goods bought from U.S. corporations. All aid programs require that most of the money be used to purchase U.S. goods ; they also require, as a condition of most foreign aid treaties, a guarantee against expropriation of U.S. corporation capital.

A third important part of the commitment to imperialism is the responsibility of the U.S. government to maintain the dollar as the world's ruling currency. The dollar's preeminent position is the monetary parallel to the dominance of U.S. military might and U.S. foreign investment. As noted in earlier U.S. corporations have profited so much from their foreign investments that the inflow of profits to the U.S. corporations has exceeded the outflow of new direct investments to other countries by about $21 billion over the past 20 years. At the same time U.S. workers have produced more goods for export than they have been able to purchase in imports. Yet, the United States had balance of payments deficits ranging from $1 to $4 billion a year in 18 of the 19 years following 1950. U.S. military expenditure abroad exceeded the total payments deficit in all but two of these years. These military expenditures abroad amounted to about $4.5 billion in 1968. Taxes on workers have financed the spread of militarism, which has made the other capitalist countries safe for U.S. corporations to build their $200 billion foreign empire. In return for U.S. military protection of U.S. imperialism, the other capitalist countries have had to increase their holdings of U.S. dollars rather than trading them for the U.S. gold stock. Workers in the other capitalist countries have not only shared the costs of U.S. imperialism by paying the profits returned to the United States and by the stagnation of their economies and their monopolization by U.S. corporations, but they also have shared the costs of the U.S. militarism to protect that imperialism by the inflation of their currencies. The ability of the United States to maintain its military presence abroad depends on the willingness of foreign governments to hold dollars as a reserve currency for international payments.

So the growing importance of militarism and war spending by the State is the result of the expanding role of the State as investment stimulator and employer within the United States and the result of the expanding role of the State in promoting U.S. capital's dominance throughout the capitalist world. Taxes on workers finance the continu-

ed profitability of both domestic and foreign investment. The development of the U.S. economy is distorted not only by the commitment to the structure of domestic monopoly capitalism but also by the commitment to an empire based on war and militarism.

But the State's ability to meet its commitments to capital is limited by the tendencies to stagnation of the system of capital itself. Internationally, the State's responsibilities to capital increasingly involve outright war with socialist forces. The imperialist system must stay at war. At the same time, however, imperialism undermines the ability of the U.S. economy to fight the wars that are necessary to preserve it. The fundamental economic contradiction of imperialism within the metropolis, then, is that imperialism leads to increasingly costly wars, but war becomes harder and harder to afford.

War is necessary to defend the empire against socialism. The military aggression of the United States in South East Asia, as well as in the Middle East and Latin America, is not accidental ; it is not mistaken ; it is not simply "logical." This agression is necessary. Economic imperialism in the underdeveloped countries stagnates their development, impoverishes their people, and engenders a cycle of increasing misery. It also engenders a response to that exploitation, the growth of a revolutionary nationalist movements to overthrow imperialism and to make national development possible. These revolutionary movements aim to overthrow their governments, expropriate foreign investments, and begin socialist development. Compromise is not possible. United States capital depends on the continued expansion of imperialism ; self-determination for the imperialized peoples requires that imperialism be defeated.

167

The U.S. government, fulfilling its imperial responsibilities, must install and maintain governments in the underdeveloped countries that will suppress their people to maintain imperialism. United States capital has a $200 billion foreign market and $65 billion in direct foreign investments that must be protected. Currently, more than 10 percent of U.S. labour is forced to be directly employed as mercenaries for U.S. capital to protect that foreign empire. Militarism and war are the substitutes for direct colonization and suppression of the people of the Third World. Taxes on U.S. workers finance the war spending ; U.S. capital profits from this war spending, both from domestic production of war goods and from the profits of empire. The expansion of imperialism meets increased resistance. The needs of U.S. capital mean that there is no retreat from militarism and war ; the needs of the peoples of the Third World mean that there is no retreat from armed struggle for self-determination and socialism. World War III is the Third World War for liberation ; there will be no peace until the imperialist system is defeated.

Imperialist wars are made necessary by the irreconcilable conflict between U.S. capital and the working people of the world. The increasing dependence on war capital and technology for executing these wars is due to the growing reliance of the monopolized domestic economy on the war industry for profits. But wars in the interest of capital can be fought only with a military that is bureaucratic and authoritarian in structure, unable to draw on the intelligence and dependability of the working people. Young workers must be literally conscripted into military service, and other workers must be given no alternatives to war production jobs. Thus, both the necessity and structure of these wars are governed by the State support of monopoly capital at home and abroad.

There can be no peace under monopoly capitalism and imperialism ; but the permanent war is becoming increasingly difficult to finance. The impoverishment of U.S. workers increases ; the inflation caused by the necessarily increasing war and other State spending erodes the domestic and international position of the dollar ; and foreign investment approaches its political and economic limits. Imperialism itself undermines the ability of the empire to continue to fight the wars that it must fight to survive.

Imperialism deforms the economies of both the imperialized and the imperialist nations. These deformations choke off the growth necessary to finance continued imperialism. As U.S. monopoly capitalism exports its stagnation via imperialism and militarism, the whole capitalist world begins to feel that stagnation. In the underdeveloped countries, imperialism not only provokes resistance but also cuts off its own further development. Foreign investment in underdeveloped countries is profitable because it is concentrated in extractive industries exploiting cheap labour and because it is not usually necessary to sell the product to the very poor people who produce it. Most important, U.S. monopoly corporations are so large and economically powerful that they dominate local capital, monopolizing the industrial and capital markets in the poor capitalist countries. The economic surplus that might be used for economic development is absorbed by the super-profits of the giant imperialist corporations which use these profits to consolidate their monopoly positions and to support local governing groups who will support the imperialist domination of their economies by suppressing their people and by tax-financing State subsidies to monopoly explotation of the imperialized countries' resources. Thus, the monopoly stagnation that is characteristic of advanced capitalist countries is exported via imperialism to backward countries that have not yet experienced economic development and will not be able to develop under imperial domination. As imperialism deepens the underdevelopment of the underdeveloped countries, the puppet governments of these stagnant economies must, because the people are resisting and because their economies are very poor, rely increasingly on U.S. military involvement to suppress the socialist forces. [64]

The limits to U.S. imperialism in the other advanced capitalist countries are more subtle than in the underdeveloped ones, since these countries are themselves imperialists in the poor countries and because they have great wealth and productivity. The other advanced capitalist countries have been junior partners in imperialism and have also adopted their own Keynesian solutions of increasing State support for their stagnating monopoly capitalisms. But their economies are weaker than the United States ; U.S. corporations have easily acquired large parts of the domestic and foreign markets of the other advanced capitalist countries. While U.S. corporations profit from expansion in the advanced capitalist countries, that very expansion itself erodes the U.S. ability to continue to finance its imperial operations. The empire requires either that the U.S. have a balance of trade surplus large enough to finance foreign investments and military expenditures abroad, or that other countries hold U.S. dollars. Foreign investments build plants abroad which compete with U.S. producers, cheapening U.S. imports and competing with U.S. exports. On the other hand, the increasing military spending to support these foreign investments leads to the neglect of productive investments in the United States. The U.S. trade balance deteriorates ; and inflation in the United States, because of the increased military spending and the decline in productive investments, limits the willingness and ability of foreign governments to hold dollars. The balance of payments problem has become so bad in recent years that the United States has had to put controls on new U.S. foreign investments to protect the existing ones. The recent erosion of the value of the dollar has increasingly challenged the entire international monetary system. The problem has become so serious that the U.S. international bankers have allowed two junior partners, West Germany and Canada, to re-value their currencies upward in an attempt to re-stabilize the system without devaluing the dollar, even though re-valuation limits the extent to which the U.S. inflation can be exported and therefore exacerbates all its domestic social and political problems.

As the external costs of imperialist expansion increase, the costs of supporting that expansion also increase within the United States. War spending has drained off resources from needed investments which were not profitable to the monopoly corporations. Even though more than a third of producers' durable goods have been purchased directly or indirectly by the federal government, primarily for war, the percentage of gross national product going for capital formation (new investment) in the United States has been the lowest of all the advanced capitalist countries. The growing war sector of the economy has meant a relatively shrinking goods producing sector of the economy. The richest country in the world is becoming impoverished by its own militarism ; yet

169

there can be no retreat from that militarism. War spending must increase not only to fight the war on socialism, but also simply to keep the crisis of stagnation from re-emerging. But further shifts of labour to the war sector of the economy are increasingly inflationary, both because labour is being shifted from the private to the public sector and because it is being shifted in the context of monopoly corporations with control over prices. As long as monopoly capitalism endures, the alternatives are clear ; increasing inflation with increasing war and other State spending increasing unemployment ; or both. Although only 10 percent of all jobs in the economy are war jobs, almost a quarter of all new jobs created in the economy over the past 20 years have been war jobs. This rate of expansion of war jobs cannot slacken, cannot increase, and cannot stay the same. With the increasing centralization of monopoly capital, tax-financed war jobs must be created on an ever expanding scale ; but the productivity of the declining number of private sector goods producing workers cannot increase rapidly enough to support this growth of wasted labour. The government fiscal machinery is increasingly inflationary as it attempts to diffuse the effects of monopoly stagnation.

Increasing militarism at home and abroad is necessary to meet the State's commitments to monopoly capital and imperialism ; financing this militarism is increasingly costly. The United States is the metropolis of a world capitalist empire. The problems of the U.S. economy, whether in the international balance of payments or in localized unemployment in one small town, are the problems of a failing empire. The State support of stagnating monopoly capitalism has spread the effects of U.S. militarism and mon-

opoly stagnation to the entire capitalist world. People in the United States experience the failing imperialism through the distortion of their economic and social life : problems of entering the labour force ; inflation ; high taxes ; increased indebtedness ; a deteriorating quality of life ; decaying cities ; housing shortages ; growing and impoverishing ghettoes ; increasing militarization of every aspect of life ; etc. The growing resistance of the many different segments of the working class to the imperialist deformations in the United States are threats to the empire.

In mid-1970, the crisis of empire seems to have become acute. Real wages of production workers have fallen for five **years : inflation** continues at a 6 percent annual rate ; unemployment is climbing beyond 5 percent ; and the job crisis is reaching recently unparalleled proportions. The job crisis for young workers looking for their first jobs has not been so bad for 20 years. Even more telling is the growing unemployment of skilled workers in the war industries. The State has tried for a year to control inflation by cutting back spending, especially in defense. The result is that in the 10 months between August 1969 and June 1970, employment fell 21.1 percent in weapons, 9.1 percent in aircraft, and 13.2 percent in motor vehicles. Employment stood still in all other goods-producing sectors of the economy, as well as in mining, construction, and agriculture. Even the services sector failed to grow between February and June 1970. [65]

The war-induced **investment boom** of the late 1960's has bred a situation in which 20 percent of total plant capacity is going unused. It is unprofitable to expand the output of goods and services ; and with so much excess capacity, the investment goods industries which produce new plant and equipment are beginning to feel the pressures of recession. Once unleashed, the collapsing structure of debt in the private sector can lead to an uncontrollable downward spiral of bankruptcy and unemployment. The expansion of the State over the past three decades has enmeshed the State in the contradictions of the capitalist economy. This expansion has decreased rather than increased the power of the State to maintain a stable economy ; the fiscal crisis, in the context of monopoly power over output and prices, is revealed by the increasingly inflationary and decreasingly anti-recessionary impact of State fiscal activities. State actions become stalemated.

The current crisis of continued inflation and sharply rising unemployment does not necessarily mean that the U.S. economy is in mortal danger. It is not likely that we are witnessing any definitive breakdown of monopoly capitalism and imperialism as an economic system, although the possibility of a serious economic collapse gets closer every day as the domestic and international monetary systems face the chronic inflation of the U.S. dollar. The economic crisis of imperialism is important not because the system will simply collapse of its own contradictions, but because growing economic problems narrow the range of policy choices available to the U.S. ruling class. When worker productivity is growing very rapidly, monopoly capital and the State together can reap plenty of surplus for further investments, private and State, and still allow the real wages of workers to rise. But when the profit rate is threatened by the economic problems of stagnation inherent in imperialism as an economic system and by the political problems of armed resistance inherent in imperialism as a system of international

political and military oppression, the priorities of capital and its State accomplice become clear. While profits are secure, capital and the State may seem to turn a benevolent face to workers. But if a choice has to be made between profits and people, the State, as the agent of capital, unhesitatingly throws its force on the side of profit. The economy can be propped up by corporatist measures such as wage and price controls. The collapse of the war industries can be staved off by State loans or even direct State intervention in an industry (such as the "nationalization" suggested by J.K. Galbraith). When the chips are down, the State drops its neutral mask and explicitly takes workers' tax money to bail out an ailing capitalism. As the problems grow in intensity, the State can no longer afford to be delicate. When people resist growing corporatization, State officials will feel less and less compunction about repressing that resistance.

The political crisis in the United States today demonstrates that the State has been forced by the failures of empire to declare itself explicitly on the side of profits and against the people who are rising up against the profit system. Blacks, youth, and women have been pushed by their experiences of the contradictions of a failing empire to oppose the State that visits those failures on them. The State, by declaring its express allegiance to capital and its wars, has forced the movement for peace to become a movement for socialism. And by trying to repress the socialist forces, the State is demonstrating that peace and socialism can only be attained by a revolution against the capitalist State. New socialist forces are being created by the failures of the empire. As blacks, youth, and women rise up against the particular bureaucratic institutions that hold them prisoners, they show

171

the revolutionary path to liberation through the destruction of the whole capitalist bureaucratic network that keeps the working people of the United States from self-determination. The new socialist forces point the way to revolution in the United States.

THE RISE OF SPONTANEOUS RESISTANCE

The imperial system is under attack. Revolutionary movements in the imperialized countries are fighting to liberate their nations from the control of U.S. capital ; revolutionaries in South East Asia are proving that the empire can be defeated. In the advanced capitalist countries a reviving socialist movement is attacking the complicity of the rulers of the sub-metropolises in the international system of domination, while workers are refusing to bear the burdens of U.S. inflation and are trying to force the State to try to ease that burden.

Inside the United States, the empire is also under attack. The black colony is waging an increasingly militant struggle for national liberation. Women are rising up against their secondary status and against the economic and political system that depends or women's oppression. Young people are in revolt against the schools and armies that imprison them in the service of the empire. These three groups are in the forefront of the resistance. The most militant blacks, youth, and women are leading the emerging revolutionary socialist movement.

These three groups are leading the active resistance because the same political economic structures and institutions that focus the costs of empire on them also offer them a way to resist. The Keynesian solution to the crisis of the 1930's and 1940's required

a major re-structuring of the social structures of monopoly capitalism to support an empire. The empire allowed capital to reap an ever greater surplus not only from workers inside the United States but also from workers throughout the capitalist world. The State helped extract that surplus, in the United States through its taxing and spending policies and in the world through its control of the international monetary system, etc. But, even more important, the State helped capital with its chronic problem of finding profitable investment outlets for the economic surplus. State investments in war channelled hundreds of billions of dollars in surplus back to capital for war industry contracts. State investments in highways kept up profits for construction, auto, oil, and other industries. State investments in education involved tremendous construction and the production of more highly trained and more profitable workers. State housing and transportation policies forced consumers to buy houses and cars and consumer durables, promoting profits in those industries.

This pattern of investment changed the life experience of workers in the United States. Blacks, women, and youth were particularly affected ; these groups, lacking social power, bore the main burdens of the changes in the social structure to uphold the empire. Therefore, as the contradictions mount in the empire's political economy, these groups are particularly subjected to those contradictions. Their resistance is generated by the contradictions of the political economy : war, the fiscal crisis, and the job crisis. It is because of these crises that blacks, women and youth have become active opponents of the State and capital. This does not mean that the issues of war, taxes, or jobs are the issues around which these groups are organizing. In fact, except for the war, the other more narrowly economic issues are largely submerged in the demands for human dignity that are animating blacks, women and youth. But it is the location of blacks, women and youth in the most contradiction-ridden institutions of the political economy that has opened up the possibility for these groups to rise up against the secondary status that capitalism has assigned to them. The mass movements of black, women and youth are movements for self-determination and equality. The most advanced elements within these mass movements are consciously fighting for socialism as the only way to achieve self-determination and equality.

The locations of black, women, and young workers in the post-World War II political economy was a consequence of the patterns of State support for the investment and debt structures of monopoly capitalism and imperialism. Black workers were pushed off the land and into urban industrial and service work during World War II to fill the labour shortage. But State support for massive construction and for war materials, industries which employ few black workers, and State absorption of surplus labour in public services, froze job opportunities in manufacturing. Labour saving automation of the increasingly monopolized production sector of the economy eliminated millions of jobs in manufacturing, mining, and construction. Black workers had no sooner gotten one foot on the ladder of the labour heirarchy than they were pushed back off, unemployed, into the growing urban ghettoes. Women were forced to work by the investment patterns that compelled workers to buy houses, cars, and other durable goods if they wanted an adequate standard of living. The expanding public sector absorbed many women ; so did clerical and service work in the private sector. At the same time the burdens of house-

work have been increased rather than reduced by single-family house construction. And the secondary status of women has been reinforced. Young workers have been located in the expanding public and services sectors of the economy ; but more importantly, they have been concentrated in the schools and the army, where the combined impact of the war, the fiscal crisis, and the job shortage has hit them particularly hard.

These three groups have experienced in particular ways the mounting crisis of imperialism and the institutions set in place to deal with that crisis. Blacks, women, and young people have always had secondary status in U.S. capitalist society ; however, each of these groups has confronted new institutions and new contradictions as a result of the temporary solutions to the contradictions of stagnation. New contradictions face these groups in the expansion of the ghettoes, the schools, the army, the welfare system, and the increase in working wives. These insituations force a new set of contradictions because of the groups' secondary status and provide a political focus and avenue of attack on that sub-human status. The crises of imperialism have been increasingly channelled into these institutions for thirty years. Blacks, women, and young workers are a substantial majority of the working class. Black workers are about 15 percent ; women make up almost 45 percent ; and workers under 25 years old are about 30 percent of the working class. Together, these groups account for about two-thirds of the working class ; their secondary status simply reveals that in fact all workers in capitalist society have secondary status. In addition, about 8 million welfare clients and 21 million high school and college students are forced into an even lowlier position ; almost all of these are either black and/or women and/or young. The failures of imperialism are increasing the pressures on these groups and the institutions that contain them. These groups are at the heart of the emerging social crisis.

The United States is in a social crisis because a large and increasing number of working class people are becoming conscious that this is not their country. A social crisis is imminent in the question : "If this is not our country, then whose is it ?" Institutions and ideologies divide the working class along race, ethnic, religious, age, and sex lines, offering a number of misleading answers to that question that do not challenge the structure of capitalist power. As the working class has grown in the United States, it has become increasingly important to capital to maintain the pluralist divisions of the working class and to make them sharper and more distinct. As long as race war can be avoided, it promotes class society for blacks and whites to remain convinced that "racism" rather than capitalism is responsible for the condition of blacks in the United States. Or again, as long as sex war is not promoted, an attack on "sexism" in this society can be tolerated if it defines political conflict in interest group rather than class terms. Racism and sexism not only exist as attitudes, but also as integral components of the institutional structures of U.S. society. Increasing group consciousness is the first sign of resistance to the divisions in the working class ; but in the first instance it leads to the true but incomplete claims that, for example, the United States is "whitey's country," or that it's "a man world," etc. But the divisions in the working class can only be transcended as part of a growing consciousness of and growing intensity of conflict among them.

The very growth of State power that fostered the present structure of the divisions in the working class has promoted the attack on and the transcendence of the divisions. Once the State took on the task of being the agent of social reform, once the State expanded its bureaucracies to become involved in virtually every aspect of life, it could no longer claim to be impotent to solve problems, nor neutral in relation to the outcome of a conflict. The State is very powerful but cannot end discrimination and black poverty and permit self-determination of the black people because it is structurally on the side of racism and private property. While the State is formally committed to equal pay for equal work for women, its actions promote unequal work for women. The State can conscript young men, but cannot offer them meaningful work. It becomes clear that the State's tremendous power is simply the political extension of the power of capital ; the State cannot respond to the needs and demands of the people. The power of the State is gained by its prostration before monopoly capitalism ; so as its power grows, the State becomes a part of the problems of working people and not a solution to those problems.

The leaders of the struggle for black liberation are leading the U.S. working class to socialist perspective. The colonial status of blacks has been reinforced in every period of U.S. history. The mass migration from country to city and from South to North has simply transformed black workers from a colonized landless rural proletariat to a colonized urban proletariat concentrated in the "native quarters" of the major cities. The black nation is imprisoned in the ghettoes. Excluded from the political forms of the country, the politics of the black nation vis-a-vis the white has been, by necessity, oppositional, confrontation, non-electoral, nationalist, and proto-revolutionary. Like the overseas colonies, the internal colony has experienced deepening underdevelopment as a result of expanding imperialism. Black workers are the bottom 15 percent of the U.S. working class. The stagnation of monopoly capitalism was hidden from other workers until very recently by visiting the stagnation on the black colony. During the apparent prosperity of the 1950's and 1960's, the jobs available to blacks declined, black incomes fell as a percent of white incomes, and black unemployment rates were two to three times as high as those of whites. The central city ghettoes grew in population and became more crowded as the invading white State demolished the ghettoes for "urban renewal." The promise of integration coincided with the reality of a more rigorous apartheid. Under the rhetoric of "equality," the U.S. ruling class has increased its oppression of the black nation.

The black movement for national liberation was led a decade and a half ago by the civil rights movement in the courts under the leadership of the tiny black bourgeoisie in the NAACP. Ironically, it was the task of the black movement to expose the country as not a democracy, even though blacks were the least likely to have illusions that it is. The challenges of younger, more radical leaders to this strategy was the beginning of the unfolding dynamics of the black struggle as a national struggle, an anti-imperialist struggle, and finally a revolutionary socialist struggle. The leaders followed the people into the streets, where the NAACP was challenged by the non-violent militance of SNCC, CORE and Martin Luther King's SCLC. These groups in turn gave rise to black power politics. At the same time, black nationalist movements like the Black Muslims gained

new adherents from the rise in mass consciousness of nationhood among black people. One of the first contemporary anti-imperialist leaders, Malcolm X, developed from a Black Muslim to a revolutionary black nationalist. The ghetto rebellions since the mid-1960's make clear that the black nation is stateless, that the ghettoes are not communities but reservations where blacks are confined but which can be and are occupied at will by the armed forces of the imperial State.

Revolutionary nationalism first found organized expression in the black nation with the formation of the Black Panther Party, which rapidly developed from an anti-imperialist to a revolutionary socialist position as the crises of the empire have made it ever more clear that the black nation will be subjected to continuing military and police occupation, that young black men will be kidnapped and forced into the imperial armies, that "public services" in the black community are simply another aspect of the invading force of bureaucrats from the metropolis, and that black workers will always remain at the bottom of the capitalist heap, the last hired, first fired. Only the liberation of the black people through socialist revolution can end racist oppression of the black people in the United States. The revolutionary leadership of the black nation is leading the attack on the state bureaucracies and social institutions that oppress blacks. But blacks have a dual role, both as an internal colony and as part of the U.S. working class, and their attack on their oppression as a nation in also an attack on their class oppression. Blacks are attacking not only the colonial institutions, such as the ghetto, but also the class institutions, such as the police, the schools, the welfare system, and the union bureaucracies. Black workers are leading these attacks on bureaucratic institutions that oppress all working people.

The black liberation movement has made U.S. workers race conscious. Blacks, long invisible, have become visible through their resistance to the State's persecution of the socialist leadership of the black movement and the increased police repression of the black community. Much of the race consciousness is promoted by State agents and the racist structures of party politics. But the main reason that race consciousness has increased is that the State can no longer confine the costs of the empire to black workers. White workers, too, are beginning to suffer. The labour union and State bureaucracies try to use the black workers as scapegoats. But it will not be possible to isolate black workers because the same processes of a failing empire that have pushed black workers into the leadership of a revolutionary movement are also pushing women and white youth into that movement at an increasing rate.

The black liberation movement is the most advanced working class struggle in the United States today ; it is the cutting edge of the mobilizing socialist forces. The newest but broadest resistance is the women's movement, which, while diverse and diffuse, is taking place in a social and economic context in which the contradictions of women's status are generating a powerful force for a revolutionary socialist movement.

Women's fight for full human status has been slow, halting, and as full of setbacks as of progress. Blacks freed from slavery, only to be forced into the lowest sectors of wage labour in a racist, capitalist society; women were freed from their pre-capitalist chattel status, only to face the contradictions of secondary status in capitalist soc-

iety. The capitalist nuclear family established a division of labour according to which wen would engage in wage labour and women would produce use values in the home, keeping house and rearing the children. Questions of the status of women as a group, the social responsibilities of the care of children, etc., were removed from politics and suppressed through the cultural forms of this division of labour. Women were forced into a secondary role, since in capitalist society use value is not ranked as equal to exchange value. At the same time the homemaker and maternal roles are glorified and women are taught from childhood to view its achievement as a goal. Women life with the contradiction of actively pursuing secondary status. This contradiction becomes acute when women are forced into the wage labour force or other collectivized experiences. When women go to work their secondary status is not left behind ; instead women's wage labour is defined as secondary to women's role in the home and women are pushed into the low wage-low productive sections of the wage labour heirarchy. Instead of overcoming their secondary status, working women find that it is reinforced.

Women have been entering the labour force at a phenomenal rate for the past thirty years. Today two-fifths of women (compared with three-fourths of men) are in the civilian labour force, even though only two-fifths of women workers (compared with two-thirds of men workers) are employed full time the year around. When we take the child rearing responsibilities of women into account, women in working class families are working outside the home on a frequency that approaches that of men. Roughly estimated, between 80 and 85 percent of women in working

176

class families work part or full time, part or all of each year. More than 70 percent of adult women work periodically : more than 90 percent of young women today will work during their lives. At the same time women are spending more time in school, itself a contradiction-ridden combination of formal equality with men in some courses (where women tend to have the higher academic achievement) and sex-role different-iation in others. The impoverishment of the family unit since World War II has now made the family so dep-endent on two wage earners that women cannot go home again. Women's secondary status is used to justify their receiving wages that aver-age 60 percent of those received by men. Further, women have not been freed of the unpaid responsibilities of housework Further, women have not housework and child rearing with-in the family, services valued at roughly one-fifth of gross national product. Monopoly capitalism attacks the nuclear family by the terms on which it includes women into the labour force. The family, which tradit-ionally has blunted working class con-sciousness, becomes a site of its rebirth as discrimination against women is exposed as discrimination against families. The dual responsibilities of women—inside and outside the home —make women acutely aware of the failures of capitalist priorities to allocate resources to meet human needs. Since mothers, 40 percent of whom work, still have the child rear-ing responsibilities, they are particul-arly aware of the inadequacies of the institutions outside the home for socializing children.

The multiple contradictions faced by women today not only force them to confront their secondary status, but also offer institutions through which they may begin ot attack it. The

specific institution of the oppression of women is the nuclear family, but it is an institution that isolates women. Women are being collectivized in school and at work, so these insti-tutions feel the first attack. The schools offer formal equality but real discrimination as they train women for the roles they will play. In high school women are tracked into commercial and homemaking courses. In college women are steered into the women's professions—teaching, nursing, social work, library science. At work single women are put into the lowest paying jobs because they do not have to support a family. Married women are put there because they are not the breadwinners in their families. The job crisis hits women before men ; unemployment rates are higher for women than for men ; women's jobs are cut back by automation. The fiscal crisis reduces the jobs available to women as public employees, and it reduces the quantity and quality of public services available to them as working mothers. As women's roles multiply they find they have second-ary status in all of them. The political and economic institutions of capitalist society are unable to take up the issues of equal status for women, the in-dustrialization of housework, the socialization of child rearing, and the democratization of the family by its abolition as a political-economic unit in capitalism. Once women begin to look for ways to transform the instit-utions that oppress them, they are forced into oppositional politics. Even though the nuclear family is the in-strument of their oppression, women are coming to oppose the State as its agent. Demands for child care facilities and equality in schools and jobs go unheeded while the war industries thrive. The State is unmasked as the enemy of women.

The women's movement is diverse ;

within it, however, a small but growing socialist nucleus is being mobilized not simply around the contradictions of their own lives but have been forced by those contradictions into an understanding that the oppression of women is a contradiction of monopoly capitalism and imperialism. The unending war on socialism has mobilized many women into opposition to the warfare state. The black liberation movement has inspired many women, black women to join it and white women to see it as an example. The women's movement is closely related to the youth movement, especially in the schools. So, although still small when compared to its potential, the women's movement is closely linked to both the black and youth movements by a shared oppression and, to some extent, a shared resistance.

The third source of spontaneous resistance in the United States has been the developing youth movement. The work-life experiences of young workers in the United States have been transformed by the establishment of the empire and its failures ; each year more young people understand that resistance is possible, even in the most bureaucratized center of the empire. Imperialist wars have expanded at the expense of other public services, while the stagnation of jobs in the economy has gotten worse. The young have been required to fight in foreign wars, to stay in schools longer simply to be able to get a job, to face high unemployment rates, etc. The young worker, the new entrant to the labour force, confronts the economic reality of stagnating monopoly capitalism in its starkest form. The developing youth movement *itself* is part of the experience of an ever increasing number of young workers ; each year, the young become increasingly opposed to things as they are and more willing to act. The black, women and youth movements overlap, inter-depend, and inter-

penetrate, which has been important for the development of each part and the whole of the new socialist opposition. The youth movement is particularly important. It is more than an aphorism that the future belongs to the young ; no old order can withstand the challenge of youth. Young men and women, young blacks and whites, have learned that the economic, social and political structures keep people powerless. Opposition to these structures, not reform within them, is the only way for working people to get democratic control over their lives. Young workers bring that understanding out of the schools and the army into the work place. As the youth movement grows up, younger workers are leading the resistance in their workplace. The illusion of the "conflict of generations" is revealed as the reality of class conflict.

The youth movement was contained at first by the schools. First the expanded high schools and then the colleges absorbed the job crisis and substituted for unemployment. Increased schooling became part of the work experience for young workers. Schools train workers in skills and ideology to meet the production and political needs of monopoly capitalism. As more young working class people went to school for longer periods, they found the schools unable to serve people because of their prior obligations to capital. However, the schools are only a part of the experience of young workers. For all young men 19 to 24 years old today, about 35 percent are in school, more than half of whom also work ; another 30 percent are in the military ; and about 35 percent are only working. More than two-thirds of young men experience both some post-secondary education and the military. Young women have overlapping school and work, school and home, home and work experiences.

School, work and the army are overlapping experiences for young men throughout their early twenties. Young workers bear the costs of militarism directly and the costs of job stagnation indirectly in the State institutions developed to serve capital. The State bureaucracies have created about two-thirds of all new jobs in the economy for 20 years ; 10 percent of all new jobs created have been as army recruits, shared on two year terms by young men. In addition, the regular expansion of education, the increasing school enrollment each year for 20 years, has freed the economy from providing a quarter more new jobs each than it has been doing. As the fiscal crisis, combined with student and soldier resistance within their institutions, leads to a levelling off of the proportions of the young people contained in the schools and the army, the job crisis will follow the youth movement into the ranks of other young workers, particularly into the already swollen ranks of the young unemployed.

The student and anti-war movements are case studies of the mounting attack on bureaucratic institutions as those institutions fail to perform their functions under the growing pressures of a failing imperialism. The schools absorbed surplus labour through taxes on workers, molding the practical and ideological skills of the future labour force to the specifications of the system. However, the school's traditional insulation from reality broke down as millions of young people from working class families flooded into the schools as part of their own work-life pattern, simply overwhelming those few whose school years were part of an elite work-life experience. The expansion changed the class base, and therefore the politics, of the schools. The schools have been transformed from liberal sanctuaries into centers of socialist education and resistance. Under black leadership and in the context of the growing war on socialism, the student movement turned from support for the civil rights movement and from narrowly defined student power to a mass student movement attacking institutional racism and the complicity of the schools themselves in promoting the empire. Interdependent with the black and student movements has been the growing intensity of the GI, draft resistance, anti-war and women's movements. The ruling institutions have shown how weak they really are by resorting to force to repress the youth movement in the schools and the army. Repression of dissenters in the military has become more and more severe. The GI movement is molilizing both young whites and blacks into active resistance to the empire ; the revolutionary army is already being trained by its enemies. Hundreds of high school and college campuses have been occupied by police and military forces. The overt police repression of the 8 million college students (equivalent to 10 percent of the total labour force) and the 13 million high school students is giving the new labour force a practical education in the nature of U.S. government. While its socialist consciousness is still small, the anti-imperialist sentiment among the young has reached mass proportions. The resistance in the high schools, colleges, and the army has reached such intensity that these youth experiences are generating each year more socialist young people who are spreading revolutionary socialist ideas and organization to fellow workers in the shops, factories, offices, hospitals, and other workplaces of the country. Militant caucuses led by young workers are springing up everywhere, defying the cautious, conservative trade unions, raising not only the demands for worker self-determination in the workplace itself, but also the demands for peace, black liberation, and the liberation of women that are the basic planks in the platform of the program for a socialist United States.

Behind the young socialist conciousness is a rising tide of youth revolt against the decadence of the economic, political, and social order of a failing imperialism. The young focus their political expression through the schools, the army, and the youth ghettoes which have been created to obscure economic stagnation. Young people have been living increasingly collectivized lives in a world without democratic, collective decision making. From these contradictions has developed a "youth culture," which is highly diverse and by no means fully revolutionary, nor fully socialist, in its content. However, from the youth has come a revival of the utopian vision, so simple yet so profound, that war, racism, sexism, and authoritarianism must and can be eliminated. The socialist vision, long tainted in this country by its association with reformism and a narrow concern with economic issues, is regaining its revolutionary, democratic, and humanist thrust.

For 30 years the U.S. working class was suffocated by the reformism and repression of the labour unions and State bureaucracies. But from the underside of the wartime "prosperity" has come a new generation of socialists to offer a new direction to working class politics. This new leadership has risen from several segments of the working class : in the black nation ; among women ; in schools and the army ; and among young workers, black and white, women and men. The leadership of each segment is itself divided and disorganized, although the struggle is more clearly focussed in the black nation than in the white. Despite the varied work-life experiences of different segments of the working class and despite the attempts by the capitalist institutions to foster racist, sexist, anti-youth conflict within the working class, workers are being unified by common struggle. The State's repression of the anti-racist and anti-imperialist movements is rapidly driving increasing numbers of workers to a socialist perspective. Since the working class can only achieve power by abolishing the existing State, corporate, and union bureaucracies, working class discontent is always distorted and perverted when expressed within the existing forms. The social pluralist institutions have attempted to set worker against worker. However, the overlapping and interdependent black, women, and youth movements, representing a majority of the working class, provides some basis for unity in struggle in the unfolding expressions of working class discontent. Excessive individualism, fear of repression, and the reality of sharp divisions in the working class still inhibit the formation of a unified revolutionary socialist program for the U.S. working class. Socialists are dispersed within both the black nation and the white, among men's and women's organizations, among community, school, army, and workplace organizations. Rather than one, or even two or three, parties ready to organize a working class revolution, today there are hundreds of parties, strategies, and groups. However, the new socialist leadership is young, not merely in age but in revolutionary experience ; as experience is gained in practice and as the metropolis comes under more severe attack from the liberation armies of the Third World, a revolutionary front will be opened by the U.S. working class within the metropolis. Of course, there cannot be a socialist revolution which places power directly into the hands of the working people of the United States until they organize and fight that revolution. However, as the socialists expand their numbers and begin to build a unified strategy and to act through disciplined revolutionary organizations, the growing spontaneous resistance of the U.S. working class will increase the mass pressure on the collapsing pluralist divisions in the working class and the decaying bureaucratic forms that are designed to contain working class resistance.

THE DECAY OF BUREAUCRATIC POWER

The failures of the United States as an economic and social system have mobilized new revolutionary forces. A failing imperialism has increased its oppression of the black nation, of women and of the young, but has done so through the very institutions through which these groups have become mobilized. The unending war, the crisis in public services and the job crisis have been imposed on two-thirds of the working class to such an extent that the most militant within these groups are awakening to the need for a socialist revolution to end the permanent war on socialism, to free the black nation, to end the oppression of women, and to offer a meaningful future to the young. At the same time that a socialist movement is growing out of the mass movement of resistance to the acute contradictions of life in the ghettoes, the schools, the army, and the nuclear family, the contradictions which had been largely contained in these institutions have recently spilled beyond them. The economic failures that had been hidden by the State subsidies, the absorption of surplus labour, and the increased exploitation of blacks, women, and youth have spilled out into the seemingly most stable institutions of the

U.S. workers' experience. Inflation, debt and unemployment have begun to erode the material standard of living of all U.S. workers. The war, the misallocation of social resources and the lack of self-determined, meaningful work and life have eroded the quality of life so badly and fostered so much social disorganization that millions of people have come to realize that they are ruled by a network of bureaucracies responding not to the needs of the people they rule but to the needs of capital. The war has mobilized not only the young men who do not want to fight it but a mass of people who see that the economic, political, and moral costs of war are improverishing the whole society. The present acute crisis in public services is a result of the allocation of resources needed by imperialism to fight the war on socialism; it is also a revolt of taxpayers whose real incomes are falling and who will not accept higher taxes. The job crisis is beginning to mean unemployment not only for the young and black workers but also for workers whose jobs depend on the State's success in staving off stagnation through purchases of construction, war goods, etc. And for more and more workers who have jobs, the job crisis looms as a confrontation with the bureaucracies that once hid and contained the contradictions and now expose them: the labour unions and the State bureaucracies themselves. The same contradictions that have made blacks, women and the young the leaders in the developing revolutionary movement are now forcing confrontations within every bureaucracy in the society. The result is mounting repression, polarization and the formation of more revolutionaries. The lines are being drawn, not only in the ghettoes, the armies and the schools, but in every workplace, in every labour union local, in every political party organization and in every State agency. The decay of bureaucratic power and the resort to force by the ruling bureaucracies reveal the breadth and depth of the crisis.

The economic crisis of imperialism reached a new level when chronic inflation, beginning in the middle 1960's, began to erode the purchasing power of U.S. workers. Until then, State support for the stagnation of monopoly capitalism and imperialism had been financed by the rising productivity of workers in the goods-producing sector, by profits on foreign investments, and by control of the international money system, which meant that U.S. inflation could be imposed on the workers in other capitalist countries. With the increased military commitment to the war against socialism in South East Asia, however, these measures were not enough to countervail against the great increase in war expenditures, and inflation became a fact of U.S. life. The real purchasing power of production workers' wages has fallen since 1965. This inflation exposes the impoverishment of each household and family, which can no longer be contained by increasing the number of earners per family, which has increased more than a third since 1950, and by increasing family debt, which has gone up twice as fast as consumption spending since 1950. Instead, the institutions of the consumer economy, which imprison workers in a network of debt and responsibilities, also increase the contradictions with which workers must live.

State support for investment in the construction of single-family homes and automobiles is an important subsidy to the goods-producing sector of the private economy. Under the auspices of a State housing and transportation policy that made is necess-ary to buy houses and cars, home ownership has expanded beyond the comfortable upper quarter of U.S. families to include more than half of the working class as well. Home owners have on the average committed more than 20 percent of their incomes to shelter, renters about 15 percent. Transportation costs are about an eighth of the consumption expenditures of an average family. The portion of income used to pay debts already contracted has risen to 23 percent today. Growing debt mortgages a family's future labour and growing debt repayments reduces its present disposable income ; the growing debt bondage increases the hardship of both inflation and unemployment, at a time when both are increasing rapidly. (The consumer economy has been based to a large extent on household debt expansion ; the control of inflation by reducing consumer credit will exacerbate the collapse of the money-debt markets.)

Probably more important than the erosion of the material standard of living is the growing evidence of the misallocation of resources, the deterioration of the quality of private and social life and the rate of social disorganization. The war is the single most glaring misuse of resources. The poorest third of the U.S. population lives on the equivalent of the U.S. war expenditures. If the trillion dollars of workers' taxes that has been spent since 1950 to buy war goods from the private economy had been spent on capital goods for the economic development of the poor countries, millions of lives might have been saved and hundreds of millions improved. The resources of this society cannot be used to industrialize and feed the world instead of maining it because the second is profitable while the first is not. The misallocation of resources is carried out by the same bureaucratic

182

institutions that imprison U.S. workers—the large monopoly corporations and their allies in the labour unions and government agencies. But the very misallocation of resources that keeps the monopoly capitalist and imperialist system going also creates its economic problems and the resistance to that system. Sixty percent of the productive resources of the capitalist world have been commandeered by U.S. capital. Yet the monopoly system is so wasteful that not only do these resources fail to provide a decent life for all the people of the world, which they could, but they do not even make the United States a society in which people are guaranteed the amenities of civilization. Instead, although annual education expenditures are about $60 billion, a Harvard study finds that more than half of the people in the United States cannot read well enough to fill out job applications or drivers' licenses. [66] Health and medical expenditures are more than $50 billion a year ; but these resources are spent on heart transplants while the level of public health deteriorates so much that life expectancy in the United States actually fell in 1969. The output of the U.S. agriculture industry could feed hundreds of millions, yet 10 million people in the United States itself and hundreds of millions elsewhere are hungry, while the government gave $3.5 billion of workers' taxes in 1969 to farmers for taking land out of production. In 1964, less U.S. land was used as crop land, 49 percent, than in 1940, 55.7 percent. Harvested acres fell from 360 million in 1949 to 294 million in 1969. Nutritionists find that less than half of the U.S. population has an adequate diet, even worse than the 60 percent figure of 1950. [67] Less milk is produced in the U.S. today than in 1955, while food technologists are busy perfecting can-sized tomatoes and smaller watermelons. Automobile production accounts for four percent of all production in the United States, about $36.5 billion in 1969, about three-quarters as much as the gross national product of India (which has more than twice the population of the United States). This wasteful and inefficient method of transportation causes 50,000 deaths in the United States every year, yet the system is so twisted that it is not possible to change to a safer method of travel. The real political importance of the erosion of the material standard of living is that it has made workers conscious of the misallocation of resources. The erosion of real wages is only one result of this misallocation ; but the reason workers are attacking it is because it is immoral and irrational.

This misallocation of economic resources leads to social disorganization and personal alienation. The number of serious crimes doubled in the 1960's. Violent deaths total nearly 100,000 a year : 50,000 in automobiles ; 21,000 suicides ; and 15,000 murders. The evidence of individual incapacity to cope with the growing social disorganization is found in the drug abuse statistics. People in the United States consume more than half a trillion cigarettes every year, 4000 per capita. They drink about 650 million gallons of distilled spirits ; 180 million barrels of beer, about 17.7 gallons per capita ; 200 million gallons of wine ; 100 million gallons of moonshine. [68] There are at least six million alcoholics ; the National Industrial Conference Board estimates that 3 to 5 percent of an average company's employees have drinking problems. [69] Chronic drunkenness is the cause of one-third to one-half of all arrests ; 20 percent of the patients in state mental hospitals suffer irreversible alcoholic psychosis ; cirrhosis of the liver is the sixth leading cause of death ; between

183

half and 70 percent of auto accident deaths and injuries are alcohol-related. [70] Drug companies manufacture annually 8 billion amphetamines, 8 billion barbiturates and 4 billion tranquilizers. [71] A study of midtown Manhattan in the early 1960's concluded that 80 percent of those interviewed showed measurable symptoms of emotional disturbance. [72]

The high level of personal distress in this society is the personal cost of powerlessness. U.S. workers, imprisoned in the strongest bureaucratic forms at the center of the imperialist system, have not been able to fight against their own helplessness. But now, as the black liberation struggle approaches the stage of open warfare, the youth movement becomes increasingly militant, and the women's movement attacks a central institution of social stability, it also becomes clear that the bureaucratic institutions that have distorted and repressed worker resistance are becoming more and more vulnerable. Under the mounting attacks of workers, led by black, young men and women workers, the labour union, corporate, political party and State bureaucracies are revealing their own weakness and that of the system. Under the pressures of the economic and political crisis, these bureaucracies drop their pretense of representing a constituency and reveal that their function is to discipline people to serve the needs of capital. If the constituency rebels, the bureaucracies resort to repression even though it means losing their legitimacy altogether. A measure of the breadth of the crisis is how widespread the attack on the bureaucracies has become ; a measure of its seriousness is the number of institutions that have begun to use force against the challengers, even at the cost of creating more and more people dedicated to their overthrow.

The United States is the most bureaucratized society in the world. Although many of the ruling institutions claim to be representative or in some way responsible to the people that they affect, in fact they are separated from the people. Bureaucracies are run by experts who keep their power by their specialized information. The people that are affected by them are clients and not constituents ; although they are perhaps formally empowered to demand responsibility, as in the labour unions, in fact the bureaucracies are independent of the people and follow the needs and logic of capital. Bureaucracies stand between the people and self-determination. The characteristic contradiction of a bureaucratic society grows out of its remoteness from the people. Unable to recognize demands until the people organize and attack the bureaucracy itself, bureaucracies respond with force and try to repress the attackers, which only increases their number and determination. Bureaucracies sow the seeds of their own destruction by acting like bureaucracies.

The labour union bureaucracies are beginning to feel the challenge. These institutions are supposed to represent about 18 million U.S. workers, but in fact they are bureaucracies, treating the membership as clients to be serviced and placated. The leadership, nominally elected, is seldom opposed ; leaders retire at 65 or 70 or die in office. Challengers run against the established leadership at the risk of their lives, as the late Joseph Yablonsky demonstrated by challenging the leadership of the Mine Workers. The leadership keeps close ties to the management of the major monopolized industries, sometimes even formalized as in the steel industry ; close ties to the political party bureaucracies through the union's political section ;

and close ties to the bureaucracies of the government at the local, state and federal level through departments of manpower, labour, etc. The functions of the unions are determined through their inter-relation with these other bureaucracies. With the corporations, the unions negotiate the rules under which labour will be exploited by capital and how much workers will be paid for that exploitation. These contract negotiations concede the power of capital to govern production and only claim a workers' right to strike if the terms of payment are not satisfactory. Even the definition of working conditions is so narrow as to lack meaning ; the unions bargain about safety rules, speedups, etc., but never over the power to set working conditions, especially to decide what to produce. Unauthorized strikes are punished by the union bureaucracies themselves as well as by law. The way that unions operate is determined largely by law, that is, by agreeing to work within monopoly capitalism and imperialism and granting legitimacy to the government in return for legal protection of the labour union bureaucracies. The unions give up any claim that workers should have self-determination ; they are then protected from challenges by other workers' organizations by law and government bureaucracies such as the National Labour Relations Board.

Political issues are carefully separated from economic issues by the labour union bureaucracies. Politically, the labour unions behave as any other interest group, lobbying through the political party bureaucracies and the lawmaking and enforcing bureaucracies of the governments. They expropriate money from their members and use it to support candidates and to lobby for measures that promote continued bureaucratic control : warfare, welfare, education programs, etc.

The union bureaucracies also wage active anti-socialist campaigns in both foreign and domestic politics, defending their bureaucratic power against the threat of a socialist workers' movement.

The labour unions claim to act for working people by taking credit for the increase in workers' real wages that was really caused by rising worker productivity since World War II. It is this narrow economic focus and the complicity with the U.S. empire that is the source of labour union vulnerability. A two fold contradiction faces the labour unions today as a result of the way that they have maintained their power. First, the economic crisis of the empire has shown that the unions can only gain economic benefits for their members in prosperous times ; since the chronic inflation began in 1965, the unions have been unable to keep up the real wages of their members. This inability unveils the complicity of the labour unions in the structure of capital. As the job crisis deepens the unions will try to preserve seniority and to share the available work among older members, sharing the hardship rather than representing the workers' interests in eliminating the whole structure of corporate power that causes the hardship. Second, because the union bureaucracies are committed to a narrow economic focus, they cannot deal with the growing social crisis of opposition to the war and to the allocation of resources, nor with the problems of blacks or women. Union members who try to get their locals to voice opposition to the war and other issues always have to fight the union leadership ; they find that the union's structures are unsuitable to the expression of opposition to the system of power because they are part of it. The labour unions can only deal with rising worker discontent over both economic and political-social issues through repression. National unions negotiate a wage settlement and then try to coerce the membership into accepting it. Union bureaucrats announce the unions' political positions in support of the war, increased spending, etc., and try to stifle members' dissent. But the result is not successful repression but increasing polarization. Wildcat strikes increase over economic issues and radical rank-and-file caucuses insist on raising political issues from which union bureaucrats recoil in horror. Young workers, black workers and women workers are attacking the union complicity with the empire, with racism, with the secondary status of women and with the impoverishment of the young. This complicity is not only on the job (through hiring practices, seniority systems, failure to press women's demands, etc.) but also as one of the system's ruling bureaucracies. As the social and economic crisis worsens, the unions will be beseiged as they retreat from the assaults of their increasingly militant membership. The unions will cooperate with capital, and the destruction of the old bureaucracies will write the end to labour union history.

Political party bureaucracies are also beginning to experience the contradictions that face institutions that are supposed to be responsible, but are not, when their clientele (to be acted upon) begins to act as if it were a constituency (to be represented). The two major political parties until recently have monopolized the legitimate channels for affecting the political system. This monopoly is reinforced by custom and also by the laws governing use of the communications facilities, "equal time" provisions, etc. Not unlike other monopolistic situations, the two parties compete only along irrelevant, non-class dimensions, field-

ing indistinguishable candidates and suppressing controversial issues by tacit or overt mutual consent, as the South East Asian war was conveniently declared "not an issue" in the 1968 Presidential campaign. When the working people, who know that this is not their political system, do not vote, they are called apathetic rather than realistic ; the poorest 40 percent of the electorate seldom if ever votes, and less than 5 percent of the voters do anything active to elect a candidate besides casting a ballot. Much more important than their function of offering the voters alternate candidates is the function of the political parties to offer corporate, union, and other interest groups alternate routes through which to pressure legislators and government bureaucracies. The political parties are another set of institutions to perpetuate the rule of capital ; they are powerful when capital has power but cannot act independent of its needs.

Because the political parties control the legitimate channels for political action, their refusal to deal with the crises of a failing imperialism forces people into other, more direct, expressions of discontent. The struggle for black liberation has been ignored so long and so consistently that the political parties can no longer win the support of even the most conservative contenders for leadership of the black nation. The anti-war movement has been so completely ignored and repressed that public demonstrations are necessary to express opposition. Taxpayer resistance to increased costs of government in the service of capital has been ignored, forcing people to reject local bond issues to ease their own financial burdens, even though it means cutting off the public services that bring them the most benefits. The growing job crisis, ignored, fuels disturbances in the black and youth ghettoes. But the political parties cannot respond to the demands for peace, freedom for the black nation, women's liberation, and a better allocation of the social resources because they are part of the structure that supports war, international and internal imperialism, waste ad monopoly capitalism. The political parties stand as intermediate bureaucracies between the people and the government bureaucracies. As the blacks, women, and youth increase their attack on the political parties and as the governments find themselves ineffectual in their pluralist bargaining as the crisis deepens, the two party monopoly will be broken and the formal politics of the nation will become increasingly fractionated, forcing the State bureaucracies increasingly to act without "consent." The political parties are forced to repress dissent, not only violently as at the Democratic convention in 1968, but subtly. But repression will not stifle the dissent; instead the political party bureaucracies continue to demonstrate by their action and their inaction that they are on the side of profits and the police in any conflict with the people.

As the crisis deepens, the State bureaucracies themselves face increasing dissent with decreasing legitimacy. The new revolutionary socialist movement is being forged out of the contradictions of particular State institutions—the ghettoes, the schools and the armed forces. It is gaining momentum as the growing repression reveals that the police and court system are in the service of capital. The bureaucracies of the welfare state are revealed as part of the structure of racism and the oppression of women. The elected decision-making bodies do not respond to popular demands because the demands for an end to war and racism are demands to dismantle the profit system. As the legitimacy of the government agencies continues to deteriorate, fewer regulations and rules are obeyed without question : more and more government resources must be channelled to police and repression to enforce the decisions in the service of capital, just as more and more people are objecting to those decisions. So to the indictment of the governments for misallocating resources to war and subsidies to business is added the indictment for spending the people's money on police to repress the people.

The State also faces a much more integral contradiction that exacerbates the deepening contradiction between the State and the people. The huge State not only rules all the people, but it also employs a fifth of all workers. The State is allied with capital to expropriate surplus value from the workers through their taxes, but it spends about half of what it expropriates ($104 billion in 1969) to hire workers itself. One out of every five workers confronts the State not only as a ruler but also as boss. The huge State bureaucracies, necessary to export, subsidize and hide the stagnation of monopoly capitalism, have created their own internal resistance from the ranks of the 18 million public employees. Public employees face the fiscal crisis as a personal experience. Many of their jobs (just as many in the private sector) are clearly surplus-absorbing, war-supporting, overtly useless. Resistance to tax increases, which they join, depresses their wages, so that they suffer from the chronic inflation. It is also difficult for public employees to win political support for wage gains since they entail tax increases. Forbidden active partisan politics by the Hatch Act and its state and local equivalents, public employees are even more clearly confined than other workers in the structures of bureaucracy. Their resistance to their confines and State attempts to repress that resistance further exposes the State's allegiances to capital. In addition to attacks from without, the State bureaucracies face growing worker threats from within (not unlike the two-front attack on the labour union bureaucracies).

Although most public employees are simply clerical and other workers with no power over others, some public employees are hired to coerce other citizens, and experience the contradictions of being themselves agents of the system. Some of these agents may continue to act as enforcers for the rulers; but others will join the anti-bureaucratic struggle. Teachers, social welfare workers and hospital personnel are particularly important: they are often black and/or young and/or women; they are the links between important oppressed groups—students and welfare recipients—and the structure of power. They are experiencing the fiscal crisis of the empire, as budgets are cut and case loads, classroom size and patient loads increase. As these public servants find that they cannot serve the people, the bureaucracies in which they work are being attacked by them as well as by their clients; increasingly the government bureaucracies face internal resistance to the war, racism and the oppression of women.

Bureaucratic power holds the United States together. Although nominally a representative government of constituencies, it is in actuality a bureaucratic government of clients. Bureaucracies govern by routine and the authority of custom; challenges to authority cannot be accommodated by bureaucratic forms of organization. As the crisis of the empire unfolds, more and more U.S. workers become anti-State and anti-bureaucratic. A revived populist consciousness is developing and with it a mounting passive resistance to bureaucratic rule: draft evasion, tax evasion, truancy, nonvoting, etc. As bureaucratic control breaks down, it becomes more centralized. Local bureaucracies thus become attacked both by the people and by the more centralized bureaucracies. The demands for "local control" are often not so much for self-determination as they are signs of interbureaucratic warfare. Nonetheless, when the people are in motion, bureaucracies are threatened. Populist sentiment can be misguided by local bureaucracies; but once unleashed, it can turn on all bureaucracy. Leaders of the socialist struggle are calling for community control of the police in the ghettoes. At the same time, populist elements in states and cities have passed resolutions telling their young men that they do not have to fight in the war in South East Asia, while throughout the country attempts are made to reassert local or states' rights against an encroaching central power. This broad anti-bureaucratic struggle is still amorphous and disparate. The decay of bureaucratic power as a social process is generating populism, local control movements, and other forms of mass efforts to gain more decision-making power for the people. But for this social process to become a revolutionary movement and not become mired in self-defeat, these spontaneous populist energies must be linked to the energies of the anti-imperialist, anti-racist movement.

The continued erosion of bureaucratic power, the increasing use of force against the ghettoes, the schools, and striking workers, private and public, forces more and more people to confront the State and to resist it. This process is going on and will continue to unfold in the context of continuing war and international crisis, continuing inflation and domestic fiscal crisis, and a continuing job crisis.

The economic and political-social problems will continue to compound each other. In the 1960's, the convergence of economic, social and political problems drove the most exploited groups of workers to mass resistance ; in the 1970's the deepening crisis will meet growing resistance and the initiative of an organized socialist movement, will move the United States toward an social revolution of the people against the government.

THE COMING SOCIALIST REVOLUTION

The proceding sections of this essay have defined the political economic context of the crisis of imperialism viewed from within the metropolis itself. In this section we explore briefly some of the developments that we think are imminent in the developing crisis and some of the implications for the future. The Third World war for liberation on is being waged throughout the imperialized world and the governing institutions within the metropolis are increasingly coming under attack by the working people of the United States. Revolutionary socialist forces are developing out of the continuing crisis. The war, the fiscal crisis, and the job crisis limit the ability of the State and its allied bureaucracies to respond to the growing demands of workers for peace and an end to the oppression of the internal black colony and of women. The State is driven to repression and the people to revolution.

The socialist revolution in the United States is developing in a context of continuing crisis—war and economic and social crisis inside the United States and throughout the capitalist world. The war against socialism and self-determination is being waged on many fronts : in South East Asia with both U.S. weapons and U.S. troops ; in the Middle East, Latin America and Africa with U.S. weapons ; and, increasingly, inside the United States itself. The ghettoes of the black nation and the schools and ghettoes of the young are under military occuption. U.S. capital must wage war against self-determination to maintain imperialism : military force is necessary to try to keep people around the world from overthrowing the tyranny of U.S. capital ; the production of military goods is the largest single industry in which U.S. capital can make investments ; and the armies hide unemployment. The stagnation of monopoly capitalism requires military production both as a political and economic necessity. Imperial expansion and monopoly profits inside and outside the U.S. are supported by the State's expropriation of a third of all products (counting purchases and transfers) and its channelling into activities that support capital, of which war is the most important. But while war spending has played an important role in postponing the stagnation crisis, that crisis has not been resolved. Instead the stagnation of monopoly capitalism and imperialism means that the war becomes more and more costly at the same time that it becomes more and more necessary. Its mounting costs are economic—chronic inflation, balance of payments deficits, growing unemployment, etc.—but also, and increasingly importantly, social and political. The misallocation of resources necessary to support imperialism has brought on a fiscal and job crisis of such proportions that it is not possible to confine its external effects to people in the underdeveloped countries and its internal effects to black, young and women workers so that a national chauvinist, racist, sexist and age dominated society can deny or ignore it. The political and economic problems coincide and reinforce each other. The costs of imperialism mount as national liberation fronts in the colonies expand the armed struggles against imperial control and as the anti-war movement in the metropolis becomes larger and more determined. Fighting through puppet governments with U.S. weapons, even when it is possible, can no longer obscure the distortion of the world economic, social and political system by the desperate need of a stagnating imperialist system for more and more war spending to prop up its profits at any cost.

Imperialism calls its own opposition into existence. In the underdeveloped countries, the processes of deepening underdevelopment set in motion by imperialist exploitation also disrupt the social and political fabric and give rise to social structures and political organizations that resist imperialism. In the United States, the processes of subsidizing and hiding the stagnation of monopoly capitalism required the continuing exploitation of the black nation, the family, and young workers. But, as in the external colonies, this exploitation has generated its own resistance—the black liberation movement, the youth movement and the movement for the liberation of women. Racism and racist structures have brought the black nation to maturity. The rulers of the white nation have put the black nation under martial law, teaching blacks the necessity of armed struggle. Millions of young men and women have been concentrated in two major work places of imperialism : the armies that fight its wars ; and the schools that absorb its unemployables, train its workforce and transmit its lies. Resistance inside these two workplaces has brought military repression there, too, again teaching that imperialism will only be defeated by force of arms. Emerging from the youth-containing institutions, young men and women are creating radical caucuses in workplaces and radical activities in communities across the country. Women have entered schools and workplaces, ending their isolation in the home and generating a women's movement that is a leading force in the conflict between the state and the people.

Continued war and the mounting resistance of blacks, women and youth to an imperialist economy's misallocation of resources goes on in the midst of a fiscal crisis which has left the State's budgetary resources inadequate to deal with its problems. The oppression of blacks, youth and women has been a structural necessity in an imperialist economy which has so distorted the economy of the metropolis that the war, the fiscal crisis, and the job crisis are now the necessary consequences. With stagnation has gone inflation and rising costs to the governments as well as to everyone else, so that public services decay and budgetary problems mount ; with the attempt to control inflation has gone unemployment and recession. Government employment and expanding school enrollment have absorbed surplus labour for 25 years ; but the fiscal crisis is also a crisis in government employment and therefore a crisis in jobs.

The job crisis is a crisis of the State. Two-thirds of all new jobs have been provided by State, hiding the stagnation of monopoly capitalism by spending workers' taxes to hire other workers who could not have been employed by a stagnating private economy. Increasing monopolization of industry, more automation, and the misdirection of resources into war rather than productive investment continue to erode the employment opportunities for new entrants to the labour force and to undermine the increases in labour productivity that had permitted increasing government spending and employment. As is becoming clearer every day, if the governments do not increase their spending at a fast enough rate to absorb surplus labour, the result is a sharp increase in unemployment. On the other hand, if they do expand government spending, they face increasing inflation that might send the whole monetary system into collapse. The prospect of economic collapse in the richest economy in the world adds to the political crises of stagnation. U.S. workers have been told that it cannot happen again ; the legitimacy of the whole political system has been staked on the permanence of prosperity. So economic crisis, which forty years ago caused people to turn to the State for amelioration of the hardships of capitalism, today is causing people to turn on the State for betraying them. Intermediate institutions are being swept aside. The political parties are collapsing. The labour unions are already under attack for their complicity in the empire and their policies of racism, oppression of women and oppression of youth, and are becoming even more embattled by the job crisis. As the crisis deepens, all the bureaucratic institutions will close ranks behind the police and military bureaucracies, in hopes that they can repress the opposition that can no longer be controlled. The militarization in its turn will sweep away the last lingering illusions that this economic and political system allows the will of the people to be expressed.

As the crisis deepens, repression will increase in extent and intensity. At the same time, however, continual efforts will be made to shore up the economy and to placate the popular unrest. The current inflation and recession will force the State to adopt wage, price, and credit controls. Public works programs will be tried to ease the unemployment ; they will be unpopular and will not end the recession. "War versus unemployment" will become a serious political issue. State loans and outright "nationalizations" of failing industries will increase. Revenue sharing schemes wil be worked out to ease the state and local fiscal crises, to keep the schools open and to meet the payrolls. Along with such reorganization will go other attempts to disguise the crisis by re-naming its parts : welfare reforms, reforms of the schools, etc. But when the people are turning on the State, the expansion of the State cannot placate them. So along with the centralization and militarization of political power, the State will try to deflect the growing popular demand for self-determination into any of a myriad of spurious "local control" plans ; in the last resort the State will try to balkanize the country, even at a high cost in efficiency, rather than allow the people to unite among themselves against the present system of power.

So here we stand in mid-1970 in the midst of the developing crisis of imperialism. While political economy does not provide a time-table for future history, it does define the context in which men will make that history ; it defines the contradictions that are throwing the economy into crisis and the people into opposition to the State ; it points to the social formations in the working class that are generating mass politics and revolutionary leadership. The preceding analysis points up several features of the political economy of the metropolis that govern the context in which revolutionary socialist organizations must operate.

First, the United States is the metropolis of world imperialism. When the

191

metropolis is overthrown, the historical epoch of capitalism and imperialism will draw to a close. So U.S. working people today play a crucial role in hastening the construction of socialism, not only in the United States but in the whole world. As the metropolis, the United States is the most militarized society in the world; a tenth of its resources and labour are devoted to war, and almost one percent to internal security. Only a mass popular revolution by an armed people can immobilize the military might of the rulers of the metropolis.

Second, the working class revolution in the metropolis will be a two nation revolution. Widespread rebellion already exists in the urban ghettoes of the black nation. The pace of revolutionary developments in the white nation must largely be determined by the course of the struggle for liberation of the black nation. On the one hand, the black struggle awakens an internally generated anti-imperialist perspective in the working people of the metropolis; on the other hand, the only defense against a State campaign of genocide against the black nation is an awakened and mobilized working class in the metropolis.

Third, women's liberation will play an unprecedented role in the socialist revolution in the United States. Women in the United States are among the most active, educated, and organized in the capitalist world. Their struggle gives rise to an internally generated demand for equality and an anti-sexist perspective inside the metropolis itself.

Fourth, the youth movement in the schools and the armies is not only a major set of recruiting institutions for the revolution, but the attack on those imperial bureaucracies is itself an important part of the revolutionary struggle. Youth are forced to be the

mercenaries of the empire; they must turn their guns around.

Fifth, the United States is an urban civilization, with tremendous concentrations of people, sophisticated communications networks, and a great dependence on technology and complex distribution patterns. Since the revolution must be fought in the cities, revolutionary strategy and tactics will be shaped both by the fragility of capital and by the vulnerability of the people.

Sixth, the United States is the most bureaucratized country in the world. Revolutionary organizations must organize in and recruit from these bureaucracies, both in the workplaces and the community, without being limited by the narrow issues those institutions allow to surface or by the means of expression they permit. The destruction of all of these bureaucracies and their replacement by the democratic structures of the working people is the task of the revolution.

The revolution will be fought for three inter-related goals—an end to imperialism, an end to racism, and an end to the oppression of women. The primary goal is to defeat imperialism because the necessities of the imperial system determine the character of the continuing war against the peoples of the world and of racism and male domination inside the United States. Opposition to the continuing Third World war generates the broadest mass-based resistance to the empire inside the metropolis. But to destroy the imperialist system of exploitation, more will be necessary than to bring home the U.S. troops. The U.S. revolution must halt the aggression against socialist struggles around the world, immediately dismantle the military machine and convert it to uses that can benefit rather than main the

192

people of the world. This transformation will only be possible if the people rather than the capitalists through their corporations and their State control production ; only socialism can bring an end to imperialism. The struggle of the black nation for liberation from imperial control is the most sharply focussed internal front of the revolution. Racist exploitation of the black working class is also imperial exploitation of the black colony. The liberation of the black nation and self-determination for the black people (and the people of other internal colonies) requires self-determination for all the working people of the metropolis. Imperialism can no more give up its internal black colony than any other ; socialists can no more perpetuate that colony than any other. Within the metropolis itself, the struggle of women against their secondary status will be the most broadly based internal issue of the revolution. Only by dismantling the imperial economy can the resources be liberated to free women from centuries of capitalist oppression.

The revolution will be a socialist revolution because only socialism can allocate resources so that they can be used for human purposes and not for profits. But millions of people will be forced by the contradictions of their own lives to support the revolution even if they do not have as comprehensive a vision of the necessary solution as the socialists. The revolution will be fought for peace, equality, and self-determination. Socialists must lead the revolution to keep alive the larger vision of the international struggle against the empire so that the revolutionary process in the United States will not bog down in national shortsightedness, slowing its progress or deforming its victories.

Socialism will unlock the productive capacity of this economy and put it at the service of the working people of the world. The tyranny of capital will be overthrown and workers will use as servants the machines that have served capitalist masters. Socialism will re-industrialize the United States and use its productive capacity to industrialize the world. A fifth of the existing plant now stands idle ; the plants will run at capacity. A tenth of production is channelled into the utter waste of war goods ; that waste will be ended and that plant and equipment retooled to produce what people need. Agricultural output can be doubled. Tens of millions of skilled trained workers can be freed from a life of wasted work in the bureaucracies of capital to be able to express their human capacities through meaningful creative work. The network of bureaucratic constraint broken, the human energy that will be released can set in motion the revolution in the production process that will follow the struggle for power and make it worth while. The victory of the armed struggle will end imperialist exploitation by war abroad and racism at home. Through socialist construction it will be possible to industrialize the ghettoes and begin real economic development in the black nation. It will be posible to end the tyranny of commodities and to industrialize housework, socialize child care, and end the oppression of women through household slavery and the nuclear family. The transportation system will be industrialized, ending the waste of resources, lives and land now swallowed by the automobile as a commodity. Liberation from commodity production will mean an end of the consumer as a category of existence and the beginning of the construction of a society in which for the first time the working people of the United States will be able to live in

193

peace and true fellowship not only with each other but with the people of the new world that the revolution will help to build.

Revolutions are made by the young, which is at it should be, since revolutions are made for the future and the future is, in the last analysis, in the hands of the young. The young in the black colony and in the metropolis are arming themselves with politics, experience, organization, and weapons, with the daring to struggle and the power to win.

ALL POWER TO THE PEOPLE!
SEIZE THE TIME!

FOOTNOTES

1. Most figures not footnoted come from or are calculated from the U.S. government's own figures as reported in the *Statistical Abstract*, 1969, or *The Annual Report of the Council of Economic Advisers*, 1970, or the *Historical Statistics of the United States*.
2. Calculated from figures in *The Fortune Directory of the 500 Largest Industrial Corporations*, May 15, 1969.
3. W. O. Douglas, *Points of Rebellion*, 1969.
4. A. M. Ross and H. Hill, eds., *Employment, Poverty, and Race*, 1965, p. 15.
5. *Ibid.*, p. 30. 6 C. Killingsworth, in Ross and Hill, p. 59.
7. Ross and Hill, *op. cit.*, p. 18.
8. U.S. Department of Labor, "The Contribution of Working Wives to Family Income," Dec. 1968 (pamphlet).
9. Andre Gorz, *Strategy for Labor*, 1967, p. 107.
10. Susan S. Baker, "The Growth and Structure of the Labor Force," in M. Herman, *et al*, eds., *Work, Youth, and Unemployment*, 1968, p. 66; B. B. Seligman, "Automation and the Work Force," *ibid.*, p. 150.
11. U.S. Department of Labor, *Handbook of Labor Statistics*, 1969.
12. Special Labor Force Report #53, cited in Killingsworth, *op. cit.*, p. 60.
13. U.S. Department of Labor, *Manpower Report of the President*, Jan. 1969, p. 44.
14. j.r.

15. A. Rees, *The Economics of Trade Unions*.
16. National Education Association, *Research Bulletin*, Oct. 1967, p. 87.
17. H. U. Faulkner, *American Economic History*, 8th ed., 1960, p. 607; and labor force participation rates from the *Historical Statistics of the United States*.
18. E. Kefauver, *In a Few Hands*, p. 84.
19. Faulkner, *op. cit.*, p. 610.
20. G. A. Steiner, *Government's Role in Economic Life*, 1953, p. 156.
21. Harry Magdoff, "Militarism and Imperialism," *Monthly Review*, Feb. 1970, p. 11.
22. Steiner, *op. cit.*
23. Faulkner, *op. cit.*, p. 698.
24. W. Adams, *Monopoly in America*, 1955, pp. 102, 120.
25. R. J. Gordon, "$45 Billion of U.S. Private Investment Has Been Mislaid," *American Economic Review*, June, 1969, pp. 221-238.
26. M. Derber and E. Young, *Labor and the New Deal*, 1959.
27. Federal Trade Commission, *Economic Report on Corporate Mergers*, GPO, 1969, p. 162.
28. *The Fortune Directory*, May 15, 1969.
29. FTC, *op. cit.*, p. 680.
30. Quoted in *Ibid.*, p. 684.
31. *Ibid.*, pp. 200 ff.
32. P.C. Dooley, "The Interlocking Directorate," *American Economic Review*, June 1969, pp. 314-323.
33. FTC, *op. cit.*, p. 199.
34. *Ibid.*, pp. 205-208.
35. *Ibid.*, p. 212.
36. *Ibid.*, p. 42.
37. Harry Magdoff, *The Age of Imperialism*, 1969, p. 178; we have drawn heavily from this valuable book.
38. *Ibid.*, p. 62.
39. G. Kolko, *The Roots of American Foreign Policy*, 1969, p. 77.
40. Judd Polk, "The Rise of World Corporations," *Saturday Review*, Nov. 22, 1969.
41. Standard Oil Company of New Jersey, *Annual Report*, 1968.
42. Figures from the Dominion Bureau of Statistics; quoted in *Business Week*, March 7, 1970; p. 103.
43. Kolko, *op. cit.*, p. 74.
44. *Ibid.*
45. E. Galeano, "De-Nationalization and Brazilian Industry," *Monthly Review*, Dec. 1969; p. 13.
46. FTC, *op. cit.*, p. 207.
47. North American-Rockwell Corporation, *Annual Report*, 1968.

48. Magdoff, *op. cit.*, pp. 74-76.
49. *Ibid.*, p. 78.
50. *Ibid.*, p. 62.
51. *Ibid.*, p. 180.
52. *Ibid.*, p. 198.
53. *Ibid.*, p. 182.
54. Actually, there was a small net outflow to Europe and Canada, and, thus, an even larger net inflow of capital from the underdeveloped countries, further impoverishing the poor.
55. The job creation estimates, while rough, are conservative. The defense-generated employment estimates were taken from the standard. Department of Labour estimates. The jobs generated in construction were assumed proportionate to public financing. The non-defense and non-construction private jobs generated by public spending are troublesome to estimate ; however, conservative estimates regarding the wages proportion of the value of these expenditures yields job creation is roughly equal to the percentage of defense purchases in total government purchases ; the low "wages" of the military are largely offset by the high profits and wages in aircraft, missiles, electronics systems parts of military procurement. The increase in the proportion of public construction and the increase in procurement as a proportion of defense expenditures between 1950 and 1968 largely are responsible for the increase in the proportion of "government-generated" jobs relative to the directly hired. Between 1950 and 1968, both the military plus government generated employment as a percentage of total employment and government purchases (excluding compensation of civilian employees) as a percentage of GNP roughly doubled ; this gives confidence in the "two-thirds of new jobs" figures.
56. *Business Week*, May 17, 1969, p. 104.
57. R. J. Gordon, "$45 Billion of U.S. Private Investment Has Been Mislaid," *American Economic Review*, June, 1969 ; pp. 221-238.
58. Harry Magdoff, "Militarism and Imperialism," *Monthly Review*, Feb. 1970, p. 12.
59. Quoted in Victor Perlo, *The New Republic*, Feb. 7, 1970.
60. The reader is referred to Paul Baran's and Paul Sweezy's *Monopoly Capital* and Paolo Sylos-Labini's *Oligopoly and Technical Progress* for more detailed discussions of these problems in monopoly capitalism.
61. Harry Magdoff, "Militarism and Imperialism," *Monthly Review*, Feb. 1970.
62. *Business Week*, March 21, 1970, p. 94.
63. Magdoff, *op. cit.*, p. 9.
64. The processes of deepening of underdevelopment in the imperialized countries are explored in Paul Baran's *The Political Economy of Growth* and A. G. Frank's *Capitalism and Underdevelopment in Latin America.*
65. *Los Angeles Times*, June 15, 1970.
66. *San Francisco Chronicle*, May 20, 1970.
67. *Los Angeles Times*, Nov. 26, 1969.
68. *Saturday Review*, March 14, 1970.
69. *San Francisco Examiner and Chronicle*, March 15, 1970.
70. *Saturday Review*, March 14, 1970.
71. *Wall Street Journal*, March 18, 1970.
72. Paul Baran and Paul Sweezy, *Monopoly Capital*, p. 364.

CONTRIBUTORS :

Rick Deaton is Assistant to the Director of Research for the Canadian Union of Public Employees. The analysis, interpretation and opinions expressed in the article published in this book are his own, and do not necessarily reflect the policies or views of CUPE or its officers. The author wishes to acknowledge his profound intellectual debt to Professor James O'Connor, Departement of Economics, San Deigo State University, for many of the germial ideas which appear in this article. Graphics courtesy of CUPE public relations department.

Lorne F. Huston is a social animator for a Montréal citizens' group, and a former research assistant at the Université de Montréal.

B. Roy Lemoine is an editor of OUR GENERATION since its founding in 1961, and has written many articles on various aspects of Québec society.

Graeme Nicholson teaches philosophy at the University of Toronto, and is an editor with the Toronto editorial collective of OUR GENERATION.

Mickey Ellinger and John Rowntree taught political science at the University of Toronto and economics at York University, respectively. They authored the widely-acclaimed "Political Economy of Youth — Youth As Class", first published in North America in OUR GENERATION. They now live and work in San Francisco.

Dimitrios I. Roussopoulos is an editor of OUR GENERATION, and works for BLACK ROSE BOOKS. His previous books include, "The New Left in Canada", and "The Case for Participatory Democracy" (with George Benello).

ESSAYS ON MARX'S THEORY OF VALUE

by Issaak Illich Rubin

According to the prevailing theories of economists, economics has replaced political economy, and economics deals with scarcity, prices, and resource allocation. In the definition of Paul Samuelson, "economics — or political economy, as it used to be called ... is the study of how men and society *choose*, with or without the use of money, to employ *scarce* productive resources, which could have alternative uses, to produce various commodities over time and distribute them for consumption, now and in the future, among various people and groups in society."

If economics is indeed merely a new name for political economy, and if the subject matter which was once covered under the heading of political economy is now covered by economics, then economics has replaced political economy. However, if the subject matter of political economy is not the same as that of economics, then the "replacement" of political economy is actually an omission of a field of knowledge. If economics answers different questions from those raised by political economy, and if the omitted questions refer to the form and the quality of human life within the dominant social-economic system, then this omission can be called a "great evasion".

Economic theorist and historian I. I. Rubin suggested a definition of political economy which has nothing in common with the definition of economics quoted above. According to Rubin, "Political economy deals with human working activity, not from the standpoint of its technical methods and instruments of labor, but from the standpoint of its social form. It deals with *production relations* which are established among people in the process of production." In terms of this definition, political economy is not the study of prices or of scarce resources; it is a study of social relations, a study of culture.

Rubin's book was first published in the Soviet Union, and was never re-issued after 1928. This is the first and only English edition. The translators are Milos Samardzija and Fredy Perlman.

275 pages/Hardcover: $7.50   ISBN : 0-919618-11-1

BLACK ROSE BOOKS No. D 13

THE GENOCIDE MACHINE IN CANADA

The Pacification of the North

by Robert Davis and Mark Zannis

The two authors examine the Canadian North thoroughly with a documentation that is impressive. This book will shock. It assesses the impact of such activities as "Project Chariot", "Icefield Ranges Project", the work of the "Defence Research Board", and the Department of Health and Welfare.

The role of the courts, legal profession, the RCMP are all critically observed as to their negative influence on the native people and their economy. The question of 'scientific' planning by various institutions like the Arctic Institute of North America is also examined in the light of the United Nations Convention on Genocide.

Publication Date : June 1973

300 pages / Hardcover $9.95 / Paperback $2.95
ISBN : 0-919618-04-9 / ISIBN : 0-919618-03-0

BLACK ROSE BOOKS No. D10

QUEBEC/CANADA AND THE OCTOBER CRISIS

edited by
Dan Daniels

This book is a collection of some of the most perceptive essays published on an event which shook the whole country. It looks at the 1970 October crisis from a number of vantage points. Included is the widely acclaimed essay by Fred Caloren, *"The War Measures Act and the Politics of Functionalism"*, *"The Roots of Extremism : State Capitalism in Canada"* by Jim Harding, *"The Urban Guerillas and the Crisis in the Western Hemisphere"* and *"Revolutionary Strategy in Québec and the Role of the Avant-Garde"* give a documentary flavour to the subject-matter. Peter Katadotis deals with the question of the relationship between the citizens movement in Montréal, FRAP, the FLQ and Mayor Jean Drapeau, while Herbert Marx gives a detailed legal background to the War Measures Act. Gérald Godin, one of those arrested, writes on how it feels to be a prisoner of war.

In addition to other essays, the book includes a preface, an epilogue and the poetry of Paul Chamberland, Gérald Godin, and Gaston Miron in both French and English.

Publication Date : June 1973

134 pages / Hardcover $8.95 / Paperback $2.25
ISBN : 0-919618-06-5 / ISBN : 0-919618-05-7

BLACK ROSE BOOKS No. D9

QUEBEC LABOUR

Preface by Marcel Pépin, president of the CNTU

What is the Confederation of National Trade Unions (CNTU) in Québec ? How did it develop from its Catholic origins into a mass militant trade union movement representing 250,000 workers ? How does the CNTU differ from the AFL-CIO affiliated Québec Federation of Labour ? How did the CNTU move beyond collective bargaining to become a unique trade movement in North America ? What is the CNTU's SECOND FRONT and what has been its effect in radicalizing both the organised labour force in Québec and the working population in general ?

Why has the CNTU now adopted a uniquely anti-imperialist, socialist, and workers' control policy ? What is the relationship of the CNTU to the national liberation movement in Québec ? How does the CNTU analyse the 'Quiet Revolution' ?

These and other questions are dealt with in this book, the content of which include :

A long historical introduction, the official translation of the document of the SECOND FRONT, and the exclusive official translation of the historic, *"Ne comptons que sur nos propres moyens"*.

224 pages / Hardcover $7.95 / Paperback $2.95
ISBN : 0-919618-14-6 / ISBN : 0-919618-15-4

BLACK ROSE BOOKS No. C6
Library of Congress Catalog Card Number : 73-76058

QUEBEC LABOUR STRIKES

edited by
BRB Collective

Since the publication of the widely acclaimed *"Québec Labour"*, the greatest General Strike in North American labour history has taken place. A Common Front of the Confederation of National Trade Unions, the Québec Federation of Labour, and the Québec Teachers Corporation while in a protracted struggle with the Québec government provoked a spontaneous revolt of some 350,000 workers in public service as well as private industry. What are the facts behind this upheaval? What has happened to the labour movement since the General Strike? What does the breakaway CSD trade union represent? What has happened to the growing radicalisation of the teachers union? How has all this affected the whole social movement consisting of the multitude of citizen committees, tenant associations, welfare recipients, unemployed workers, community medical and legal clinics and so on? These and many other related questions are examined in this thoroughly documented book.

Publication Date : June 1973

225 pages / Hardcover $9.95 / Paperback $2.95
ISBN : 0-919618-1 / ISBN : 0-919618-07-3

BLACK ROSE BOOKS No. D11